Paris 1 ͻͷ0S

Paris Bistros

A GUIDE
TO THE 100 BEST
BISTROS IN PARIS

Robert and Barbara Hamburger

Absolute Press

Published by Absolute Press (Publishers), 14 Widcombe Crescent,
Bath BA2 6AH

First published in 1991 by the Ecco Press, 100 West Broad Street,
Hopewell, NJ 08525, USA

First published in the UK by Absolute Press in April 1992

© Robert and Barbara Hamburger 1991

Designed by Richard Oriolo

Printed by the Longdunn Press, Bristol

ISBN 0 948230 52 5

In memory of our dear friend
Ingrid Abrams,
a most delightful traveling companion
and connoisseur of food and
wine who introduced us to
the pleasures of
the table.

ACKNOWLEDGMENTS

We would like to thank
Richard Abrams, Ellen and Joel Baumwoll,
Sue and Jerry Fine, Michael Hamburger, David Hamburger,
Sofula Novikova, Nicolas Ranson,
Meryl Salzinger and Liz Wolter.

Paris Bistros

CONTENTS

Introduction   1

PART I
The Bistros
by Arrondissement   5
Ratings   11
1erArrondissement   15
2e Arrondissement   33
3e Arrondissement   47
4e Arrondissement   53
5e Arrondissement   67
6e Arrondissement   79
7e Arrondissement   99
8e Arrondissement   115
9e Arrondissement   129
10e Arrondissement   137
11e Arrondissement   143
12e Arrondissement   157
13e Arrondissement   161
14e Arrondissement   169
15e Arrondissement   177
16e Arrondissement   189
17e Arrondissement   195
18e Arrondissement   211
19e Arrondissement   215
20e Arrondissement   221

PART II
Bistro Cuisine   229
La Carte   233
Carte des Vins   235
Hors d'Oeuvres/Entrées   237
Les Plats   245
Desserts   261
Glossary   265

PART III
Ratings of the
Best Bistro Dishes   269
Books of Interest   287
Index of Bistros   289

INTRODUCTION

Paris Bistros: A Guide to the 100 Best Bistros in Paris is written for the food-conscious traveler who wants to discover small, unpretentious neighborhood restaurants which serve traditional French food, in an intimate atmosphere, with as little fuss as possible. For a while it looked as if the bistro might disappear as fast-food chains became popular and nouvelle cuisine emerged to dominate the culinary world, but today the bistro is undergoing a significant revival. The famous old bistros, many still run by the original owners or their families, are more in demand and better than ever. Responding to this trend, several successful chefs and restaurateurs have opened bistro-style second or third establishments, abandoning the formal, luxury atmosphere of their "starred" restaurants for more intimate and convivial surroundings. A new brand of bistro has emerged alongside the classic ones and become immensely popular. These new bistros offer the perfect combination of intimacy and reasonable prices while maintaining the highest standards of fresh produce, traditionally prepared but adapted to today's diets. There are no heavy sauces or excessive flavors, just fresh old-fashioned food, simply cooked and generously served.

Dining out remains an integral part of Parisian life. People from every social stratum spend a good part of their time and income in restaurants. Lunch can last two hours; dinner is often longer, requiring thoughtful planning, consultations with waiters and much savoring of each dish and each ingredient. Every meal has a touch of ceremony, with carefully laid-down rules governing the choice and order of courses. The famous starred restaurants lend glamour to Parisian life, but it is the neighborhood bistros which give the city its character and color. A few bistros have become ultra chic, trendy and expensive, but the majority remain simple and casual where you can have an affordable meal of remarkable quality.

The word "bistro" supposedly dates from 1815, after Napoleon's defeat at Waterloo. Russian occupation troops camped out on the Champs-Élysées, hungry and thirsty, crowded into the city's cafés crying "Bystro! Bystro!" meaning "QUICK! QUICK!"

It first appeared in general usage around the turn of the century and was used to describe a place for public drinking (as opposed to a café, which was for coffee). Bistro probably stems from the word "Bistouille," meaning coffee mixed with eau-de-vie. Whatever the word's derivation, the bistro is a Parisian phenomenon and traditionally a family business. Its classic image is of a cozy neighborhood spot with a bar at the entrance. The postage-stamp dining area in the back, lined with dark wood and leather banquettes, is brightened by a few brass fixtures, red-checkered cloths, lace curtains and green potted plants. The proprietor-chef dashes between the front door to greet an important guest and the kitchen to finish the daily specials. His wife, acting as hostess-manager, sits behind the bar at the *caisse* where she can keep an eye on the accounts and the customers. At mealtimes the tables are filled with neighborhood regulars who love to eat. Everything is clean and cheerful. The menu is small but varied, offering a good choice of substantial dishes low in price but of excellent quality. The latest culinary chichi is ignored and the best traditions of French cooking are maintained. The choice of wine is limited but carefully made. Crusty bread is brought to the table by an amiable waiter who is proud of the food being served. Delicious smells waft into the dining room as a beef stew that has been simmering for hours in aromatic liquids makes an appearance. Everyone is talking and eating at the same time, chatting gaily back and forth from table to table. Suddenly the chef emerges in tall hat and clean apron to pass among the tables asking if everything goes well, making conversation, shaking hands, sometimes offering suggestions but never insisting. Some bistros may have been modernized but most have not changed for years and it is this consistency which brings patrons back week after week, month after month, year after year.

How do you distinguish a top bistro from a lesser one? A difficult question. The answer lies mostly in the quality of the ingredients and the preparation of the dishes. However, a bistro is defined not only by the food or even its price. It has an ambience; it's a place of a certain character; a place where you may find yourself sitting *coude à coude* (elbow to elbow) with perfect strangers, sharing a taste of food, listening to stories from regulars about the "old days," or to the chef tell how a new specialty was conceived, or perhaps chatting over a crowded bar with the owner about the "little" wines he has discovered. There is always an atmosphere of good cheer and well-being.

Books are written about Paris restaurants regularly, but few focus on the more obscure places unfrequented by tourists. Listed in the pages that follow is a cross section of what we consider to be the *best* bistros in Paris; where good food, nothing complicated or elaborate, is the most important factor. They range from expensive to inexpensive, from illustrious to unknown and from chic to unpretentious, but one thing is constant: the quality of the cuisine. In compiling this directory we have relied on firsthand experience, the recommendations of numerous guidebooks and the advice of both American and Parisian friends. As there are sure to be some omissions, we have included a list of sources for further reference.

This book is divided into three parts. Part I begins with a list of the bistros grouped by their overall ratings according to our system of "stars." This is followed by a brief description of the 20 districts or *arrondissements* into which Paris is divided. Finally, the bulk of this section is devoted to a more complete review of each bistro, and is arranged by *arrondissement*.

Part II explains the dishes most commonly encountered on a bistro menu. We do not provide actual recipes, but describe the ingredients and preparation of each dish so you can have a general idea of what you would like to order. This listing includes some regional dishes as well as important menu terms and phrases. A short glossary at the end offers other useful terms.

Part III contains a rating of what we consider to be the best bistro dishes and where to find them. We propose a list in descending order of where, in our estimation, the best or most interesting renditions of the dishes are presented. The overall rating of any establishment does not necessarily indicate the merits of every dish served there. A one- or two-"star" bistro may prepare a dish of four-star quality because it is a house specialty and connoisseurs will flock there seeking that particular item. Some of the most enjoyable dining experiences we have had are trying these wonderful foods in the lesser-known places. This section is followed by an index of the establishments described in this book.

There are many hundreds of bistros and bistro-type restaurants scattered throughout Paris. Not every one of them is run with the same pride and respect for cuisine or customers. In many the food is delicious while in others it is only mediocre. We hope this guide will help in your selection and provide you some of the pleasure bistro dining has given us.

PART I

The Bistros by Arrondissement

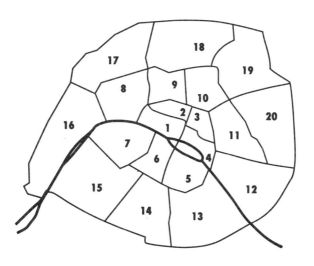

**A Diagram of Paris
Showing the Arrondissements**

*P*aris is divided into twenty *arrondissements* (districts) spiraling clockwise around the first, which marks the center of the city. Each *arrondissement* has its own atmosphere and distinctive landmarks, so to know the number of the *arrondissement* is to know the style and character of the district.

The 1ᵉʳ (meaning Premier) includes part of the Île de la Cité and the areas around the Louvre and Palais Royal. This is a tourist, shopping and business district with many hotels, restaurants, travel agencies, specialty shops, banks and government buildings. It is busy with commercial traffic during the day but quiet at night.

The 2ᵉ, 3ᵉ, and 4ᵉ (Deuxième, Troisième and Quatrième) include the areas of Les Halles (the old produce markets long-since demolished and moved to an area near Orly airport), Beaubourg and the Marais. These are among the oldest and most historic parts of the city but have undergone an astounding transformation during the last twenty years. The narrow, slummy streets and courtyards of Beaubourg and Les Halles have been turned into a large pedestrian area with a shopping mall, a large leisure center, and many new apartments, all dominated by the gigantic glass-and-steel Pompidou Center. The fine old *hôtels* (mansions) of the Marais, of which almost one hundred remain, are being cleaned and restored. Many are of great historic and architectural interest. Some are used to house museums, schools, libraries and cultural centers; others are being converted into luxury apartment houses. Trendy boutiques, antique shops, cafés and restaurants attract a yuppie crowd.

The 5e and 6e (Cinquième and Sixième) on the left bank comprise the areas of St.-Michel and St.-Germain-des-Prés. They are among the liveliest and most picturesque sections of the city but very different from one another. The 5e is student Paris, the Quartier Latin, "Boul' Mich'" and the Sorbonne. The 6e is intellectual and literary Paris; snobbish and avantgarde. The narrow mazes of streets are lined with book shops, publishing houses, antique stores, art galleries and boutiques of every description. Tourists, artists, writers, publishers, students, teachers, actors, models and others who simply live in the neighborhood crowd into the cafés morning, noon and night to talk, think, read, write, eat and drink.

The 7e (Septième) is on the left bank but has nothing in common with the 5e or 6e. It is mainly residential; an area of high rents and smart people; conservative and wealthy. There is little to attract the tourist except the historic monuments of the Tour Eiffel, the Invalides, Napoleon's Tomb, and the Musées d'Orsay and Rodin. The most interesting spots are the sections around the Rue Cler and Rue St.-Dominique.

The 8e (Huitième) is the most diverse *arrondissement*. It is the district of the Étoile, Arc de Triomphe, and Place de la Concorde. It encompasses the luxury areas around the Madeleine and Faubourg-St.-Honoré; the Avenues Montaigne and de Marigny with their expensive hotels, shops, restaurants and embassies; the champs-Élysées with its banks, airline offices, car showrooms, cinemas, nightclubs, cafés and fast-food joints; and the middle-class student and commercial areas around Gare St.-Lazare and Boulevard Haussmann.

The 9e (Neuvième) is the *arrondissement* of the Gaillion-Opéra, Pigalle and the Grands Boulevards (an area of about three miles leading from the Opéra to the Place de la République and Bastille). It is a shopping, theater and business district with banks, insurance companies and diamond merchants. The Grands Boulevards are solid with big department stores, boutiques, cafés, brasseries and movie houses. The smart end is near the Opéra; it gets seedier as you go east. The areas around Place Pigalle abound with sex shops, prostitutes, porn films and bookstores.

The 10e (Dixième) is largely unspoiled and dominated by two large train stations; the Gare du Nord and the Gare de l'Est. It doesn't have much to offer tourists, but the Rue de

Paradis is worth a visit if you're interested in glass and china. Baccarat is at No. 30 bis.

The 11e, 12e and 13e (Onzième, Douzième, and Treizième) are middle- and working-class areas, crowded with high-rise developments and small industries such as printers, mechanical enterprises, hide and leather shops and furniture manufacturers. A visit to the Bois de Vincennes is certainly worth a detour to the 12e. Some *quartiers* have large immigrant populations and each group maintains its characteristic shops, cafés and restaurants. The Asian restaurants in the 13e are the best in Paris.

The 14e and 15e (Quatrozième and Quinzième) are the old districts around Montparnasse and have in the last several years undergone much development. No longer the historic refuge of famous writers, poets and artists, the cafés, brasseries and movie houses continue to attract a lively and "hip" crowd. You can still get the flavor of the past at La Coupole or Closerie de Lilas. There are no great monuments to see among the quiet residential sections, but you can get glimpses of the way things once were.

The 16e (Seizième) contains the *quartiers* of Passy and Auteuil. Here the rich and super chic live on private, tree-lined streets, behind closed doors and ivy-covered walls. There are many parks, quiet gardens, embassies, museums, small villas and discrete hotels.

The 17e (Dix-Septième) is also a luxury area, although not as posh as the 16e. It is not a tourist area, but a visit to the Quartier Batignolles is interesting. In Rue Poncelet there is a lively market with an astounding choice of produce.

The 18e (Dix-Huitième) contains the slopes of Montmartre. The area is overshadowed by the great white basilica of Sacré-Cœur. There is still a country atmosphere here despite the hordes of tourists that crowd into the streets day and night. It is one of the most fascinating sections to visit and has largely survived reconstruction due to the steep and narrow streets of the Butte, which either come to an abrupt end or are connected by flights of steps. Small gardens, orchards and even a vineyard remain as reminders of what this charming old village once looked like. Another historic village of the 18e is la Goutte d'Or (The Drop of Gold). This is a commercial and working-class area of mixed nationalities mainly from North Africa, Morocco, the Ivory Coast and the French Antilles. The Arab groceries and the Afro-Antilles restaurants are among the best in the city.

The 19e and 20e (Dix-Neuvième and Vingtième) are the most remote *arrondissements*. They are the foreign *quartiers* of Paris. Waves of immigrants have settled here: Russian and Polish Jews, followed by Armenians, Greeks, Arabs, North Africans, Yugoslavs, Turks, Sephardic Jews and Orientals. There is an exotic mixture of food, shops, newspapers, cafés, etc. Among the new apartment blocks and large-scale developments can still be seen tiny houses, gardens and *impasses*. The main tourist attractions are the Parc des Buttes-Chaumont in the 19e and Père-Lachaise cemetery in the 20e.

Ratings

★ ★ ★ ★ THE BEST

★ ★ ★ EXCEPTIONAL

★ ★ VERY GOOD

★ ABOVE AVERAGE

★ ★ ★ ★

CHEZ PAULINE 1er
RESTAURANT PIERRE AU PALAIS ROYAL 1er
L'AMI LOUIS 3e
BENOÎT 4e
JOSÉPHINE (CHEZ DUMONET) 6e

JEAN DE CHALOSSE 8e
AUBERGE PYRÉNÉES CÉVENNES (CHEZ PHILIPPE) 11e
LE PETIT MARGUERY 13e
CHEZ GEORGES 17e

★ ★ ★

LE CHÂTELET GOURMAND 1er
LA FERMETTE DU SUD-OUEST 1er
LA TOUR DE MONTHLÉRY (CHEZ DENISE) 1er
CHEZ LA VIELLE 1er
CHEZ GEORGES 2e

À L'IMPASSE (CHEZ ROBERT) 4e
L'OULETTE 4e
CHEZ RENÉ 5e
ALLARD 6e
LA CAFETIÈRE 6e
LA FOUX 6e
CHEZ MAÎTRE PAUL 6e
LE PETIT ZINC 6e

AUX FINS GOURMETS 7e
CHEZ EDGARD 8e
SAVY 8e
LA GRILLE 10e
À SOUSCEYRAC 11e
ASTIER 11e
CARTET 11e
LE CHARDENOUX 11e
CHEZ MARCEL
(ANTOINE) 12e

LA CAGOUILLE 14e
PIERRE VEDEL 15e
LE BISTROT DE
L'ÉTOILE 17e
CHEZ GORISSE 17e
À LA POMPONNETTE 18e
LE POUILLY-REUILLY
(PRÉ-ST.-GERVAIS) 19e

★ ★

LESCURE 1er
PAUL 1er
LA VIGNE (CHEZ
SABINE) 1er
LE BRIN DE ZINC . . . ET
MADAME 2e
LE BRISSEMORET 2e
AUX LYONNAIS 2e
CHEZ PIERROT 2e
LE ROND DE SERVIETTE
2e
AU GOURMET DE L'ISLE
4e
LE MONDE DES
CHIMÈRES 4e
LE TRUMILOU 4e
MOISSONNIER 5e
AU MOULIN À VENT
(CHEZ HENRI) 5e
LA RÔTISSERIE DU
BEAUJOLAIS 5e
CHEZ TOUTOUNE 5e
LE CAMÉLÉON 6e
AUX CHARPENTIERS 6e
CHEZ L'AMI JEAN 7e
LA FONTAINE DE MARS
7e

AU PIED DE FOUET 7e
LA POULE-AU-POT 7e
THOUMIEUX 7e
CHEZ ANDRÉ 8e
L'ARTOIS (ISIDORE) 8e
AU PETIT RICHE 9e
LE ROI DU POT-AU-FEU
9e
CHEZ CASIMIR 10e
CHEZ FERNAND (LES
FERNANDISES) 11e
LE BOEUF BISTROT 13e
LES PETITES
SORCIÈRES 14e
RESTAURANT BLEU 14e
AU PASSÉ RETROUVÉ 15e
LE PETIT MÂCHON 15e
PIERRE LE LYONNAIS 16e
LE BISTROT D' À CÔTÉ
"FLAUBERT" 17e
CHEZ FRED 17e
LES GOURMETS DES
TERNES 17e
L'OEUF À LA NEIGE 17e
LE SANCERRE 19e
AUX BEC FINS 20e

★

CHEZ CLOVIS 1er

AUX CRUS DE BOURGOGNE 2e

AU DUC DE RICHELIEU 2e

CHEZ RABU 3e

BISTROT DE CLÉMENCE 4e

PERRAUDIN 5e

LE BISTROT D'HENRI 6e

LA LOZÈRE 6e

POLIDOR 6e

LA CIGALE (CHEZ PIERRE ET MICHELINE) 7e

CHEZ GERMAINE (BABKINE) 7e

LE MONTALIVET 8e

LES BACCHANTES 9e

CHEZ GRAND-MÈRE 13e

L'AUBERGE DU CENTRE 14e

LE BISTROT D'ANDRÉ 15e

LA GITANE 15e

CHEZ YVETTE 15e

LE SCHEFFER 16e

LE PETIT SALÉ 17e

LE BISTROT DU XXe 20e

BOEUF GROS SEL 20e

CHEZ ROGER 20e

1er

LE CHÂTELET GOURMAND

CHEZ CLOVIS

LA FERMETTE DU SUD-OUEST

LESCURE

PAUL

CHEZ PAULINE

RESTAURANT PIERRE AU PALAIS ROYAL

LA TOUR DE MONTHLÉRY (CHEZ DENISE)

CHEZ LA VIELLE

LA VIGNE (CHEZ SABINE)

1er *Arrondissement*

Louvre– Les Halles–Palais-Royal

PLACES OF INTEREST

Centre National d'Art et de Culture Georges-Pompidou
(Beaubourg)
L'Église Saint Eustache
L'Église Saint Germain l'Auxerrois
Fontaine des Innocents
Forum des Halles
Île de la Cité (1er, 4e)
Jardin des Tuileries (and Arc de Triomphe du Carrousel)
Le Louvre des Antiquaires
Musée des Arts Décortifs
Musée du Louvre & l'Orangerie
Opéra (1e, 2e, 9e)
Palais de Justice (Conciergerie, Sainte Chapelle)
Palais-Royal (and Gardens)
Place du Châtelet
Place Dauphine
Place and Colonne Vendôme
Place des Victoires (1er, 2e)
Pont-Neuf, Square du Vert Galant
(Bateaux Mouches or Vedettes)
Quai de la Mégisserie (bird, flower and animal market)
Rue St. Honoré
Rue de Rivoli

LE CHÂTELET GOURMAND ★ ★ ★

M. Guy Girard

ADDRESS: 13, rue des Lavandières Ste.-Opportune, 75001
CLOSED: Sun., Mon. and August 1–21
PRICE RANGE: Fairly expensive
TEL: 40-26-45-00
METRO: Châtelet-Les Halles
CREDIT: Amex, Visa, MasterCard and Diners

Chef Guy Girard offers an interesting menu which revolves around tasty spit-roasted meat and poultry. During the winter months, game is included and there is always a pêche du jour *(fish of the day) and a* broche du jour *(spit of the day).*

M. Girard, the chef who made Le Galant Vert and the Petit Coin au Bourse famous, has opened his own place in a picturesque old Les Halles wine bistro once known as Le Rouge et le Blanc. The eclectic decor is a little kitschy, with masks of Bacchus hung above the long marble bar and bunches of plastic grapes and vines dangling from the ceiling and light fixtures. An old copper coffee maker and fresh flowers add a nice touch and the well-spaced tables are covered with linen cloths. Everyone eats from one of the fixed menus which vary in price and length and include supplements "justified by market prices." There is usually a choice of seven or eight grilled meats, delicious fresh foie gras and the light and tasty fish preparations which might include turbot or sole fillets in light lobster sauce. The *prix-fixe* lunch includes a carafe of Gamay or Touraine. The desserts are nothing special and the wine a bit expensive, although there are some nicely priced Beaujolais.

RECOMMENDED DISHES

Foie Gras Frais de Canard. Duck foie gras.
Salade de Calamars Farcis. Stuffed-squid salad.
Escargots de Bourgogne. Vineyard snails in garlic sauce.
Homard Rôti en Brioche. Roast lobster meat served in a
  rich bun.

Côte de Boeuf Bordelaise. Ribs of beef served with a wine and shallot sauce.

Gigot d'Agneau des Pyrénées. Roast leg of lamb.

Pintade Rôtie au Verjus. Roast guinea hen cooked in the juice of unripe grapes.

Rognons de Veau au Coulis d'Echalotes et Vin Rouge. Lamb kidneys in a thick shallot-and-red-wine sauce.

Tarte aux Pommes. Apple tart.

Clafoutis. Custard tart with fresh figs.

Nougat Glacé. Candied fruit in nougat ice cream.

WINE

Expensive, however, there is a small selection of reasonably priced Beaujolais and Rhône wines available.

CHEZ CLOVIS ★

M. Claude Cornut

ADDRESS: 33, rue Berger, 75001
CLOSED: Sun.
TEL: 42-33-97-07
PRICE RANGE: Moderate
METRO: Louvre or Halles
CREDIT: Amex and Visa

The perfect old-time bar-bistro with an animated atmosphere, a gracious patron, some good wines by the glass and copious portions of unpretentious food.

Chez Clovis is one of a line of bistros facing the gardens of the Forum des Halles and Saint Eustache. A profusion of plants and flowers, red moleskin seats, copper handrails and photographs of old Les Halles create a friendly, brasserie-like atmosphere. The Cornut family is from the Auvergne, and so a number of their tasty traditional preparations reflect that region's cuisine. The classic *potée,* the sausages and an excellent *clafoutis* can be recommended. In addition there is game in season and wine served by the glass.

RECOMMENDED DISHES

Foie Gras Frais Maison. Duck foie gras.

Salade Folle. Mixed salad of curly lettuce, green string beans, bacon, chicken gizzards and duck foie gras.

Pied de Veau Entier Vinaigrette. Veal foot in a cold oil-and-vinegar dressing.

Charcuteries Maison. Large and varied selection of prepared and cooked pork products.

Papillote de Saumon aux Petits Légumes. Salmon pieces baked in a pouch with vegetables.

Potée à l'Auvergnate. Braised-cabbage soup with pork and sausage.

Tête de Veau Sauce Gribiche. Calf's head served in a vinaigrette.

Plat de Côte aux Légumes. Beef ribs in court bouillon with vegetables.

Boeuf à la Fichelle aux Trois Légumes. Poached fillet of beef served in its own broth with a complement of mixed vegetables.

Civet de Cerf aux Pâtes Fraîches. Deer stew served with fresh pasta.

Andouillette "A.A.A.A." Grillée. Grilled pork sausage.

Clafoutis Maison. Custard tart with fruit filling.

Tarte-Tatin. Upside-down apple pie.

WINE

Wines specially bottled for Chez Clovis.

LA FERMETTE DU SUD-OUEST ★ ★ ★

M. Jacky Meyer

ADDRESS: 31, rue Coquillière, 75001
CLOSED: Sun., holidays and August
PRICE RANGE: Fairly expensive
TEL: 42-36-73-55
METRO: Halles
CREDIT: Visa and MasterCard

Authentic regional specialties from the Gironde and Landes regions of Southwestern France are served in an authentic auberge *atmosphere.*

The decor is simple and pleasant but the ambience smart and intimate in this untouristy bistro near the Église Saint Eustache. The dining areas are located on two levels and decorated with regional memorabilia. Everything, from the foie gras to the *boudin,* not to mention the *cassoulet* and the *confit,* is cooked to perfection.

You can begin with a *pousse-rapière,* a lovely Southwestern apéritif made with Armagnac brandy and Champagne. It is especially good here.

RECOMMENDED DISHES

Cochonnailles. Assorted pork products.
Jambon de Campagne. Country ham.
Palette de Cochon Confite. Preserved pork shoulder.
Andouillettes. Grilled pork sausages.
Gras-Double Fenouillard. Ox tripe with fennel.
Boudin Paysan. Grilled blood sausage served with onions and bacon.
Cassoulet à l'Ancienne. Bean-and-meat stew cooked in an earthenware pot.
Pintade au Chou. Guinea fowl with cabbage.
Cailles Farcies au Foie Gras à l'Armagnac. Stuffed quail with foie gras and Armagnac.
Magret de Canard aux Cèpes. Fattened duck breast with mushrooms.
Crème Caramel. Vanilla-flavored flan.
Île Flottante. Poached egg whites (meringue) floating in vanilla-custard sauce.

WINE

Côtes-de-Buzet, Madiran and Cahors.

LESCURE

M. Lascaud

ADDRESS: 7, rue de Mondovi, 75001
CLOSED: Sat. evening, Sun., December 23–January 2 and August
PRICE RANGE: Moderate
TEL: 42-60-18-91
METRO: Concorde
CREDIT: Visa

A rustic atmosphere and generous helpings of simple French home-cooking are the attractions in this charming little bistro tucked away in a corner just off the Rue de Rivoli. The specialties vary from day to day and if you come early enough, you may find a seat among the tourists and faithful regulars who fill the place for lunch.

Customers have been sitting *coude à coude* (elbow to elbow), at tiny tables, under hanging garlands of garlic, onions, sausages and herbs since 1919 when Leon Lescure opened here. The place is still owned and operated by the second generation of his family, which continues the tradition of serving bourgeois plates at prices in the middle range. The service is a little harried but when the food arrives, it's always good. A fine *beouf bourguignon,* spareribs with red cabbage and a copious *poule-au-pot* (boiled, stuffed chicken) are among the choices. A few items from the Limousin region are also listed. If you want to wait for a place, there is a little zinc bar at the entrance, and during the summer, tables are set out onto the narrow sidewalk.

RECOMMENDED DISHES

Maquereau Frais à la Marinade. Mackerel fillets poached in white wine and served cold as a first course.
Pâté en Croute Chaude Salade. Pâté nestled in a hollowed-out slice of bread, served over salad.

Poule-au-Pot Farcie Henri IV. Stuffed chicken poached with vegetables.

Boeuf Bourguignon Garni. Beef cooked in red wine with bacon, small onions and mushrooms.

Confit de Canard "Comme en Limousin." Preserved duck grilled and accompanied by sautéed potatoes in oil.

Poularde au Riz Sauce Basquaise. Chicken served with rice and covered with tomato-and-green-pepper sauce.

Haddock Poché à l'Anglaise. Poached haddock English-style.

Filet de Canard Sauce au Poivre Vert. Fattened duck breast grilled with green peppercorns.

Vacherin aux Fraises ou Framboises. Meringue ring filled with cream and either strawberries or raspberries.

Tartes Maison. Fruit tarts (especially apricot).

Les Cabécous des Causses de Roc-Amadour. Special small round goat cheese from the Southwest.

WINE

Cahors or Macon Blanc.

PAUL

Mme. Dunand

ADDRESS: 15, place Dauphine, 75001
CLOSED: Mon., Tues. and August
PRICE RANGE: Moderate
TEL: 43-54-21-48
METRO: Pont-Neuf or Châtelet
CREDIT: Visa and Diners

A delightful old Parisian standby located on the Île de la Cité. There is nothing fancy here, but the food is good for the price. Sit at one of the wrought-iron and marble tables facing the Seine and you will know what old-fashioned bistro dining is all about.

Paul is a well-known antique, quietly situated among the lovely brick houses and dense chestnut trees on the historic Place Dauphine. The long, low room with terra-cotta-and-white-checked tile floor opens on both ends; one side facing the river on the Quai des Orfeures, the other the square. There is an attractive bar at the entrance and a subdued atmosphere is created by dark maroon painted walls stenciled with scenes of Paris. Brass pots, fresh flowers and fruit add a few bright touches. It is said that nothing has changed here for fifty years except possibly the prices. The menu still lists, among the array of time-tested classics, the *éscalope en papillote* and *baba au rhum,* two favorites probably a century old. The place can get crowded, for it is one of the most agreeable bistros to be found in the city. The terrace in summer is an unforgettable delight.

RECOMMENDED DISHES

Terrinette de Foie de Volaille. Chicken liver pâté.
Foie Gras de Canard. Duck foie gras.
Escargots de Bourgogne. Vineyard snails in garlic butter.
Sole Meunière. Fillet of sole coated with flour and fried in butter.
Escalope de Veau en Papillotte. Slices of veal baked in a pouch.
Quenelles de Brochet Nantua. Pike dumplings in a rich cream sauce with puréed crayfish, butter and truffles.
Haricot de Mouton. Mutton stew.
Tripes à la Mode de Caen. Tripe cooked with cider.
Tête de Veau Échalote. Calf's head with shallots.
Baba à la Confiture Flambé au Rhum. Yeast cake steeped in rum, filled with jam and set alight.
Mousse au Chocolat. Chocolate mousse.

WINE

Beaujolais, Côte-du-Rhône, Muscadet.

CHEZ PAULINE

M. Andre Génin

ADDRESS: 5, rue Villedo, 75001
CLOSED: Sat. lunch (summer), Sat. evening, Sun., December 24–January 2. Usually last two weeks of July and first two weeks of August
PRICE RANGE: Expensive
TEL: 42-96-20-70
METRO: Pyramides
CREDIT: MasterCard and Visa

One of the finest bistros in Paris; everything is top quality. Its location is convenient, the decor lovely, the service friendly and professional and the cuisine incredible. It is a very comfortable place, polished and expensive.

Located just in back of the Palais-Royal not far from the Comédie Française, this upscale bistro is one of the most popular with chic Parisians and knowledgeable tourists. Chef Génin's mouth-watering cuisine is a mixture of Burgundian classics with some nouvelle touches. The menu, which changes several times a year, offers everything you might want: pâtés, foie gras, wonderful hot oysters, frogs' legs, grilled sole and *rouget* (red mullet), *langoustines* and fabulous Bresse chicken with truffles. During the autumn and winter fresh game is a specialty. Rabbit stews, wild ducks and succulent wild boar are exquisitely prepared. There are wonderful cheeses and desserts, including homemade sherbets, petit fours, a superb rice pudding and a *millefeuille* with strawberries which is something special. The wine list includes a number of outstanding bargains, but the house wines, usually a Brouilly or Chiroubles, are fruity and inexpensive. An extensive selection of imported coffees is also offered.

RECOMMENDED DISHES

Salade Tiéde de Tête de Veau Sauce Gribiche. Calf's-head salad served warm with a vinaigrette dressing.

Jambon Persillé Comme en Bourgogne. Cold pressed ham with parsley in a white wine aspic.

Terrine de Foie de Volaille. Chicken liver pâté.

Terrine de Lapereau en Gelée de Pouilly. Rabbit pâté in Pouilly wine aspic.

Foie Gras Frais de Canard. Fresh duck foie gras.

Chou Farci "Paysanne." "Peasant style" stuffed cabbage.

Raie au Chou Nouveau. Skate with green cabbage.

Ris de Veau en Croûte. Calf's sweetbreads served as a filling in a hollowed-out pastry.

Boeuf Bourguignon Garni de Pâtes Fraîches. Beef stewed in burgundy wine with onions and mushrooms served with fresh pasta.

Côte de Boeuf Grillée et Son Gratin Dauphinois. Ribs of beef served with sliced potatoes baked with cream and browned on top.

Poularde de Bresse Rôtie (served for two). Roasted Bresse chicken.

Lièvre à la Royale (in season). Hare, boned and stuffed with foie gras and truffles, then braised in red wine and brandy.

Gâteau de Riz de Madame Ducottet. Rice pudding with fruit *confit* and vanilla custard sauce.

Crème Brulée à la Vanille. Custard, topped with brown sugar browned to a hard coating under a grill.

WINE

Beaujolais, Sancerre, Burgundy.

RESTAURANT PIERRE AU PALAIS ROYAL ★ ★ ★ ★

Mme. Nicole & M. Daniel Dez
Chef: Roger Leplu

ADDRESS: 10, rue de Richelieu, 75001

CLOSED: Sat., Sun., August and most holidays

PRICE RANGE: Fairly expensive

TEL: 42-96-09-17

METRO: Palais-Royal

CREDIT: Amex, Visa, Diners and MasterCard

*This admirable establishment, once known as Pierre Trai-
teur, remains one of the most distinguished and best bistros in
the city. The menu features finely executed classics and some
flavorful, more modern, fish preparations.*

The setting of this old house is calm and comfortable, consisting of brown-velvet banquettes, wood paneling, raw-silk-
covered walls and pictures of the nearby Palais-Royal. There
are two rooms, separated by a wooden bar, which are always
packed, but the friendly service makes you feel immediately at
home. The inspiration for the cuisine comes from the
provinces, but you will find some of the most flavorful bourgeois cooking in Paris here. Fresh fish is flown in from Normandy each day, the Roquefort is superb and the desserts are
ambrosia. There are two preparations that should not be
missed: the *gratin dauphinois,* which may not appear on the
menu but which can, nevertheless, be ordered, and the mackerel in cider, which is always on the menu.

RECOMMENDED DISHES

Saucisson Chaud Lyonnais Poché au Beaujolais. The
    Jésu de Morteau sausage poached in Beaujolais wine.
Terrine de Foie Gras de Canard. Pâté of duck foie gras.
Filets de Maquereaux Frais au Cidre. Mackerel fillets
    poached in cider and apples and served cold.
Jambon Persilée. Cold pressed ham with parsley in white
    wine aspic.
Andouillette en Fricassée à la Lyonnaise. Pork sausage
    sautéed with potatoes and onions.
Estofinade Rouergate. Codfish stew.
Chou Farci à la Bourguignonne. Stuffed cabbage.
Raie au Beurre Noisette. Skate in black butter.
Coquilles Saint-Jacques. Scallops.
Filet de Bar Grillée au Beurre Blanc. Grilled fillet of sea
    bass in white-wine butter sauce.
Galette de Boudin aux Oignons. Blood sausage with
    onions.
Boeuf Ficelle à la Menagiere. Poached fillet of beef in its
    own broth served "housewife style" with vegetables and
    onions.
Rognon de Veau à l'Echalote Confite. Veal kidneys in a
    shallot *confit.*
Gratin Dauphinois. Sliced potatoes baked with cream, sea-

soned with garlic, sprinkled with Gruyère cheese and browned on top.

Râble de Lièvre (in season). Roast saddle of hare.
Tarte à la Pamplemousse. Grapefruit tart.
Tarte-Tatin. Upside-down apple pie.
Crème Renversée au Caramel. Caramel flan.

WINE

Sancerre, Chinon, Bourgueil, Beaujolais (all the important growths).

LA TOUR DE MONTHLÉRY (CHEZ DENISE) ★ ★ ★

Mme. Denise Benariac

ADDRESS: 5, rue des Prouvaires, 75001
CLOSED: Sat., Sun. and July 15–August 15
PRICE RANGE: Fairly expensive
TEL: 42-36-21-82
METRO: Louvre, Halles, or Châtelet-Les Halles
CREDIT: Visa

"Chez Denise" is an old all-night Les Halles institution which continues to maintain an atmosphere of conviviality and good cheer. Sour-dough bread from Poilâne, the famous Parisian baker, the Brouilly and the pot-au-feu *are as unchangeable as the place itself.*

An interesting mix of customers keeps this wonderful place busy day and night, so reservations are a must except possibly at 4 A.M. The decor is nicely warm. Celebrity portraits, lithographs, photographs and posters clutter the old stone walls. Overhead, wooden rafters are lined with hams and sausages undisturbed by little hanging lamps. A black-and-white tile floor, brass rails, a long bar at the entrance, old subway seats as banquettes, and red-and-white checkered cloths complete the scene. The hearty, straightforward cuisine includes sausages, stews, *ongelet* (steak) and delicious tripe served Normandy-style steaming hot in an enormous tureen. This is one of the most consistently popular bistros in Paris; a great early-morning "hangout."

RECOMMENDED DISHES

Cochonnailles (Assiette de Charcuterie). Assorted pork products.
Terrine de Foie de Volaille. Chicken liver pâté.
Tripes au Calvados. Tripes cooked in cider brandy.
Chou Farci. Stuffed cabbage.
Boeuf Gros Sel (Pot-au-Feu). Boiled beef with vegetables and beef broth.
Haricot de Mouton. Mutton stew with potatoes, turnips and onions.
Pied de Porc Grillé. Grilled pigs' feet.
Lapin à la Moutarde. Rabbit in mustard sauce.
Andouillette. Grilled pork sausage served hot with mustard and vegetables.
Onglet de Boeuf, Frites. Flank steak grilled with shallots and served with outstanding french fries.
Oeufs à la Neige. Egg whites poached in milk, served with vanilla custard.
Tarte aux Pommes. Apple tart.

WINE

Sancerre, Bordeaux, Brouilly, Provençal rosé and Muscat.

CHEZ LA VIELLE ★ ★ ★

Mme. Adrienne Biasin

ADDRESS: 1, rue Bailleul or 37, rue de l'Arbre-Sec, 75001
OPEN: Open for lunch only
CLOSED: Sat., Sun. and August
PRICE RANGE: Fairly expensive
TEL: 42-60-15-78
METRO: Pont-Neuf or Louvre
CREDIT: Amex

Adrienne Biasin, distinguished chef, hostess and renowned bistro personality, prepares everything herself in a tiny kitchen across the hall from her delightful little six-table bistro. Simple home cooking is the specialty here and everything is of exceptional quality. Reservations should be made at least two weeks in advance.

Everything is *formidable* chez Adrienne. You'll begin with a choice of six or seven superb hors d'oeuvres, which arrive at your table on a cart. You are urged to help yourself from heaping bowls of stuffed tomatoes, sausage and potatoes, pâtés, *rillettes,* beets or celery root salad. The menu that day might include a lamb stew, beef with carrots, calf's liver, ratatouille or *boeuf à la mode.* It's all good and so are the desserts, especially the chocolate mousse and apricots or prunes. Located on the corner of Rue Bailleul and Rue de l'Arbre Sec, the cozy dining room with a timbered ceiling and lovely tile floor is homey and inviting. There is a bar behind which two motherly waitresses wait to serve the next course.

RECOMMENDED DISHES

Tomatoes Farcies. Stuffed tomatoes.
Terrines de Grand-Mère. Rustic country pâtés.
Céleri Rémoulade. Shredded celery root in spicy mayonnaise.
Rognon de Veau. Veal kidneys served minced.
Navarin d'Agneau. Lamb stew.
Boeuf Miroton. Slices of beef with a sweet onion sauce.
Boeuf à la Mode. Beef, pot roasted in red wine with vegetables.
Boeuf en Daube. Wine-flavored beef stew.
Sauté d'Agneau. Sautéed lamb.
Haricot de Mouton. Mutton stew with potatoes, turnips and onions.
Hachis Parmentier (order in advance). Minced-meat shepherd's pie.
Pot-au-Feu (order in advance). Boiled beef with vegetables and broth.
Ratatouille Parfumée. Eggplant stew with tomatoes, onions, peppers and garlic stirred in oil.
Gâteau au Chocolat. Chocolate cake.
Mousse au Chocolat. Chocolate mousse.
Gâteau de Riz. Rice pudding with fruit *confit* and whipped cream.

Country Wines, Saumur Champigny, Brouilly.

LA VIGNE (CHEZ SABINE)

Mme. Sabine Collin

ADDRESS: 30, rue de l'Arbre-Sec, 75001
CLOSED: Sat. lunch, Sun.
PRICE RANGE: Moderate
TEL: 42-60-13-55
METRO: Pont-Neuf or Louvre
CREDIT: Visa

The atmosphere is young and merry, as is the clientele of this intimate little bistro with a flowery vineyard-like motif. The solid bistro menu is well priced and the daily specials are prepared from the finest ingredients. The place merits its popularity.

A lovely wood and zinc bar, an old iron stove and music greet you as you enter the door of La Vigne. The long, narrow room is decorated with big bouquets of silk flowers, botanical prints and hanging overhead lights covered with lace doilies. However, the delicate touch is reserved for the decor, not the cuisine of owner-chef Mme. Collin. The dishes, sometimes bourgeois, sometimes *canaille* (peasant), are fresh and delicious featuring hearty stews, grilled meats, some spectacular seafood and a good selection of well-chosen little wines including a Ménétou Salon or a Givry. Her specialty for dessert is an extravagant soufflé laced with Grand Marnier *à commander* (which must be ordered at the beginning of the meal).

RECOMMENDED DISHES

"Demoiselle la Vigne" Tarte de Pommes de Terre au Foie Gras. Little potato tart with foie gras.
Oeufs en Meurette. Poached eggs in red-wine sauce.

Sauté de Veau aux Fines Herbes. Veal browned with finely chopped herbs.

Blanquette de Veau (Thursdays). Veal stew in a white sauce made from cream and egg yolks.

Rognon de Veau Grillée Henry IV. Grilled veal kidneys garnished with artichoke hearts and served with a béarnaise sauce.

Coquilles Saint-Jacques à l'Échalote. Grilled scallops with shallot sauce.

Cotriade à ma Façon (Fridays). Bretagne white-fish stew with mussels, onions and potatoes.

Haddock au Beurre Blanc Nantais. Haddock with white-wine butter sauce garnished with vegetables.

Andouillette à l'Ancienne Sauce Moutarde. Pork sausage in mustard sauce.

Magret de Canard à l'Orange. Fattened duck breast grilled in orange sauce.

Pieds de Porc Sauce Ravigote. Pigs' feet in a spicy vinaigrette with mustard, *cornichons* and capers.

Nougatine Glacée au Gingembre. Nougat ice cream with ginger.

Soufflé au Grand Marnier. Soufflé of orange-flavored brandy (must be ordered at start of meal).

WINE

Excellent inexpensive choice of little wines, particularly whites. Sancerre, Gigondas, Saumur Champigny.

2^e

LE BRIN DE ZINC . . . ET MADAME
LE BRISSEMORET
AUX CRUS DE BOURGOGNE
AU DUC DE RICHELIEU
CHEZ GEORGES
AUX LYONNAIS
CHEZ PIERROT
LE ROND DE SERVIETTE

2e Arrondissement

BOURSE–TURBIGO

PLACES OF INTEREST

La Bourse (Stock Exchange)
Cabinet de Médailles (Museum of coins, medals,
artifacts, and royal treasures)
Covered passages *(Vivienne, du Grand-Cerf,
du Bourg-l'Abbé de la Trinité, Basfour, Beauregard,
des Panoramas, des Princes)*
Place du Caire
Quartier de la Presse
Rue des Petits-Carreaux and *rue Montorgueil*
Sentier (Garment District)
Tour de Jean-Sans-Peur

LE BRIN DE ZINC . . . ET MADAME ★ ★

M. Yvon Levaslot

ADDRESS: 50, rue Montorgueil, 75002
CLOSED: Sun.
PRICE RANGE: Fairly expensive
TEL: 42-21-10-80
METRO: Étienne-Marcel, Halles or Sentier
CREDIT: Amex, Visa and MasterCard

You'll immediately feel at home in this attractive new bistro created on the premises of a famous old Les Halles bistro called La Grille. The menu is a mixture of traditional bourgeois dishes with some more modern inventions.

Many Parisians considered the opening of Le Brin de Zinc as the reopening of La Grille, a celebrated bistro when Les Halles was at its peak. La Grille originally opened as a wine shop in 1830 and continued in business as a bistro until about ten years ago. Recently the space was taken over and, without destroying the decor or greatly modifying the spirit of the cuisine, the old doors reopened. The pretty curved bar at the entrance dates from 1911. There are lovely mirrors, red banquettes and old fixtures and grilles that give one the feeling of going back in time as do dishes like onion soup, oxtails braised in red wine and stuffed pigs' feet. There is a cabaret next door, called "Et Madame," which opens around 10:30 P.M. and where you can hear French songs from the 50s until dawn.

RECOMMENDED DISHES

Poêlée d'Escargots en Ratatouille. Snails served over a stew of eggplant, zucchini and tomatoes.
Oeufs Pochés Toupinel. Poached eggs in baked potatoes.
Soupe à l'Oignon Gratinée. Onion soup served in its own pot with a thin crust of browned cheese.
Terrine de Gibier. Game pâté (in season).
Queue de Boeuf Mitonée Braisée au Vin Rouge. Braised oxtail simmered in red wine.

Boeuf Miroton. Slices of beef in broth with mustard and onions.

Entrecôte à la Moelle. Rib steak with bone marrow sauce.

Tête de Veau Avec Langue et Cervelle, Sauce Gribiche. Calf's head with tongue and brains in a cold vinaigrette of *cornichons* and capers.

Pieds de Porc Farcis. Grilled, stuffed pigs' feet.

Pavé de Cabillaud en Bourride. Fresh codfish stew served with *aïoli* (garlic mayonnaise).

Clafoutis aux Poires. Custard tart with pears.

Pot de Crème à la Vanille. Vanilla cream pot.

Marquise au Chocolat, Sauce Café. Chocolate mousse cake topped with coffee sauce.

WINE

St. Nicolas de Bourgueil/Chez Bruneau, Chinon Saint-Amour, Bandol, Bourgogne Aligoté.

LE BRISSEMORET

M. Claude Brissemoret

ADDRESS: 5, rue Saint-Marc, 75002

CLOSED: Sat. and Sun.

PRICE RANGE: Moderate

TEL: 42-36-91-72

METRO: Bourse or Montmartre

CREDIT: Visa

A strange, slightly decrepit but charming little "hole in the wall" with excellent food seasonally fresh and nicely prepared. There are some fabulous homemade desserts. Reservations must be booked well in advance, as this is an "in" Bourse restaurant.

Located directly behind Paris's stock exchange, across from the *Passage des Panoramas,* the beautiful old facade of Brissemoret simply says *"VINS-RESTAURANT-A LA CARTE*

ET PLAT DU JOUR." Inside, the small rectangular dining room has lace curtains, modern posters, a tile floor, old wine-colored velour banquettes, and a large central mirror. There is a stairway leading up to the w.c., but no longer an upstairs dining room. A small zinc bar at the entrance, simply set with a bouquet of fresh flowers, hides the antique kitchen beyond. Very white tablecloths and napkins of heavy linen cover the nine or ten marble-topped tables, each of which is set with a saltcellar and pepper mill. Homemade foie gras, mushrooms in cream sauce, hot goat cheese salad, marinated baby lamb chops served in a red wine sauce, *entrecôte* with marrow, guinea fowl with fruits and lamb kidneys in a fabulous mustard and onion sauce are served on handsome stoneware plates. Each main dish is carefully prepared and accompanied by an outstanding sauce. The house wine is a red Gamay de Touraine and there is a very fine and reasonably priced Calvados available.

RECOMMENDED DISHES

Filets de Maquereau Pochés au Vin Blanc. Poached fillets of mackerel in white wine.

Foie Gras Frais Maison. Fresh duck foie gras.

Salade de Foies de Volaille. Chicken liver salad.

Côtes d'Agneau en Chevreuil. Lamb chops cooked like venison.

Fricassée de Pintade aux Fruits. Light guinea fowl stew with fruits of the season.

Entrecôte Bordelaise et Moelle. Rib steak in bone marrow sauce.

Rognons d'Agneau Sauce Robert. Lamb kidneys in an onion-and-mustard sauce.

Saumon Frais Cru, aux Herbes. Fresh raw salmon with herbs.

Gâteau au Chocolat. Chocolate cake.

Tarte aux Pommes. Apple tart.

WINE

Crozes Hermitage/A. Graillot, Pouilly Fumé/Joseph Ballard, Gamay de Touraine.

AUX CRUS DE BOURGOGNE ★

M. & Mme. Bouvier

ADDRESS: 3, rue Bachaumont, 75002
CLOSED: Sat., Sun. and August
PRICE RANGE: Fairly expensive
TEL: 42-33-48-24
METRO: Sentier or Halles
CREDIT: Visa and MasterCard

Rich, traditional first-rate Burgundian specialties and wine are served in a bright, lively, rustic atmosphere. A very popular place with a young branché *(hip) clientele, so reservations are advisable.*

The only thing that has changed in this charming establishment is its owner, now the nephew of the vibrant Mme. Larcier, who reigned for more than forty years from behind her wooden bar. You will still find a lovely dining room painted bistro blood-red-and-yellow and decorated with mirrors, prints and posters, long red-and-white drapes at the windows and red-checkered cloths and napkins on the tables. Red banquettes and brass rails divide the room into cozy sections. There is also still fresh goose foie gras and lobster with mayonnaise on the menu as well as intensely flavored *coq-au-vin, boeuf bourguignon* and wild boar in season. There is a fine selection of little-known first-class Burgundies that are good but a bit expensive. The least expensive wines are a Corsican red and a Côtes-de-Brouilly.

RECOMMENDED DISHES

Filets de Hareng. Marinated herring fillets.
Demi-Langouste, Mayonnaise Frâiche. Spiny lobster, steamed, split open and served in its shell with fresh mayonnaise.
Foie Gras d'Oie Frais. Fresh goose foie gras (best accompanied by a moderately priced glass of excellent Sauternes).
Gibiers en Saison. Game served in the fall and winter months.

Raie au Beurre Nantais aux Pâtes Fraiches. Skate in a white-wine butter sauce served with fresh pasta.

Coq au Brouilly et aux Cèpes. Chicken simmered in Beaujolais wine with wild mushrooms.

Boeuf Bourguignon. Beef cooked in red wine with onions and mushrooms.

Pieds de Porc Panées Grillés. Pigs' feet coated in bread crumbs and grilled.

Millefeuilles. Puff pastries.

Gâteau au Chocolat Maison, Crème Anglaise. Rich chocolate cake served in a light egg custard.

Tarte au Citron. Lemon tart.

WINE

Large selection of reasonably priced wines from Beaujolais and Burgundy, Brouilly.

AU DUC DE RICHELIEU

M. Paul Georgé

ADDRESS: 110, rue de Richelieu, 75002
CLOSED: Sun. and August
PRICE RANGE: Moderate
TEL: 42-96-38-38
METRO: Richelieu–Drouot
CREDIT: Visa

A young, rather upscale clientele keeps a bright and boisterous atmosphere going in this classic wine bistro where one can come day or night to drink good wine and enjoy honest home-cooking with some Lyonnaise specialties.

M. Paul Georgé, who has been the *patron* here for more than forty years, loves his trade and his customers. The old-time regulars come to the delightful bar to drink his excellent Beaujolais—the Chenas, the Brouilly, the Saint-Amour, the Moulin-à-Vent and a fresh and effervescent Fleurie. The younger crowd comes to enjoy delicious country ham, snails, grilled *andouillettes* (pork sausages), *pot-au-feu* or *coq-au-Beaujolais*. The late-19th-century dining room is unpretentious in decor, with burgundy leather banquettes, globe lights, hanging plants and little tables covered with checkered cloths and paper. Posters, prints and certificates are casually hung around the tawny walls.

RECOMMENDED DISHES

Saucisson de Lyon aux Pommes Chaudes à l'Huile. Large slicing sausage with potatoes in oil.
Terrine de Canard Sauvage. Pâté of wild duck.
Daube au Chénas. Braised beef in Beaujolais wine.
Coq au Beaujolais. Chicken stewed in Beaujolais wine.
Pot-au-Feu. Boiled beef with vegetables and broth.
Petit Salé aux Lentilles. Slightly salted pork served with lentils.
Civets de Biche. A ragout of deer meat.
Potée Auvergnate. A thick salt-pork and cabbage soup with mixed vegetables and meats added.
Andouillette au Pouilly Grillée. Grilled pork sausage in white Burgundy wine.
Filet de Daurade Dieppoise. Fillet of sea bream poached in white wine with mussels, shrimp and mushrooms served in a cream sauce.
Crème Caramel. Vanilla-flavored flan.
Mousse au Chocolat. Chocolate mousse.
Gâteau aux Pommes. Apple cake.

WINE

House Wine/Fleurie, Saint-Amour, Brouilly, Pouilly Fumé, Muscadet, Châteauneuf-du-Pape.

CHEZ GEORGES ★ ★ ★

M. Georges Constant
M. Brouillet

ADDRESS: 1, rue du Mail, 75002
CLOSED: Sun., holidays and August
PRICE RANGE: Fairly expensive
TEL: 42-60-07-11
METRO: Sentier
CREDIT: Amex, Visa, Diners and MasterCard

Very popular, delightful old bistro with pushy waitresses, a fine wine cellar with many bargains and a menu offering all the bistro classics carefully and skillfully prepared. Reservations are advisable.

Chez George is a wonderful place with a simple hospitable look that typifies restaurants of the old style. The entrance is a kind of passageway and bar decorated by a wall painting of young couples and minstrels strolling through a medieval garden. Rows of mahogany-colored banquettes, closely spaced tables and giant arched beveled mirrors run along the walls on each side of the small alley-like dining room. A communal coat rack in the center breaks the monotony of the starkly simple tile floor. The long and varied handwritten menu rarely changes, to the delight of everyone who comes here. Among the nineteen appetizers available are eggs in a red-wine sauce with truffles. These can be followed by a choice of several classic fish or meat preparations, including such famous specialties as the *sole au pouilly*, the *pavé* (steak) *du mail* and the duck with *cèpes*. The house has an extraordinary cellar of fine old Burgundy and Bordeaux wines, but you can also order Beaujolais served by the pitcher.

RECOMMENDED DISHES

Salade de Museau de Boeuf. Beef headcheese salad.

Jambon Persillé. Parslied ham in white wine aspic.

Terrine de Foie de Volaille. Chicken liver pâté.

Oeufs en Meurette aux Truffes. Poached egg in red-wine sauce with truffles.

Steak de Canard aux Cèpes. Grilled duck fillet with sautéed wild mushrooms.

Gigot d'Agneau Rôti, Gratin Dauphinois. Roast leg of lamb with sliced potatoes baked with cream and browned on top.

Pavé du Mail. Thick slice of beef served with a mustard sauce.

Rognon de Veau Grillée Henri IV. Grilled veal kidneys with artichoke hearts.

Raie au Beurre Noisette. Skate in black butter sauce.

Sole au Pouilly. Fillet of sole cooked in white Burgundy wine.

Charlotte aux Poires. Baked custard pudding with buttered bread and sliced pears.

Baba au Rhum. Yeast cake steeped in rum syrup.

Beaujolais wines served by the pitcher, Côtes-de-Brouilly, Morgon.

AUX LYONNAIS

M. Pierre Vallée

ADDRESS: 32, rue Saint-Marc, 75002
CLOSED: Sat. lunch, Sun., holidays and August
PRICE RANGE: Moderate
TEL: 42-96-65-04
METRO: 4-Septembre, Bourse or Richelieu–Drouot
CREDIT: Amex, Visa, Diners and MasterCard

A lovely fin-de-siècle bistro which commands a faithful following. The quality of the food, the cooking and the service are absolutely dependable. Its location in the Bourse area assures it is usually busy, so reservations are suggested.

A few steps from Place Boïeldieu, just behind the Bourse is the lovely old red-and-cream facade of Aux Lyonnais. A picture of two provincial women welcomes you into the picturesque dining room. White and rose motif tile dados and arched mirrors adorn attractive turn-of-the-century walls molded with roses and garlands. Brass globe lights, lovely tile floors, etched glass windows, lace curtains and potted palms enhance the well-kept decor.

All the great wine villages of Beaujolais are to be found on what is described as the "Route de Beaujolais," and you will have no difficulty choosing a wine to accompany the basic bistro cuisine with some Lyonnais specialties. A 77F lunch menu includes *confit* and *cassoulet,* and a friendly all-female staff provides efficient and helpful service.

RECOMMENDED DISHES

Petits Pâtés Chauds, Enrobés d'Herbes Dans la Crépine. Pâtés served hot, enriched with herbs and wrapped in pig's membrane.

Saucisson Chaud Lyonnais, Pommes à l'Huile. Large slicing sausage with potatoes in oil.

Salade Frisée au Lard Avec Saucisson Chaud. Chicory salad served with bacon and slices of hot sausage.

Oeufs en Meurette. Poached eggs in red-wine sauce.

Pieds de Mouton à la Rémoulade. Sheep's feet in a mustard-mayonnaise sauce with chopped *cornichons,* egg and capers.

Poule Gros Sel avec Ses Légumes. Poached chicken with vegetables.

Gras-Double à la Lyonnaise. Ox tripe sliced and fried with onions, vinegar and parsley.

Pieds de Porc Grillés. Grilled pigs' feet.

Quenelles de Brochet au Beurre Blanc. Pike dumplings in a white-wine butter sauce.

Raie au Beurre Brun. Skate cooked with brown butter, lemon and parsley.

Tarte-Tatin, Crème Fraîche. Upside-down apple pie served with slightly soured cream.

Oeufs à la Neige. Egg whites poached in milk and served with vanilla custard sauce.

WINE

"ROUTE DE BEAUJOLAIS" complete list of Beaujolais Crus served in full and half bottles.

CHEZ PIERROT ★ ★

M. Pierre Losson

ADDRESS: 18, rue Étienne-Marcel, 75002
CLOSED: Sat., Sun. and July
PRICE RANGE: Fairly expensive
TEL: 45-08-17-64
METRO: Étienne-Marcel
CREDIT: Amex, Visa, Diners and MasterCard

Two lovely dining rooms in brown and cream, brightened by white globe chandeliers and mirrors, are usually filled with regulars from the fashion world. Waiters dressed in long aprons and polka-dot ties serve very generous portions of traditional food.

Pierre Losson began life in Les Halles as a waiter at a famous restaurant called Monteil. In those days butchers and vegetable vendors started work at midnight and great appetites were stimulated by hard work in the stalls. Restaurants opened at 5 A.M. and it was not unusual to serve a whole rabbit or chicken as a single portion. Giant plates of boiled beef, pigs' feet, veal and lamb stews were washed down by rough red wine, bought by the barrel and bottled in the street. Monteil was torn down in 1969 with the rest of the buildings in that part of Les Halles, but Losson retained the old phone number, moved into an old grain shop a few blocks away, installed a fine zinc-topped bar and opened in 1972. Today Chez Pierrot, a diminutive of Pierre, is a bustling business which carries on the Les Halles tradition of good eating. There are always a dozen or so hors d'oeuvres from which to choose, followed by hearty stews, sausages, *fricassées* and sautés. There is a huge selection of cheeses, and the wine list includes some fine Burgundies, Bordeaux and Loire Valley whites. You can finish the evening with a Monte Cristo or Churchill from the house humidor.

RECOMMENDED DISHES

Salade de Crevettes Rosés aux Champignons. Shrimp and mushroom salad.

Petits Maquereaux au Vin Blanc. Tiny mackerel marinated in white wine.

Filets de Soles Farcis. Stuffed fillets of sole.

Escalope de Bar en Papillote. Slices of sea bass baked in a pouch with herbs.

Pieds de Porc Grillés. Grilled pigs' feet.

Boeuf Bourgignon. Beef cooked in red wine with onions and mushrooms.

Tripes à la Mode de Caen. Tripe cooked in cider with onions, carrots and leeks flavored with Calvados brandy.

Pigeon Rôti Grand-Mère. Roast pigeon cooked with onions, mushrooms and potatoes.

Tarte aux Questches. Plum tart.

Crème Caramel. Vanilla-flavored flan.

WINE

Chénas, Brouilly, Côtes-de-Buzet.

LE ROND DE SERVIETTE ★ ★

M. André Genin

ADDRESS: 16, rue Saint-Augustin, 75002
CLOSED: Sat. lunch and Sun.
PRICE RANGE: Moderate
TEL: 49-27-09-90
METRO: 4-Septembre or Bourse
CREDIT: Visa and MasterCard

A popular and attractive new bistro recently opened by M. André Genin, one of the most well-known and respected bistro chefs in Paris. The menu offers familiar dishes mi-bourgeois, mi-canaille *(half-bourgeois, half-peasant). There are good wines by the carafe and excellent coffee.*

Le Rond de Serviette is a modest annex to the celebrated Michelin-starred Chez Pauline (see 1er Arrondissement). The appealing dining room, once a brasserie, is now outfitted with lovely upholstered chairs and banquettes printed with a tapestry pattern. Comfortable tables are set with individual paper napkin rings designed by decorator Patrick Frey. Red moiré walls provide the backdrop for a collection of Daumier prints and modern lantern-like fixtures softly spotlight the tables. The *plats* and desserts of the day are scripted on slate menus and you will find all the classics richly prepared. More modern ideas are seen in the fish and seafood dishes. The cellar offers anything you could wish for with small but well-chosen selections. All are excellent companions to the food.

RECOMMENDED DISHES

PLATS DU JOUR
Tête de Veau et Langue, Sauce Ravigote (Mondays). Calf's head and tongue in vinaigrette.
Petit Salé aux Lentilles (Tuesdays). Lightly salted pork with lentils.
Jambon Braisé aux Epinards (Wednesdays). Braised ham with spinach.

Pot-au-Feu (Thursdays). Boiled beef with vegetables and broth.

Brochette d'Agneau Grillée (Fridays). Skewered and grilled marinated lamb.

Terrine de Lapereau en Gelée Comme "Chez Pauline." Rabbit pâté in white-wine aspic.

Salade Tiède de Tête de Veau, Sauce Gribiche. Warm calf's-head salad served in a vinaigrette with *cornichons* and capers.

Filets de Maquereau Marinés au Vin Blanc. Marinated mackerel fillets in white wine.

Hachis Parmentier du Rond de Serviette. Meat-and-potato casserole (shepherd's pie).

Blanquette de Veau. Veal stew in a white sauce made from cream and egg yolks.

Profiteroles. Ice-cream-filled pastries covered with chocolate.

Crème Brûlée. Cream custard topped with brown sugar burned under the grill to form a hard coating.

WINE

Small but varied selection from most French wine regions. Bordeaux/Carafe Le Maison, Château Vignolles Peyroulet/ Graves, Saumur Champigny, Sancerre, Pouilly Fumé.

3^e

L'AMI LOUIS
CHEZ RABU

3ᵉ Arrondissement

MARAIS–TEMPLE

PLACES OF INTEREST

Centre Culturel du Marais
Hôtel de Guenegaud (Musée de la Chasse et de la Nature)
Hôtel de Libéral-Bruand (Musée de la Serrure—locksmithing)
Hôtel Rohan
Hôtel Salé (Musée Picasso)
Le Marais (the northern half)
Musée Carnavalet
Musée du Conservatoire National des Arts et Métiers
Palais de Soubise
(Archives Nationales—Musée de l'Histoire de France)
Rue des Gravilliers
Rue des Rosiers (Old Jewish quarter)
St. Nicolas-des-Champs (Abbey)

L'AMI LOUIS

M. de la Brosse

ADDRESS: 32, rue de Vertbois, 75003
CLOSED: Mon., Tues., July and August
PRICE RANGE: Very expensive
TEL: 48-87-77-48
METRO: Temple
CREDIT: Amex, Visa, Diners and MasterCard

The most illustrious bistro in Paris, drawing a clientele from around the world. The dining room is dark and dingy, the waiters indifferent, but the food is sublime. Extravagant portions with prices to match.

This famous eating place with its little oval mirrors, its iron-legged marble-topped tables and its worn-out Art Deco trompe l'oeil ceramic tile floors was named after the restaurant's original maître d'hôtel, Louis Pedetos. It became the domain of the legendary Antoine Magnin during the 1930s. Magnin, a quiet man who always wore a red scarf tied under his thin white beard, was Paris's most renowned roasting chef, and as his reputation spread, L'Ami Louis became celebrated. When he died a few years ago, three members of the staff continued to manage the place. They have faithfully preserved its picturesqueness, its popularity and its prices. Everything here is superb, but people come for the outrageous slabs of Landes foie gras served with Bayonne ham, the best roast chicken in existence, the marvelous fresh snails, frogs' legs, Breton scallops and, in season, the game with mushrooms. An evening could cost you as much as at Le Taillevent, but here you will have the satisfaction of seeing mink coats tossed overhead to lay against the ancient walls' flaking paint.

RECOMMENDED DISHES

Foie Gras Frais de Landes. Fresh duck foie gras from the Landes region in Gascogne (four large slices).

Escargots de Bourgogne. Vineyard snails in garlic butter.

Confit de Canard Froid. Preserved duck *confit* served cold.

Cèpes Rôtis en Saison. Roasted wild mushrooms available from fall to early spring.

Gibiers en Saison. Game available from fall through the middle of April.

Coquilles Saint-Jacques à la Provençale. Scallops sautéed with garlic and tomatoes.

Côte de Veau Grillée à la Crème. Grilled veal chop served with a rich cream sauce.

Pigeon Rôti aux Petits Pois. Roast pigeons with tiny green peas.

Rognon de Veau Grillé à la Crème. Grilled veal kidneys in a rich cream sauce.

Côte de Boeuf Grillée Avec Pommes Allumettes. Grilled ribs of beef with shoestring potatoes.

Poulet Rôti (for two). Roast free-range chicken.

Gigot d'Agneau de Lait Rôti. Roast leg and hindquarter of suckling lamb.

Gâteau de Pommes de Terre à l'Ail. Potato cake with garlic and parsley.

Nougatine Glacée. Sweet walnut ice cream.

WINE

Fleurie.

CHEZ RABU ★

Mme. Rabu

ADDRESS: 10, rue des Haudriettes, 75003
CLOSED: Evenings, Sun. and August
PRICE RANGE: Moderate
TEL: 42-72-10-43
METRO: Rambuteau or Arts–et–Métiers
CREDIT: Amex, Visa, Diners and MasterCard

*A quiet little lunch-only spot in the heart of the Marais, ideally suited for a leisurely meal. Pleasant, cozy and very **popular, so you will need a reservation.*

Mme. Rabu takes special care to maintain the quality of the food and service in her very congenial little bistro. There is an old-fashioned wooden bar on the left as you enter the first of two small, softly lit rooms with brown leather booths and little square tables. The cream-colored walls are brightened by bevel-edged mirrors, copper pots and caricatures by Sem, but the atmosphere is quiet and denlike. Fresh, quality products are used to prepare the simple menu, which begins with a good potted *terrine* and omelettes followed by lamb stew, salt pork with potatoes and the house specialty of calf's brains in browned herb butter. There is a small wine list, including some Alsatian crus and a superior Calvados. Coffee is served in a pot, and the bittersweet chocolate mousse is rich and creamy.

RECOMMENDED DISHES

Moules de Bouchot à la Crème. Tiny mussels in cream sauce.

Rilletes du Mans. A spread of preserved pork from Le Mans in the Loire Valley.

Omelette au Lard. Omelette with bacon.

Tomates Farcies Provençales. Stuffed tomatoes with garlic.

Gigot de Pré-Salé Agneau Rôti. Roast leg of salt marsh lamb.

Hachis Parmentier (Plat du Jour). Meat-and-potato casserole (shepherd's pie).

Navarin de Mouton. Mutton stew with potatoes and onions.

Gras-Double à la Lyonnaise. Ox tripe, sliced and fried with onions, vinegar and parsley.

Andouillette de Troyes Vert Pré. Pork sausage garnished with potatoes and parsley butter.

Tarte aux Quetches. Plum tarts.

Profiteroles au Chocolate Chaud. Ice-cream-filled pastries covered with hot chocolate sauce.

WINE

Côtes-du-Rhône, Bourgueil.

4^e

BENOÎT

BISTROT DE CLÉMENCE

AU GOURMET DE L'ISLE

À L'IMPASSE (CHEZ ROBERT)

LE MONDE DES CHIMÈRES

L'OULETTE

LE TRUMILOU

4e Arrondissement

HÔTEL-DE-VILLE

PLACES OF INTEREST

Bastille (July Column)
Cathédral de Notre-Dame (Musée Notre-Dame)
Église Saint-Paul–Saint-Louis
Hôtels de Sully, Sens, Beauvais, Lambert, Lauzin, Aumont
Hôtel-de-Ville
Île de la Cité
Île Saint Louis
Le Marais (Southern half)
Musée Victor Hugo
Notre-Dame-des-Blancs-Manteaux
Odéon (Théâtre de France)
Place du Marché Sainte-Catherine
Place des Vosges (3e, 4e)
Pont-Marie
Rue Saint-Antoine, Rue des Lions Saint Paul, Rue Pavée
Tour Saints Gervais et Protais

BENOÎT

M. Michel Petit

ADDRESS: 20, rue Saint-Martin, 75004
CLOSED: Sat., Sun. and the first three weeks of August
PRICE RANGE: Expensive
TEL: 42-72-25-76
METRO: Châtelet
CREDIT: None

A beautiful old bistro opened in 1912 and run today by the grandson of its original owner. You will be charmed by the perfect old-world decor and the superb bourgeois Lyonnais cuisine. This is one of the finest bistros in the city and very popular with Americans. Reservations are essential.

Ignoring all fashions of the time, Benoît has preserved its French character and old-world charm for over three-quarters of a century. A five-minute walk from the Pompidou Center, located on a pedestrian street near the Tour St.-Jacques, the red-and-gold-trimmed awning and polished wooden facade contrast with lush potted evergreens. Inside, the light oak paneling is set off with mirrors, old photographs, brass globe lights, red banquettes and etched-glass wall dividers. A polished marble-topped bar near the entrance is crowded with glistening glasses and bottles. Fresh flowers and potted palms are scattered about. The menu, presented in an old leather frame, lists such famous specialties as salad of beef and brawn, mussel soup, beef with carrots (*boeuf mode*), grilled *boudin* (blood sausage) with apples, calf's tongue with herb sauce, roasted Bresse chicken and the *cassoulet maison* made with asparagus and white beans. There is an additional menu of daily specials. Desserts are delicious, with such delights as chocolate *marquise* with coffee-flavored *crème anglaise,* pear tart, apples in light puff pastry with *crème fraîche* and vanilla ice cream flavored with Grand Marnier and served with candied orange slices. The house Beaujolais is an excellent Brouilly.

RECOMMENDED DISHES

Saucisson Chaud de Lyon. Hot poached sausage.
Soupe de Moules. Large *terrine* of mussel soup.

Compotiers de Boeuf en Salade à la Parisienne. Beef salad served with a large and varied choice of hors d'oeuvres.

Marmite Dieppoise du Pêcheur. Fish and shellfish stew with leeks, white wine and cream.

Boeuf à la Ficelle. Beef, first quickly roasted, then tied with a string and suspended in broth to poach.

Boeuf Mode Braisé à l'Ancienne. Marinated beef braised in Beaujolais wine and served with carrots, mushrooms, turnips and onions.

Tête de Veau Sauce Ravigote, Avec Langue et Cervelle. Calf's head, brains and tongue in vinaigrette.

Rognon de Veau Entier en Cocotte. Whole veal kidney, pot-roasted in a casserole.

Cassoulet Maison. White-bean-and-meat stew cooked and served in an earthenware pot.

Lièvre à la Royale. Whole boned hare stuffed with foie gras and truffles and braised in red wine and brandy.

Blanquette de Veau à l'Ancienne. Veal stew in a white cream sauce served with white rice.

Boudin Grillé aux Pommes. Large blood sausage served with apples and potatoes.

Feuilletée Chaude aux Pommes Avec Crème Fraîche. Hot puff pastry with apples and slightly soured cream.

Soufflé Glacé au Grand Marnier. Iced soufflé with Grand Marnier brandy.

Mousse au Chocolat. Chocolate mousse.

Marquise au Chocolat. Mousse-like chocolate sponge cake with butter cream filling.

WINE

Chiroubles, Morgon, Brouilly.

LE BISTROT DE CLÉMENCE ★

M. Stéphane Blanchet

ADDRESS: 4, Quai d'Orléans, 75004
CLOSED: Sun., Mon. lunch
PRICE RANGE: Moderate
TEL: 46-33-08-36
METRO: Pont-Marie
CREDIT: Visa, Diners and MasterCard

The inventive and personal cuisine created by owner-chef Stéphane Blanchet is one of the best values on the Île-St. Louis. A cozy bistro atmosphere is created by beamed ceilings, lace curtains, small tables and a lovely bar.

M. Blanchet's cooking is basically bourgeois with some modern touches, and everything is outstandingly fresh. He offers some unique specialties such as pasta salad, oysters with broccoli sauce, scallops with lime, and red mullet with red cabbage that are delicate and flavorful. There are two *prix-fixe* menus that change weekly depending on market produce. The first includes a choice of four main courses (*plats*), while the other, less expensive, one has a choice of two *entrées,* two *plats* and cheese or dessert. The pretty little wine list was designed by painter Jean-Pierre Rémon and wines by the glass are served at the bar, where you can look out across the Seine to the Tour d'Argent, a restaurant which claims to be the oldest eating-place in Paris, an inn of this name having been opened on the present site in 1582.

Recommended Dishes

Saumon Fumée Sur Son Lit de Framboises. Smoked salmon on a bed of raspberries.

Flan de Truite Saumonée. An open sea trout tart.

Soupe à l'Oignon Gratinée. Onion soup poured over a slice of bread and topped with browned grated cheese.

Salade de Pâtés Fraîches. Fresh pasta salad.

Émincée de Saint-Jacques au Citron Vert. Sliced scallops in lime sauce.

Filet de Rouget au Beurre de Vin Rouge et Choux Rouge. Red mullet in red-wine sauce served with red cabbage.

Pot-au-Feu Clémence Avec Son Os à Moelle. Beef boiled with vegetables and served with bone marrow.

Blanquette de Veau à la Crème d'Herbes Fines. Veal stew in a white cream sauce with fine herbs.

Mousse au Chocolat Trop Sucrée. Sweetened chocolate mousse.

Charlotte du Jour. Hot fruit pudding with seasonal fruit.

Gratin de Poire au Pralin. Pears browned in a custard sauce coated with almond caramel.

Wine

House Bordeaux (Carafe).

À L'IMPASSE (CHEZ ROBERT)

M. André Collard

ADDRESS: 4, Impasse Guéménée, 75004
CLOSED: Sat. lunch, Sun., Mon. eve. and August
PRICE RANGE: Moderate
TEL: 42-72-08-45
METRO: Saint-Paul or Bastille
CREDIT: Visa

A small, unostentatious family bistro with a most imaginative and refined menu reflecting the best of the market and the season. The clientele is a mix of chic Parisian regulars and American tourists. Reservations are advised in the evening.

Chez Robert is very much a family affair with all the Collards dividing their efforts. "Deedee" is in the kitchen, "Papa" is at the bar and Robert and his wife welcome and serve their guests with unfailing charm. The simple dining room has the look of a hospitable country inn with stone walls, tile floors, wrought-iron sconces, ladderback chairs with rush seats and wooden tables freshly set with white linen. In an adjacent room there are a few more tables and a wooden bar. Considering the remarkably high quality of the food, the prices are quite reasonable. *Blanquette de veau* (veal stew in cream sauce), *chou farci* (stuffed cabbage) and *civet de lapin* (rabbit stewed in wine) are marked as specialties, but everything is good. Among the dozen appetizers are a *terrine* of skate with mint, gazpacho and fresh salmon marinated in dill and lemon. Stuffed fillets of chicken and duck in a bilberry and vinegar sauce make an outstanding main course. The fish, always fresh, are simply prepared but flavorful. There are several desserts, but the tarte-Tatin (an upside-down caramelized apple tart, native to the Sologne region and reputedly named for the two sisters who invented it) is delicious.

RECOMMENDED DISHES

Terrine de Girolles. Mushroom mousse served cold.
Terrine de Lapin en Gelée aux Concombres. Rabbit pâté in a wine-vinegar aspic with cucumbers.

Foie Gras Frais de Canard en Terrine, Maison. Fresh duck liver pâté served in a *terrine.*

Filet de Cabillaud Sur Compotée de Tomate à l'Huile d'Olive et au Basilic. Fresh cod fillet on a bed of stewed tomatoes in olive oil and basil.

Pavé de Volaille aux Myrtilles. Breast of duck and stuffed chicken breasts in a bilberry (similar to blueberry) sauce.

Civet de Lapin. Rich rabbit stew.

Blanquette de Veau à l'Ancienne. Veal stew in a white sauce of cream and egg yolks served with white rice.

Chou Farci. Stuffed cabbage.

Tournedos de Veau à la Crème de Ciboulette. Veal steaks, stuffed with baby vegetables and foie gras, served in a chive-seasoned cream sauce.

Île Flottante à la Fleur d'Oranger. Orange meringue floating in vanilla cream custard.

Tarte-Tatin. Very generous upside-down apple pie.

WINE

Château Bellevue-la-Foret, Côtes-de-Frontonnais.

AU GOURMET DE L'ISLE ★ ★

M. Jean-Michel Mestivier

ADDRESS: 42, rue Saint-Louis-en-l'Île, 75004
CLOSED: Mon., Tues. and August
PRICE RANGE: Moderate
TEL: 43-26-79-27
METRO: Pont-Marie
CREDIT: Amex

A very picturesque establishment with a rustic 16th-century dining room and an international clientele. The generous classic dishes are supplemented by a few Auvergnat and Limousin specialties. An interesting selection of "little" country wines is offered at reasonable prices.

M. Jules Bourdeau, a young octagenarian, sold this famous old bistro a few years ago, but nothing has changed since his departure. Reservations are still indispensable; the incomparable *andouillettes "A.A.A.A.A."* are never greasy and still steeped in red wine with pork rinds and served with red beans. The fresh artichokes are accompanied by poached eggs in an herbal sauce, and the *charbonnée de l'Isle* (pork in red wine with bacon, baby onions, croutons and potatoes) is still the winning house specialty. There is now a *prix-fixe* tourist menu at 100F which includes an *entrée,* a main course, salad or cheese, and dessert or ice cream selected from the à la carte menu. The *crème limousine* is a caramel custard in warm chocolate sauce. You will be served by candlelight in a 300-year-old vaulted stone "cave" with hand-hewn beams and tapestries characteristic of the Île-St.-Louis cellars of old.

RECOMMENDED DISHES

Fond d'Artichaut Frais Saint-Louis. Fresh hearts of artichoke in vinaigrette.

Boudin de Campagne Pommes Fruits. Large slicing sausage, grilled and served with apple slices.

Moules Farcies Beurre Échalotes. Stuffed mussels in shallot butter.

Tête de Veau Remoulade. Calf's head in a mustard-mayonnaise sauce with chopped *cornichons* and capers.

Cervelle Beurre Fondu et Pommes Vapeur. Brains in melted butter with steamed vegetables.

Charbonnée de l'Isle au Marcillac (Civet de Porc). Grilled pork stew with bacon and onions in a rich wine sauce. The outstanding specialty of the bistro.

Andouillette (A.A.A.A.A.) Rognons de Coq. Grilled pork sausage served with kidney beans in white sauce.

Pintadeau Grillé aux Lentilles Vertes du Puy. Grilled guinea fowl served with small green lentils.

Poires Cuites au Vin. Pears cooked in red wine.

Profiteroles. Ice-cream-filled pastries covered with melted chocolate.

WINE

Very inexpensive little country wines. Gaillac, Marcillac.

LE MONDE DES CHIMÈRES ★ ★

Mme. Cecile Ibane

ADDRESS: 69, rue Saint-Louis-en-l'Île, 75004
CLOSED: Sun., Mon., holidays and last two weeks in February
PRICE RANGE: Fairly expensive
TEL: 43-54-45-27
METRO: Pont-Marie or Cité
CREDIT: Visa

A most picturesque stone-and-beam bistro installed in a 17th-century maison where the owner, Cécile Ibane, creates splendid bourgeois specialties to the delight of local Saint-Louis residents.

The Monde des Chimères is a well-known address to many Parisians but not to many tourists. Pretty paintings and pleasant lighting brighten the little dining room filled with well-spaced tables and chairs. The cooking is as appealing, with many items not usually found on a classic bistro menu. Chicken roasted with garlic, sliced duck breast with figs and honey, lamb baked with onions and potatoes, skate in sherry vinegar, and *poule-au-pot Henri IV* (so named for Henry of Navarre who has been quoted as saying "I wish that every Sunday my peasants of France may have a 'poule-au-pot'"—a chicken in the pot). There are so many marvelous homemade desserts that it's often hard to know which to choose, but if you have a sweet tooth, try the frosted mandarin oranges—they are a real treat.

RECOMMENDED DISHES

Feuillées d'Escargot à la Crème d'Ail. Snails in garlic cream sauce.
Petit Ragoût de Moules au Pistou. A light mussel stew with basil.
Bouillabaisse Foide en Gelée. Cold jellied fish soup.
Foie Gras de Canard Maison. Fresh duck foie gras.
Terrines de Maison. Various pâtés served in terrines.

Poulet aux Quarante Gousses d'Ail. Chicken roasted with
40 garlic cloves.

Poulet-au-Pot Henry IV. Stuffed chicken poached with vegetables.

Côtes de Mouton Champvallon. Sautéed mutton cutlet.

Brandade de Morue. Creamed salt cod.

Veau Braisé à l'Estragon. Braised veal with tarragon.

Magret de Canard aux Fruits et au Miel. Grilled, fattened
duck breast with fresh fruit and honey.

Pigeon Rôti à l'Estragon. Roast pigeon with tarragon.

Mandarine Givrée au Coulis Chaud. Frosted mandarin
orange in a thick hot sauce.

Tarte aux Pommes Chaude et à la Cannelle. Hot apple
tart with cinnamon.

Baba au Rhum. Spongy yeast cake steeped in rum syrup
served with a quartered orange.

WINE

Fine selection of little wines from most of the wine regions of
France. Côtes-de-Buzet, Saint-Nicolas-de-Bourgueil, Gamay
de Touraine.

L'OULETTE ★ ★ ★

M. Marcel & Mme. Noelle Baudis

ADDRESS: 38, rue des Tournelles, 75004
CLOSED: Sat., Sun., August 5–21 and December 23–January 2
PRICE RANGE: Moderate
TEL: 42-71-43-33
METRO: Bastille, Chemin Vert or Saint-Paul
CREDIT: Visa

*The rather modest appearance of this tiny establishment belies
what you will find in terms of cuisine, as the owners are en-
thusiasts of food and wine from their native Quercy. The succulent dishes, though basically modern inventions, are
inspired by that region and are so outstanding that reservations must be made days in advance.*

A few years ago l'Oulette was just a little neighborhood bistro, but the cooking was so good that it is now, though still small and modest, one of the best bistros in the city. The decor is very understated. A simple white-painted entrance, with a tiny bar on the right, leads into a narrow room neatly arranged with little tables, white-lacquered bentwood chairs and *art moderne* sconces. Quercy is not fish country, but owner-chef Marcel Baudis prepares wonderful marinated mackerel with tomatoes and basil, freshly marinated sardines, delicious salmon trout with tarragon, hake with artichokes, a *fricassée* of sea trout with lentils and fried squid with potatoes. Main dishes include braised oxtail with foie gras and stuffed tomatoes, beef braised in Cahors wine with carrots, *gras-double* (ox tripe) with saffron, rabbit with chestnuts or saffron rice and roast duckling and *confit* with turnips. Regional desserts, including a walnut ice cream parfait, and wines, such as a nice Cahors, round out the menu.

RECOMMENDED DISHES

Salade Quercynoise. Regional salad with chicken livers, gizzards and walnuts.

Blancs de Sardines Fraîches Marinées. Fresh sardines marinated in white wine.

Escabèche de Calamars aux Pommes de Terre Tièdes. Fried squid served with potatoes.

Croustade de Petits Gris aux Noix. Pastry shell filled with tiny creamed gray snails and walnuts.

Petit Pâté de Canard aux Épices. Duck liver pâté with spices.

Gigotin de Lapin au Riz Safrané. Roasted hind leg of rabbit with saffron rice.

Merlu Rôti à l'Artichaut et aux Épices. Roast hake with artichokes and spices.

Râble de Lièvre aux Châtaignes. Saddle of hare with chestnuts.

Chartreuse de Queue de Boeuf Braisée au Foie Gras en Tomates Farcies. Oxtail braised in Chartreuse liqueur with foie gras and stuffed tomatoes.

Filet de Rascasse aux Pois Gourmands et à l'Anis. Fillet of scorpion fish with a pea purée flavored with anise.

Daube de Boeuf aux Vieux Cahors. Beef braised in Cahors wine with vegetables.

Cassolette de Gras-Double au Safran. Ox tripe baked in a *cassolette* dish with saffron.

Pastis du Quercy aux Pommes et aux Pruneaux.
Exceptional flaky pastry with apples and prunes.
Parfait Glacé aux Noix. Whipped walnut ice cream.
Île Flottante et Crème au Caramel. Meringue topped with
burnt caramel floating in vanilla cream custard.

WINE

Fine selection of Southwest regional wines. Gaillac (*rouge* or
blanc), Côteaux-de-Quercy.

LE TRUMILOU

M. Jean-Claude Dumond
Chef: Raymond

ADDRESS: 84, Quai de l'Hôtel-de-Ville, 75004
CLOSED: Monday
PRICE RANGE: Moderate
TEL: 42-77-63-98
METRO: Pont-Marie or Hotel-de-Ville
CREDIT: None

*There is an old-time Parisian atmosphere in this delightful
quayside bistro offering generous helpings of very good home
cooking at reasonable prices. Request a window table with a
view of the Seine and Notre-Dame. The sidewalk tables are
not recommended because of the traffic.*

Located on the *quai* between the Pont d'Arcole and the Pont
Louis-Philippe, Trumilou is a pleasant spot for a homespun
meal. It is a rather large place with three dining rooms. Two
are rustic in decor. The larger of these, crowded with tables
and decorated with bucolic scenes, is less cozy than the
smaller of the two, which is simply outfitted with banquettes, a
crystal chandelier and fresh flowers. The third is a no-frills bar
with a pinball machine. No matter where you eat, opt for one
of the *prix-fixe* menus. The most expensive one offers a good
choice of *entrées*, including pâté, herring, sausages and a deli-

cious *salade Niçoise*. Poultry is a specialty, so there are several excellent selections. A delicious *poulet Provençal* (chicken in tomato sauce) and roast guinea fowl with sautéed potatoes can be recommended. Sautéed lamb is another good choice. In addition to these, the à la carte menu lists three or four fish dishes. Desserts are typical, but the Cantal cheese and coffee ice cream are excellent.

RECOMMENDED DISHES

Filets de Hareng. Marinated herring fillets.

Assiette de Cochonnailles. Platter of assorted pork products (*saucisson, rillettes, pâté*).

Moules Marinière. Mussels cooked with wine wine, shallots and parsley.

Crudités. Lavish helpings of fresh raw vegetables.

Pot-au-Feu (Avec Os à Moelle et Légumes). Boiled beef with marrow bones, vegetables and broth.

Étouffade de Boeuf. Beef casserole with vegetables in a wine sauce.

Piperade. Scrambled egg omelette with tomatoes, peppers and onions.

Poulet Provençal. Roast chicken with onions, garlic and tomatoes.

Canard aux Pruneaux. Grilled duck with prunes.

Ris de Veau Grandmère. Sweetbreads cooked with onions, mushrooms and potatoes.

Sauté d'Agneau. Sautéed lamb.

Gigot d'Agneau, Haricots Blancs. Roast leg of lamb with white beans.

Gâteau de Riz Avec Un Sabayon. Rice pudding with fruit *confit*, in an egg-yolk-and-wine mixture.

Pêche Melba. Cold peaches served on ice cream with raspberry purée.

WINE

Saint-Pourcain, Saumur Champigny.

5^e

MOISSONIER

AU MOULIN À VENT (CHEZ HENRI)

PERRAUDIN

CHEZ RENÉ

LA RÔTISSERIE DU BEAUJOLAIS

CHEZ TOUTOUNE

5ᵉ *Arrondissement*

QUARTIER LATIN–PANTHÉON

PLACES OF INTEREST:

Boulevard Saint-Michel (Place St.-Michel)
Églises de Saint-Séverin, Saint Étienne-du-Mont, St. Médard
et St. Julien-le-Pauvre
Église du Val-de-Grâce
Hôtel le Brun
Institut du Monde Arabe
Le Jardin des Plantes et Muséum National d'Histoire
Naturelle
La Mosquée de Paris (The Paris Mosque)
Musée de l'École Superieure des Beaux-Arts
Musée de Sculpture en Plein Air
Musée des Thermes et l'Hôtel de Cluny (The Cluny Museum)
Le Panthéon
Quai de la Tournelle
Rue Mouffetard and Place de la Contrescarpe
La Sorbonne

MOISSONNIER ★ ★

M. Louis Moissonnier

ADDRESS: 28, rue des Fossés-Saint-Bernard, 75005
CLOSED: Sun. eve, Mon. and August
PRICE RANGE: Fairly expensive
TEL: 43-29-87-65
METRO: Cardinal-Lemoine or Jussieu
CREDIT: None

Widely known, very popular, family-run bistro with down-to-earth, substantial, old-fashioned food inspired by Lyonnaise cuisine.

Appearing in every guidebook and "best" list, Moissonnier is well known for its copious portions of partly Lyonnaise, partly traditional food. A large menu (the one in English is not as complete as the one in French) begins with *les saladiers Lyonnais* at 50F per person. The *saladier* is a rolling cart of hors d'oeuvres consisting of large bowls of lentils, kidney beans, pickled calf's feet, sausages, *museau* (beef brawn), red cabbage, herring, *rillettes, rosettes,* white sausages and cold beef in salad. Following this, a long list of choices includes such favorites as beef with a sweet onion sauce (*boeuf miroton*), grilled pigs' feet with red kidney beans, tripe, steak, salt pork with lentils, chicken in raspberry vinegar and several freshly made desserts. The atmosphere downstairs is gay with a typical bistro ambience and decor: a zinc bar at the entrance, elbow-to-elbow tables, little chairs, banquettes, fresh flowers and pleasant lighting. Upstairs is hot, noisy and smoky, decorated with tacky fake-white-brick walls, wine kegs, and bright lights. Don't expect fabulous food, but you will certainly eat well in picturesque surroundings.

RECOMMENDED DISHES

Saladiers Lyonnais. Choice of a dozen fish, meat and vegetable salads brought to the table in large bowls.
Rosette de Lyon. Large dry pork sausage, sliced and eaten cold.

Saucisson Chaud Pommes à l'Huile. Hot Lyon sausage with sliced potatoes in oil.

Oeufs en Meurette. Poached eggs in red-wine sauce.

Quenelles de Brochet. Pike dumplings in cream sauce.

Pieds de Porc Panés, Grillés aux Haricots Rouges. Grilled breaded pigs' feet with red kidney beans.

Boeuf Miroton. Slices of beef in broth with onions and mustard.

Gras-Double Sauté Lyonnaise. Ox tripe sliced and fried with onions, vinegar and parsley.

Tablier de Sapeur Sauce Gribiche. Breaded ox tripe served with spicy mayonnaise sauce.

Andouillette au Vin Blanc et Échalotes. Grilled pork sausage with white wine.

Boudin Noir. Large grilled blood sausage.

Mousse au Chocolat aux Zestes d'Oranges. Chocolate mousse with orange rind.

Gâteau de Riz. Rice pudding.

WINE

Wines available by the pitcher: Macon Villages Blanc, Arbois Blanc, Saint-Nicolas-de-Bourgueil, Brouilly, Morgon, Arbois Rouge.

CHEZ HENRI (AU MOULIN À VENT) ★ ★

❧

M. Gerard & Mme. Josette Gelaude

ADDRESS: 20, rue des Fosses-Saint-Bernard, 75005

CLOSED: Sun., Mon. and August

PRICE RANGE: Fairly expensive

TEL: 43-54-99-37

METRO: Cardinal-Lemoine or Jussieu

CREDIT: Visa

An authentic old-time neighborhood wine bistro specializing in beef and Beaujolais. It is widely known and very popular, so reservations are suggested.

The mill which gives this restaurant its name stands on one of the rolling hills of the Beaujolais vineyards. Moulin-à-Vent, a deeply colored red wine, is the most prestigious of the crus from the region. At Chez Henri the wine-bar decor hasn't been changed in years and the original zinc counter still sports little half-barrel wine kegs to match the half-barrel overhead lights. The handwritten *carte,* with specials marked in red, begins with a few salads, Burgundy snails, foie gras, many sausages including a selection from the Ardèche and the famous house Provençal frogs' legs. Huge cuts of steak and a hefty *boeuf bourguignon* are the favored main courses, but there are also a few veal, duck and lamb selections. Desserts like *tarte-Tatin,* chocolate *charlotte* and *île flottante* are typical, but the prunes stewed in Armagnac are special and a fruity Berthillon sherbet is always refreshing.

RECOMMENDED DISHES

Foie Gras de Canard Maison. Fresh duck foie gras.

Andouillette Grillée au Vin Blanc. Pork sausage grilled with white wine.

Escargots de Bourgogne. Vineyard snails in garlic butter.

Jambonnette de l'Ardéche, Pommes à l'Huile. Dried salt pork sausage shaped like a ham, served with sliced potatoes in oil.

Grenouilles Fraîches Sautées à la Provençale (October to May). Sautéed frogs' legs with tomatoes, garlic and onions.

Coquilles St.-Jacques Fraîches à la Provençale (October to May). Scallops sautéed with tomatoes, garlic and onions.

Boeuf Bourguignon. Beef stewed in red wine with onions and mushrooms.

Le Boeuf Saignant "Dit à la Ficelle." Beef lightly roasted, then tied with string and lowered into simmering broth. Served rare.

Côte de Boeuf Bourguignonne (for two). Roast ribs of beef.

Châteaubriand, Entrecôte, Faux-Filet. Several outstanding varieties of superb-quality beef cuts.

Tarte-Tatin Chaude. Upside-down apple pie served hot.

Gâteau de Riz Crème à l'Anglaise. Rice pudding in vanilla custard sauce.

WINE

Vast selection of top-quality Beaujolais. St.-Amour.

PERRAUDIN

M. Hubert Gloaguen
Mme. Marie-Christine Kvella

ADDRESS: 157, rue Saint-Jacques, 75005
CLOSED: Sun. evening
PRICE RANGE: Inexpensive
TEL: 46-33-15-75
METRO: Luxembourg or Odéon
CREDIT: None

Simple good-quality food in an authentic bistro atmosphere frequented by a mixed clientele of regulars, tourists and yuppies. Sunday brunch is served, after which you may choose to walk up to the Panthéon where such notables as Victor Hugo, Louis Braille and Zola are laid to rest.

Herbert Gloaguen, the new *patron* (who also owns Bistrot d'André in the 15e), and his sister, Marie-Christine Kvella, continue to run this popular old Sorbonne haunt in the style of the past. An old barroom with bistro brownish-red-and-cream walls, dark wood and tile floor is brightened by mirrors, posters and lace doilies draped over hanging lights. The large zinc bar is adorned with fresh flowers and the tables set with red-and-white cloths covered with paper. *Entrées,* which include salads, eggs, ham, quiches and soup, range in the evening from 16F to 25F unless you choose a dozen very good Burgundy snails. The *plats* from 45F to 60F include simple meats, sausages, poultry and poached salmon. A salad, string beans or *frites* are extra, and *crème fraîche,* for a supplement of 5F, is a nice accompaniment to the typical desserts. A *dégustation* menu of wines keeps the bar busy and the 68F Sunday brunch menu includes fresh-squeezed juice, toast, bacon, pancakes and eggs.

RECOMMENDED DISHES

Escargots Vrais de Bourgogne. Vineyard snails in garlic butter.

Quiche Lorraine de Mamie. Custard tart with bacon, eggs and cream.

Rollmops et sa Crème Fouettée et Citronnée. Marinated, rolled herring fillets with thick cream.

Gigot d'Agneau et Gratin Dauphinois. Roast leg of lamb with sliced potatoes, baked in cream and browned on top.

Navarin. Lamb stew.

Boeuf Bourguignon à l'Ancienne. Beef stewed in red wine with onions and mushrooms.

Petit Salé. Lightly salted cooked pork.

Andouillette de Vouvray, Sauce Moutarde et Pommes Frites. Grilled pork sausage with Vouvray wine served in a mustard sauce with french fries.

Compote de Pommes du Jardin. Stewed apples.

Crème Caramel à l'Orange. Vanilla-and-orange-flavored flan.

WINE

Cahors de Domaine, Saint Amour, Sauvignon Blanc.

CHEZ RENÉ ★ ★ ★

M. Jean-Paul & Mme. Jacqueline Cinquin

ADDRESS: 14, blvd. Saint-Germain, 75005

CLOSED: Sat., Sun., August and Christmas week

PRICE RANGE: Moderate

TEL: 43-54-30-23

METRO: Cardinal-Lemoine

CREDIT: None

A steady clientele frequents this unpretentious old bistro which has been serving copious portions of straightforward Burgundian specialties and wine for decades.

On warm nights a few sidewalk tables are set under the light-blue awning of Chez René, which spans the corner at Blvd. Saint-Germain and Quai Saint-Bernard. The atmosphere is engaging as waiters in long aprons open bottles of the house Chénas and Juliénas to accompany hearty portions of parslied ham, burgundian snails, frogs' legs, pike dumplings, eggs in red-wine sauce, hot sausages, red meats, beef stews, *coq-au-vin* and an excellent steak in *Bercy* butter with *frites*. There are brass rails above the moleskin banquettes, simple wooden bistro chairs and tables, each set with a pepper mill and mustard jar, scattered about the linoleum floors of the unpretentious dining room. Prints, posters and paintings add a cheerful note to the darkening cream-colored walls. A small bar faces the entrance and the owners are always ready with a warm and friendly welcome.

RECOMMENDED DISHES

PLATS DU JOUR

Pot-au-Feu (Mondays). Boiled beef with vegetables and broth.

Haricot de Mouton (Tuesdays). Mutton stew with white beans.

Gras-Double (Wednesdays). Ox tripe, sliced and fried with onions, vinegar and parsley.

Boeuf à la Mode (Thursdays). Braised beef simmered in red wine with vegetables.

Blanquette de Veau (Fridays). Veal stew in white cream sauce, served with white rice.

Assiette de Cochonnailles. Assorted pork products.

Saucisson Chaud Pommes à l'Huile. Hot sausage with sliced potatoes in oil.

Quenelles de Brochet à la Crème. Pike dumplings in butter cream sauce.

Coq au Vin. Chicken stewed in red wine with onions and mushrooms.

Cuisses de Grenouilles à la Provençale. Sautéed frogs' legs with tomatoes, garlic and onions.

Boeuf Bourguignon. Beef stewed in red Burgundy wine with onions and mushrooms. The outstanding specialty of the bistro.

Entrecôte Bercy Pommes Sautées. Sautéed rib steak in a shallot-and-bone-marrow sauce served with sautéed potatoes.

Andouillette au Pouilly. Grilled pork sausage in white Burgundy wine.

Crème Caramel. Vanilla-flavored flan.

Gâteau de Riz Maison. Rice pudding with fruit *confit.*

Mousse au Chocolat. Chocolate mousse.

Extensive selection of first-rate Beaujolais. Chénas, Juliénas.

LA RÔTISSERIE DU BEAUJOLAIS ★ ★

M. Alain Robert

ADDRESS: 19, Quai de la Tournelle, 75005
CLOSED: Mon. and Tues. lunch
PRICE RANGE: Moderate
TEL: 43-54-17-47
METRO: Maubert-Mutualité or Cardinal-Lemoine
CREDIT: Visa

Run by Alain Robert, but the brainchild of Claude Terrail, this stylish new bistro is located across the street from its most famous sister, La Tour d'Argent, and has developed a winning formula: a splendid list of Beaujolais wines, a small menu of well-prepared Lyonnais sausages and enticing rotisserie meats and poultry, all at very good prices.

Whether you choose a sidewalk table with a view of Notre-Dame, the bar room to the left of the entrance or the dining room to the right, you will need to book ahead as this popular spot is usually filled with an upscale crowd. Begin with the house *kir* made with Macon wine and select one of the daily specials listed on a large blackboard. You will find things like roast pigeon or quail, veal chops, saddle of lamb, grilled Lyonnais sausages or chicken stewed in Beaujolais wine. Fresh cheese and delicious fruit tarts are also enjoyable.

RECOMMENDED DISHES

Saucisson Chaud, Beurre. Little hot sausages served with
  sliced potatoes in oil and bread and butter.
Foie Gras de Canard. Fresh duck foie gras.
Filets de Hareng, Pommes à l'Huile. Marinated herring
  fillets accompanied by potatoes in oil.

Caille Rôti. Quail roasted on the spit.

Pigeonneau de la Bresse aux Petits Pois. Bresse squab roasted on the spit and served with tiny peas.

Piece d'Agneau Rôti. Lamb roasted on the spit.

Andouillette Grillée (A.A.A.A.A.) Sauce Moutarde. Grilled pork sausage with mustard sauce.

Sabodet Rôti au Beaujolais. Grilled pigs'-head sausage from the top-rated House of Bobosse, served hot in slices.

Coq-au-Vin du Beaujolais. Chicken stewed in Beaujolais wine with onions and mushrooms.

Filet de Dorade en Bouillabaise. Fillet of red sea bream in a hearty Provençal fish soup.

Crème Caramel. Vanilla-flavored flan.

Mousse au Chocolat. Chocolate mousse.

Savarin aux Fruits. Cake ring drenched with brandy and filled with fruits.

WINE

Featuring all the Duboeuf Beaujolais crus.

CHEZ TOUTONE ★ ★

Mme. Colette Dejean
Chef: Jean-Louis Huclin

ADDRESS: 5, rue de Pontoise, 75005
CLOSED: Sun. and Aug. 5–Sept. 5
PRICE RANGE: Moderate
TEL: 43-26-56-81
METRO: Maubert-Mutualité
CREDIT: Visa and MasterCard

A small, crowded, cheerful little bistro serving giant-sized portions of country-style cuisine with a light Provençal touch. Everything is freshly prepared, and based on market availability.

Mme. Colette Dejean, better known as "Toutone," has created a landmark in the 5ᵉ *arrondissement* with her popular canteen-like restaurant and home-style cooking. There are no reservations accepted, but regulars line up to claim one of the 50 or so places in the brightly lit dining room crowded with tables. Eclectic artwork and posters decorate the white-plaster walls along with café curtains, a blackboard menu, red-and-white cloths and napkins providing a young and gay ambience. The *prix-fixe* menu begins with a large *soupière* steaming with the soup of the day (all you can eat) followed by a large choice of *entrées*, including a superb duck *terrine*. Main courses of beef, lamb, veal, rabbit, tripe and duck are accompanied by freshly baked baguettes and fresh noodles. There is a takeout shop, Toutone Gourmande, located at 7, Rue de Pontoise, carrying many of her best products.

RECOMMENDED DISHES

Soupière Chaude ou Froide. Warm or cold soup tureen.
Pain de Cervelle Sauce Grelette. Calf's-brain loaf served with a cold whipped-cream sauce.
Bulots à l'Aïoli. Sea snails with garlic mayonnaise.
Quiche aux Poireaux. Custard tart with leeks.
Pieds de Veau aux Lentilles. Grilled stuffed calf's foot served on a *beignet* (fritter) with lentils.
Estouffade Provençale. Meat stewed in a sealed pot with tomatoes, garlic and *aubergines* (eggplant).
Agneau de Pré Salé au Gratin Dauphinois. Roast leg of lamb (pastured in salt fields) served with sliced potatoes cooked in cream and browned on top.
Tête de Veau aux Légumes Vinaigrette aux Herbs. Calf's head served hot with baby vegetables in vinaigrette.
Andouillette. Superb-quality grilled pork sausage.
Pièce du Boucher à l'Échalote. Marinated braised rump of beef with shallot sauce.
Feuilletée de Pommes Tièdes. Hot apple puff pastry.
Mousse au Chocolat. Chocolate mousse.
Soufflé au Chocolat. Chocolate soufflé.

WINE

Minervois, Sancerre, Gamay Rouge de Touraine.

6ᵉ

ALLARD

LE BISTROT D'HENRI

LA CAFETIÈRE

LE CAMÉLÉON

AUX CHARPENTIERS

LA FOUX

JOSÉPHINE (CHEZ DUMONET)

LA LOZÈRE

CHEZ MAÎTRE PAUL

LE PETIT ZINC

POLIDOR

6e Arrondissement

SAINT-GERMAIN–LUXEMBOURG

PLACES OF INTEREST

Boulevard Saint-Germain, Place St.-Germain, and the
Église Saint-Germain-des-Prés
École des Beaux-Arts and *l'Hôtel de Conti*
Église Saint-Sulpice (*Delacroix* mural)
Fontaine des Medicis
Hôtel des Monnaies (the mint)
Institut de France
Jardin et Palais du Luxembourg (Musée Luxembourg)
Musée de la Poste
Musée Zadkine
Place Furstenberg (Atelier Eugène Delacroix)
Place de l'Odéon
Quais Malaquais-de-Conti and *Grands-Augustins*
Rue de Rennes
Rues de Seines, St.-Andres-des-Arts, Buci, Jacob

ALLARD ★ ★ ★

M. Bernard Bouchard

ADDRESS: 41, rue Saint-André-des-Arts, 75006
CLOSED: Sat., Sun., August and December 23–January 1
PRICE RANGE: Expensive
TEL: 43-26-48-23
METRO: Saint-Michel
CREDIT: Amex, Visa, Diners and MasterCard

One of Paris' most famous bistros, situated on one of the most colorful corners in the Latin Quarter. Good classic cooking with an accent on Burgundian specialties and wine. The entrance is located at 1, rue de l'Éperon.

Allard is still one of the most congenial bistros on the Left Bank. Established in 1931, it was the first of its kind to gain international fame. A few years ago it lost a *Michelin* star and its reputation began to slip. Happily, the new owner has lavished attention on the decor and the cuisine. He has spruced up the two small period dining rooms, the old floors, the tin ceilings, the open kitchen and the zinc bar. The menu, which is still written in purple ink, retains the famous old Allard specialties. Generous portions of country ham, sausages, snails, foie gras, frogs' legs, Toulousian-style *cassoulet,* veal stew and the delicious duck with olives washed down with the house Brouilly, are still the house favorites.

RECOMMENDED DISHES

Jambon Persillé. Parslied ham in aspic.
Cochonnailes. Selected pork products, sausages, *fromage de tête,* etc.
Escargots de Bourgogne. Vineyard snails in garlic butter.
Pintade aux Lentilles (for two). Roast guinea foul with lentils.
Boeuf à la Mode (Mondays). Beef braised in red wine with carrots.
Canard aux Navets/Olives (for two). Duck with turnips, in

the spring, and with olives during the rest of the year. The outstanding specialty of the bistro.

Sole Meunière. Fillet of sole, coated with flour, fried and served with brown butter.

Poissons au Beurre Blanc (Coquilles Saint-Jacques ou Turbot). Scallops or turbot in a white-wine butter sauce.

Cassoulet Toulousain. White-bean-and-meat casserole with sausage, pork and goose.

Gras-Double. Ox tripe, sliced and fried with onions, vinegar and parsley.

Petit Salé aux Lentilles. Lightly salted cooked pork with lentils.

Navarin aux Pommes (Fridays). Lamb stew with potatoes and onions.

Coq-au-Vin (Wednesdays). Chicken stewed in red wine with onions and mushrooms.

Charlotte au Chocolat. Baked custard pudding on molded bread filled with chocolate.

Tarte-Tatin. Upside-down apple pie.

WINE

Sancerre, Meursault, Hermitage, Pouilly.

LE BISTROT D'HENRI ★

M. Henri Poulat

ADDRESS: 16, rue Princesse, 75006
CLOSED: Sunday
PRICE RANGE: Moderate
TEL: 46-33-51-12
METRO: Mabillon
CREDIT: Amex, Visa, Diners and MasterCard

A modest place with no sign on the white facade to indicate its presence. The atmosphere is relaxed and the cuisine skillfully prepared by owner-chef M. Henri Poulat.

This bright restaurant on pretty little Rue Princess is very much a neighborhood favorite. Crowded tables fill the tiny dining room, gaily decorated with an amusing modern fresco. A long window in the rear opens onto the kitchen and a small bar serves as a waiter's station and cashier's desk. The *carte,* written on file cards, lists about a half-dozen *entrées* and eight main courses. The *entrées* include hot goat cheese salad, mozzarella with tomatoes, country ham, *terrine* and Coréze sausage. The next line on the *carte* reads *GRATIN DAUPHINOIS avec: romsteck* followed by calf's liver with onions, duck with peaches, free-range chicken in vinegar sauce and a lamb stew Moroccan-style. Desserts change each day, but there is always *patisserie* and a splendid fruit compote.

RECOMMENDED DISHES

Assiette de Jambon de Campagne. Platter of cured and smoked country ham.

Os à Moelle. Bone marrow spread, served with toasted slabs of country bread.

Saucisse Sèche de Corrèze. Poached country sausage.

Pavé de Coeur de Romsteck Avec Gratin Dauphinoise. Thick piece of grilled rumpsteak served with sliced potatoes baked in cream and browned on top.

Foie de Veau Confiture d'Oignons. Grilled calf's liver on a bed of onion preserves.

Gigot Rôti au Four. Roast leg of lamb.

Veritable Poulet Fermier au Vinaigre. Roast free-range chicken in a vinegar sauce.

Rognons de Veau de Lait Nature. Grilled lamb kidneys.

Crème Caramel. Vanilla-flavored flan.

Compote Grandmère. Stewed apples and pears.

Mousse au Chocolat. Chocolate mousse.

WINE

Saumur-Champigny, Beaujolais.

LA CAFETIÈRE ★ ★ ★

M. Louis Diet
M. Jean Romestant

ADDRESS: 21, rue Mazarine, 75006
OPEN: Daily
PRICE RANGE: Fairly expensive
TEL: 46-33-76-90
METRO: Odéon, Mabillon or Pont-Neuf
CREDIT: Visa and MasterCard

The quality of the cuisine is as remarkable as the collection of coffee pots scattered about this sophisticated spot where chic customers enjoy refined food, champagne by the carafe and chocolate mousse served in a huge soup tureen.

The name means "The Coffee Pot" and the place lives up to it by displaying coffee pots collected over the 25 years this charming restaurant has been in business. Two cozy, dimly lit dining rooms with Provençal wallpaper and simple wooden chairs and tables provide a nostalgic setting where you will enjoy such delights as brioche with beef marrow, eggs with truffles, lentils with shallots, marinated mushrooms, gazpacho, cold salmon, grilled sausage, chicken in hot sauce, red mullet with anchovy butter, fillet of beef with a sauce made of Meaux mustard and fresh vegetables in season. Reserve a table on the ground floor for dinner at 8 after gallery-hopping and a relaxing apéritif at one of the neighborhood's famous cafés.

RECOMMENDED DISHES

Plats du Jour. Specialties of the day are determined by the availability of meats and vegetables in the produce markets.

Langue de Boeuf Sauce Piquante (Plat du Jour). Beef tongue in hot sauce.

Canard aux Olives (Plat du Jour). Duck with olives.

Petit Salé aux Lentilles (Plat du Jour). Lightly salted cooked pork with lentils.

Boudins aux Pommes (Plat du Jour). Grilled blood sausage with fried apples.

Pot-au-Feu (Plat du Jour). Boiled beef with vegetables and beef broth.

Sauté d'Agneau (Plat du Jour). Pan-fried lamb.

Concombres à la Crème. Sliced cucumbers in a delicious cream sauce.

Moules Marinière. Mussels cooked with white wine, shallots and herbs.

Oeufs en Meurette. Poached egg in red-wine sauce.

Moelle de Boeuf en Brioche. Bone marrow spread in a rich, buttery bun.

Rougets Grillés Beurre d'Anchois. Grilled red mullet in anchovy butter.

Andouillette au Muscadet. Pork sausage cooked in white Loire wine accompanied by french fries.

Côte de Veau au Citron. Grilled veal chop with lemon.

Carré d'Agneau Rôti au Tomates à la Provençale (for two). Roast rack of lamb with cooked tomatoes Provence-style.

Mousse au Chocolat "Cafetière." Chocolate mousse.

Oeufs à la Neige. Poached egg whites (meringue) in vanilla custard sauce.

Tarte aux Pommes. Apple tart.

Charlotte au Melon. Baked custard pudding on molded bread with melon.

WINE

Champagne en Carafe, Sancerre, Brouilly, Saint-Nicolas-de-Bourgueil, Chinon, Graves, Côtes-du-Rhône.

LE CAMÉLÉON ★ ★

M. Raymond Faucher

ADDRESS: 6, rue de Chevreuse, 75006

CLOSED: Sun., Mon. and August

PRICE RANGE: Moderate

TEL: 43-20-63-43

METRO: Vavin

CREDIT: None

The cuisine is basically bistro, but every item on the menu is prepared with originality and imagination. Listen to the owner's advice before ordering one of the Loire wines.

A bar, old-fashioned flowery wallpaper, multicolored tile floors, marble tables, high-backed wooden booths, brass wall lights, pastel drawings and dozens of photographs provide a vibrant setting for some interesting food. Both traditional and more inventive dishes are prepared by chef Thierry Thibault. Fresh pâté, poached oysters in a red-wine butter sauce with mushrooms and a superb shredded oxtail salad with chicory are some of the marvelous starters.

Salt cod is a specialty and served in several ways: cold in a vinaigrette, *à la Provençale* with a bold *aoïli*, or simply with a fresh-tomato-and-herb sauce. There is duck *confit* with roasted potatoes and sorrel sauce, veal in tomato sauce with noodles and breast of chicken with a sweet and sharp green-pepper sauce. Everything is done with a certain flair. Desserts are delicious and, if it's on the menu, you might like to try the tea soufflé in a cool mint sauce.

Recommended Dishes

Salade de Queue de Boeuf Tiède. Shredded oxtail salad. One of the specialties of the bistro.

Cochonnailles. Selection of first-quality pork products.

Pâté de Campagne. Coarse country pâté.

Frisée aux Lardons. Chicory salad with bacon.

Tendron de Veau aux Pâtes Fraîches. Stew made from the cartilage-filled rib meat of veal, accompanied by fresh pasta. The other outstanding specialty of the bistro.

Boeuf en Daube. Beef braised in red wine with vegetables, slow simmered and served in an earthenware pot.

Morue Provençale en Aïoli. Creamed salt cod with garlic mayonnaise.

Foie de Canard Maison au Bonnezeaux. Duck livers cooked in a sweet white wine from Anjou.

Bavette du Boucher. Skirt steak served butcher's style with bone marrow.

Crème Caramel. Vanilla-flavored flan.

Mousse au Chocolat Blanc. White-chocolate mousse.

Tarte-Tatin. Upside-down apple pie.

Wine

Saumur-Champigny, Sancerre, Chinon.

AUX CHARPENTIERS ★ ★

M. Pierre Bardèche

ADDRESS: 10, rue Mabillon, 75006
CLOSED: Sun. and between Christmas and New Year's
PRICE RANGE: Moderate
TEL: 43-26-30-05
METRO: Mabillon, St.-Sulpice or St.-Germain-des-Prés
CREDIT: Amex, Visa, Diners and MasterCard

Historically a carpenters' canteen, today a b.c.b.g.("bon chic, bon genre"—i.e. Yuppie) hangout, but still serving solid plates of bourgeois cuisine with an emphasis on meat. Drinks are dispensed from behind the long old-fashioned zinc bar in authentic bistro style.

Aux Charpentiers is one of the best-known and popular Saint-Germain-des-Prés bistros with a long and colorful history. The carpenters for which it is named formed an organization of "companions" dating back to the medieval guilds. The members—master carpenters and cabinetmakers—made the restaurant their rendezvous. Today there is no trace of them left in the area except in the two large dining rooms here, which are decorated with prints and photographs commemorating those days. Located steps away from the lovely Square and Church of St.-Sulpice, the bistro continues to thrive, serving the traditional *plats du jour* for which it is famous. With a few new salads, *ratatouille* and gazpacho added to the *entrées,* and only one or two fish specialties, the *carte* offers basic, uncomplicated food with good, but rather expensive, wine.

RECOMMENDED DISHES

PLATS DU JOUR
Sauté de Veau (Mondays). Pan-fried veal.
Boeuf Mode aux Carrottes (Tuesdays). Braised beef simmered in red wine with carrots.
Petit Salé aux Lentilles (Wednesdays). Lightly salted cooked pork.

Jarret de Veau et Ses Legumes (Thursdays). Veal knuckle served with a garnish of vegetables.

Aïoli de Morue et Ses Legumes (Fridays). Creamed salt cod with garlic mayonnaise and vegetables.

Chou Farci Campagnard (Saturdays). Stuffed cabbage.

Fromage de Tête aux Echalotes. Headcheese with shallot sauce.

Salade de Chèvre Chaud. Hot-goat-cheese salad.

Foie Gras de Canard Frais Maison et Son Verre de Sauternes. Fresh duck foie gras accompanied by a glass of Sauternes.

Boeuf à la Ficelle. Beef, slightly roasted, tied with a string and lowered to poach in broth with vegetables.

Boeuf en Daube. Braised beef with vegetables slow-simmered and served in an earthenware pot.

Pied de Porc Ste. Ménéhould. Pigs' feet grilled in breadcrumbs.

Côtes de Boeuf (for two). Roast ribs of beef.

Andouillette de Troyes à la Ficelle. Poached pork sausage.

Boudin. Large blood sausage.

Caneton Rôti, Sauce Olives et Porto. Roast duckling in a port-wine sauce with olives.

Mousse au Chocolat. Chocolate mousse.

Tarte Pralinée aux Poires. Pear tart with almonds.

WINE

Vins de Bordeaux, Côtes-du-Rhône, Vins de Loire.

LA FOUX ★ ★ ★

M. Alex Guini

ADDRESS: 2, rue Clément, 75006
CLOSED: Sun., Mon. lunch and holidays
PRICE RANGE: Fairly expensive
TEL: 43-54-09-53
METRO: Mabillon or Odéon
CREDIT: Amex, Visa, Diners and MasterCard

One of the most likeable places of the Saint-Germain quarter, with a modern decor and an easygoing, comfortable atmosphere created by patron *Alex Guini, who comes from Lyon, and his charming wife Simone, who is Niçoise. The menu reflects both regions, but the daily specials are always from among Alex's own recipes.*

Saturday lunch at "Chez Alex" has become a tradition. The elegant table linen and crystal are replaced with oilcloths and water tumblers in preparation for a unique meal. In the summer it's a Niçoise luncheon with *pissaladière,* an onion-and-olive pizza, *salade Niçoise,* and stuffed vegetables (onions, eggplant, peppers and tomatoes) from the Comté de Nice. During the winter a Lyonnais *mâchon* (brunch) is presented with sausages, *pied de mouton,* cold trotters in a pickle sauce, pork shoulder with chopped cabbage, hot salmon and a ripe selection of regional goat cheeses.

RECOMMENDED DISHES

Rosette de Lyon. Large, dry pork sausage sliced and eaten cold.

Soupe au Pistou. Provençal vegetable soup with basil.

Brouillade aux Truffes. Scrambled eggs with truffles.

Pieds de Mouton, Rémoulade. Sheep's feet in a mustard mayonnaise with chopped *cornichons* and capers.

Tripes à la Niçoise. Tripe cooked with white wine, onions, carrots and garlic.

Tablier de Sapeur. Ox tripe, sliced and fried with onions, vinegar and parsley.

Pot-au-Feu d'Alex (Wednesdays). Boiled beef with vegetables in a unique recipe from the chef's grandmother.

Andouillette de Fleury. Poached pork sausage in mustard sauce.

Quenelles de Brochet. Pike dumplings in cream sauce.

Poulard de Bresse (Tuesdays). Free-range Bresse chicken wrapped in a pig's bladder and cooked in bouillon.

Bavarois aux Fruits. A molded bavarian cream with fresh fruit.

Mousse au Chocolat. Chocolate mousse.

WINE

Brouilly Maison, St.-Joseph, Fleury, Medoc (Bordeaux) wines.

JOSÉPHINE (CHEZ DUMONET) ★ ★ ★ ★

M. Jean Dumonet
Chef: Marc Amory

ADDRESS: 117, rue du Cherche-Midi, 75006
CLOSED: Sat., Sun., July and Christmas week
PRICE RANGE: Expensive
TEL: 45-48-52-40
METRO: Falguière
CREDIT: Visa and MasterCard

A perfect neighborhood eatery featuring superb foie gras, fresh seafood that arrives daily from Normandy, extraordinary wines and an authentic Parisian bistro atmosphere. In season, the truffle adds its subtle flavor to many dishes: truffles in puff pastry with eggs, shredded over fresh foie gras or in a ragoût *with Champagne sauce.*

Otherwise known as Chez Dumonet after its proprietor, M. Jean Dumonet, this charming family restaurant is amazingly unspoiled by its popularity. The long, bright dining room is sectioned into three distinct areas by etched-glass-and-wood dividers. There is a long bar at the entrance, tastefully decorated with a huge floral arrangement echoed by fresh flowers set on each table. Old tile floors, blond-oak paneling, beveled mirrors and cream-colored walls covered with nautical prints, posters and paintings complete the simple decor. The meal begins with an *amuse-bouche,* followed by wonderful *terrines,* stuffed mushrooms, artichoke hearts with fresh vegetables, sliced duck breast with mustard sauce, flaky sole in a smoky butter sauce, or grilled foie gras. Desserts are also delicious, and a light *millefeuille* or a Grand Marnier soufflé may be enjoyed by two people if ordered before dinner.

RECOMMENDED DISHES

Jambon des Landes. Cured and mildly smoked Landes ham.
Foie Gras de Canard Frais. Fresh duck foie gras served in
　　a variety of ways: "natural" with black truffles, "block"
　　with raisins, garnished with sorrel or grilled with ar-
　　tichoke or celery.

Pied de Veau Vinaigrette. Slices of calf's foot in a spicy vinaigrette.

Compote de Lapin Champenoise. Hot rabbit *terrine.*

Boeuf Bourguignon aux Nouilles Fraîches. Beef stewed in red wine, onions and mushrooms served with fresh noodles.

Navarin d'Agneau. Lamb stew with potatoes and onions.

Gigot d'Agneau Duranton aux Haricots Blancs (Wednesday lunch). Roast leg of lamb with white beans.

Tournedos Rossini. Heart of the beef fillet grilled with truffles.

Andouillette Truffée Feuillitée. Grilled and truffled pork sausage in a puff pastry.

Cassoulet. Meat-and-white-bean casserole with sausages, pork, garlic and preserved goose.

Confit de Canard. Preserved duck seasoned with duck fat and served with sautéed potatoes.

Ris de Veau aux Morilles. Braised sweetbreads with wild mushrooms.

Gigot de Lotte à l'Ail en Chemise. Encased monkfish cooked in a garlicky white-wine-and-cream sauce.

Turbot Grillé Béarnaise. Grilled turbot with a hollandaise sauce of shallots, tarragon and white wine.

Tarte Fine Chaud aux Pommes. Hot, thin apple tart.

Suprème au Chocolat Albertine. Brioche hollowed-out and filled with chocolate sauce.

Soufflé au Grand Marnier (for two). Light, puffy whipped egg dessert flavored with Grand Marnier brandy.

WINE

Beaujolais and a superb selection of Bordeaux wines—one of the richest in Paris.

LA LOZÈRE ★

Mme. Elisabeth Almeras
Chef: Alice Guelle

ADDRESS: 4, rue Hautefeuille, 75006
CLOSED: Sun., Mon. and August
PRICE RANGE: Moderate
TEL: 43-54-26-64
METRO: Saint-Michel or Odéon
CREDIT: Visa

An authentic Provençal maison, *the property of the Lozère tourist office, serving only the specialties of that area, including* aligot, *a thick purée of creamy mashed potatoes and melted Cantal cheese flavored with garlic.*

Very near the entrance of the Place Saint-Michel and Rue Saint-Andre-des-Arts is the friendly green-and-glass exterior of Maison de la Lozère. This is not a quick place for lunch, but while you relax you can browse through the brochure of products sold in their store nearby at 1 *bis* Rue Hautefeuille. The dining room has stone walls with rustic furniture and artisan's works from the Lozère, a department in south-central France west of the Rhone. There are three set menus; one at 76F which offers soup, salad or pâté, the *plat du jour,* cheese or dessert; one at 94F with crudités, pâté or a Roquefort salad, the *plat du jour,* cheese and dessert and the last at 115F offering a few of the region's specialties like sausages, *tripoux* (tasty little packets of stuffed tripe in tomato sauce sprinkled with parsley), and *aligot,* plus salad, a cheese plate and dessert. The à la carte menu features omelettes and vegetables. Dark, crusty bread shipped from the region and local wines are perfect complements to the food.

RECOMMENDED DISHES

Assiette de Cochonnailles du Pays. Assorted regional pork products.
Salade au Cantal et Lardons. Salad greens with bacon and Cantal cheese.
Assiette de Jambon Cru. Cured regional ham.
Omelette aux Cèpes. Omelette with large wild mushrooms.
Pélardon Chaud Sur Salad. Soft nutty-flavored little goat cheese served hot in a salad.
Entrecôte Garnie. Rib steak with Roquefort sauce.
Aligot d'Aubrac (Thursday dinner only). Mashed potatoes with garlic and Cantal cheese. The outstanding specialty of the bistro.
Pain de Campagne. Great crunchy loaves of rye bread imported fresh from the Lozère.
Chou Farci. Stuffed cabbage.
Tripoux de Lozère. Stuffed veal tripe with heavy seasoning in a tomato sauce sprinkled with fresh parsley and accompanied by pan-fried potatoes.
Confit de Porc Froid. Preserved pork served cold.

Plateau de Fromages. Fine assortment of Auvergne cheeses.

Gâteau Lozère (Amelou). Honey, hazelnut and almond cake.

Clafoutis. Custard tart filled with batter poured over fruit and baked until brown.

WINE

Vin du Tarn (in the pitcher), Vin de Gaillac, Cahors.

CHEZ MAÎTRE PAUL ★ ★ ★

M. A. Gaugain

ADDRESS: 12, rue Monsieur-le-Prince, 75006
CLOSED: Sun., Mon. and August
PRICE RANGE: Moderate
TEL: 43-54-74-59
METRO: Odéon or Luxembourg
CREDIT: Amex, Visa, Diners and MasterCard

A friendly, family-run bistro resembling a cozy mountain inn, serving delectable regional food and wine from the Jura and Franche-Comté, areas east of Burgundy.

Armand and Jacqueline Gaugain welcome a clientele of regulars and connoisseurs to their half-timbered little nook, a short walk from the Odéon. For thirty years their tiny kitchen has been turning out generous portions of specialties made with regional products and wines. You might like to try the *saucisse de Montbéliard,* a grilled cumin-flecked pork sausage served with potatoes and garnished with parsley and a dash of vinegar, followed by either the *ris de veau au vin de paille* (calf's liver in straw wine) or *poulet au vin jaune* (chicken in a rich wine sauce with mushrooms and tomatoes). There is a marvelous fish stew (*marlotte d'anguilles au vin d'Arbois*) and *sandre* (pike-perch) in a heady wine sauce with garlic, shallots and cream. There are two dining rooms, but you will have to call in advance to reserve one of the seven tables on the ground floor, where provincial charm abounds.

RECOMMENDED DISHES

Jambon Cuit du Jura. Cooked Jura ham.

Escargots au Vin d'Arbois. Snails in a Jura-wine sauce.

Saucisse de Montbéliard Chaud, Pommes à l'Huile. Grilled cumin-flavored sausage with sliced potatoes in oil.

Cochonnailles. Excellent-quality pork products (*rosettes, terrines, jambon, saucisses*, etc.).

Saumon Sauvage Beurre Blanc. Wild salmon cooked in a white-wine-butter sauce.

Filet de Sole au Château Chalon. Fillet of sole cooked in a white-wine sauce.

Filets de Sandre à la Comtoise. Fried pike-perch fillets.

Foie de Veau au Vin de Paille. Grilled calf's liver cooked in a Jura-wine sauce.

Poulet au Vin Jaune. Chicken cooked with mushrooms, tomatos and white Jura wine.

Entrecôte à la Vigne Ronne (for two). Rib steak cooked with grapes and *marc* (brandy).

Plateau de Fromages. Outstanding selection of regional cheeses (*Cancoillote, Comté, Vacherin, Morbier*).

Gâteau aux Noix. Walnut cake.

Tarte aux Pommes. Apple tart.

WINE

Arbois/Pupillin, Château-Chalons, Vin Jaune, Vin de Paille (dessert wine).

LE PETIT ZINC   ★ ★ ★

Layrac Brothers

ADDRESS: 25, rue de Buci, 75006

OPEN: Daily

PRICE RANGE: Moderate

TEL: 46-33-51-66

METRO: St.-Germain-des-Prés, Mabillon or Odéon

CREDIT: Amex, Visa, Diners and MasterCard

The enormously popular bistro annex of the Restaurant Muniche, next door, owned by the Layrac brothers who also own a caterer at 29, rue de Buci and l'Echaude at 21, rue de l'Echaudé. Open until 3 A.M.

In addition to its picturesque location in the Buci food-and-flower market, Le Petit Zinc is famous for well-cooked, reasonably priced food. The oysters, fish and shellfish are celebrated, but there are also fine meat specialties. *Boeuf bourguignon, poule-au-pot,* duck *confit,* lamb with kidney beans, a variety of sausages, and calf's liver—listed as the house specialty and prepared three different ways—are all delicious. Request a table outside if you can get one: it will offer a startling contrast to the rather dark interior, with black moleskin banquettes and elbow-to-elbow seating. Little lamps, engravings and posters add a nice touch to the room. A Poitou Gamay is the house red and a pleasant Sauvignon is the house white.

RECOMMENDED DISHES

Huîtres, Coquillages. Fresh oysters and assorted shellfish.

Fois Gras de Canard Maison. Duck foie gras prepared by the chef.

Salade de Filets de Canard Fumes. Smoked-duck-breast salad.

Soup du Pêcheur Avec Rouille, Croutons et Fromage. Fish soup with spicy mayonnaise, croutons and grated cheese.

Sardines Fraîches Grillées. Grilled fresh sardines.

Saumon Cru Mariné aux Baies Roses. Marinated raw salmon with pink peppercorns.

Cuisse de Canard Confite, Pommes Sarladaise. Preserved duck leg with sliced, sautéed potatoes.

Boudin. Grilled blood sausage with fried apples.

Gigot de Petit Agneau Barronet du Limousin aux Flageolets. Roast leg of young lamb with white beans.

Poule-au-Pot Avec Ses Legumes Dans Son Bouillon. Stuffed chicken with vegetables and broth.

Foie de Veau. Calf's liver prepared three different ways. Natural, Meunière and Venetian-style. The outstanding specialty of the bistro.

Gibier Game in season (wild boar and deer).

Darne de Saumon Grillée Sauce Choron. Thick slice of grilled salmon in a béarnaise sauce with tomato purée.

Filet de Rascasse au Velouté de Baies Roses. Filet of
scorpion fish in a creamy white sauce with pink peppercorns.

Marquise au Chocolat. Lady fingers layered with rich chocolate bavarian cream and covered with whipped cream and
syrup.

Tarte Chaude aux Pommes. Hot apple tart.

WINE

Saint-Pourcain (Rouge), Vins du Pays (Country Wines), Poitou
Gamay (Rouge), Sauvignon Blanc.

POLIDOR

M. André Maillet

ADDRESS: 41, rue Monsieur-le-Prince, 75006
OPEN: Daily, all year
PRICE RANGE: Inexpensive
TEL: 43-26-95-34
METRO: Odéon, Luxembourg or Cluny
CREDIT: None

*An ancient left-bank landmark with a great tradition of serv-
ing low-cost meals. The long menu is almost as famous as the
roster of notables who have eaten here.*

Crémerie Restaurant Polidor was opened in 1845 and by 1890
was a real bistro or *bouillon,* serving low-cost meals and bowls
of soup, coffee, chocolate or rice with boiled milk. Located
near the Sorbonne, it still attracts many students, professors,
bohemian types and tourists from all over the world. The
menu, written in both English and French, offers home-style
bistro classics including a famous pumpkin soup, chicken in
cream sauce, *tripe à la mode de Caen* and an enormous *tarte-
Tatin.* On Friday the *plats du jour* are fish and include skate in
butter sauce, calamaries and a good fish soup. Reservations
are not necessary as one can usually find a seat at one of the

long communal tables. Except for the installation of electricity, nothing has been changed since 1910.

RECOMMENDED DISHES

Saucisson Chaud. Small country sausages, served hot.

Terrine de Campagne aux Herbs. Coarse country pâté.

Véritable Escargots de Bourgogne. Vineyard snails with garlic butter.

Soupe de Potiron à la Crème. Creamed pumpkin soup.

Pintade aux Lardons et aux Choux. Guinea fowl with bacon and braised cabbage.

Blanquette de Veau au Riz. Veal stew in white sauce with white rice.

Poule-au-Pot Sauce Supréme. Stuffed chicken with vegetables in a creamy sauce.

Boeuf Bourguignon. Beef stewed in red wine with tiny onions and mushrooms.

Ragoût de Porc Mijoté à l'Ancienne. Slow-simmered pork stew.

Sauté d'Agneau aux Flageolets (Thursdays). Pan-fried lamb with small green kidney beans.

Lapin à la Moutarde (Saturdays). Rabbit in mustard sauce.

Petit Salé aux Lentilles (Tuesdays). Lightly salted cooked pork with lentils.

Tripes à la Mode de Caen. Tripe with kidney fat, cider, calf's feet and Calvados simmered in a heavy casserole, served steaming hot with boiled potatoes.

Baba au Rhum Avec Crème Anglaise. Yeast cake drenched with rum syrup and served in vanilla custard sauce.

Gâteau de Riz aux Raisins de Smyrne. Rice pudding with raisins in egg custard.

WINE

Beaujolais Villages, Cahors, Sancerre, Côtes-du-Rhône, Château Magondeau.

7e

CHEZ L'AMI JEAN

LA CIGALE (CHEZ PIERRE ET MICHELINE)

AUX FINS GOURMETS

LA FONTAINE DE MARS

CHEZ GERMAINE (BABKINE)

AU PIED DE FOUET

LA POULE-AU-POT

THOUMIEUX

7e Arrondissement

TOUR-EIFFEL

PLACES OF INTEREST

*Égouts de Paris (*Paris sewer tours leave from the *Place de la Résistance)*
Hotel Biron (Musée Rodin)
Invalides, Tombeau de Napoléan and the *Musée de l'Armée*
Musée d'Orsay
Palais Bourbon
Pont Alexandre III (7e, 8e)
Pont d'Iena
Rue du Bac
Tour Eiffel, Champs-de-Mars and the *École Militaire*

CHEZ L'AMI JEAN ★ ★

M. Pierre Paqueguy

ADDRESS: 27, rue Malar, 75007
CLOSED: Sun. and August
PRICE RANGE: Inexpensive
TEL: 47-05-86-89
METRO: La Tour–Maubourg or Invalides
CREDIT: Visa

Opened in 1931 as a Basque restaurant, this popular neighborhood spot continues to provide a good selection of regional specialties and wines. The cooking is still basically Basque, but not exclusively, so many traditional bistro plats *are included on the menu.*

This rustic little bistro is filled with Basque sports memorabilia, in particular from the world of rugby. The walls are covered with team pictures, trophies, banners and all manner of mementos. The sports theme is carried over into the bar area, where central casting has skillfully placed wonderful old characters noisily extolling the virtues of this or that rugby team. The cuisine is unpretentious but l'Ami Jean does serve some truly Basque dishes, practically impossible to find outside the region. Most outstanding is the spicy Béarn vegetable soup *garbure,* the paella, the tiny squid with tomatoes (*chipirons*) and of course the Basque scrambled eggs, *piperade,* which comes with cured Bayonne ham. The perfect wine to go with this hearty fare is red Irouléguy. With an alcohol level of 14%, this wine is full of fruit and has that spicy *goût du terroir* which complements the food, including the egg dishes. Save room for either the *crème caramel* or the *gâteau Basque,* a marvelously rich cream-filled cake. After the meal stroll down to the nearby Seine and across the lovely Pont de l'Alma.

RECOMMENDED DISHES

Jambon de Bayonne. Cured Bayonne ham.
Anchois Frais Marinés. Marinated anchovies, served cold.

Garbure (dinner only). Béarn vegetable soup served in an earthenware *toupin.*

Bloc de Foie Gras de Canard. Fresh duck foie gras.

Terrine de Lapin au Foie de Canard. Rabbit and duck liver pâté.

Piperade. Basque omelette with tomatoes, peppers and onions. Served with sliced Bayonne ham.

Poulet Basquaise. Chicken cooked with tomatoes, peppers, *chorizo* (sausage), mushrooms and red wine.

Confit de Canard des Landes, Pommes Sarladaises. Grilled preserved duck served with sliced sautéed potatoes and truffles.

Paëlla Valenciana (dinner only). Chicken, seafood and sausage mélange cooked with rice and saffron.

Chipirons à la Basquaise. Tiny stuffed squid (calamaries) stewed in their own ink with tomatoes.

Coq-au-Vin du Chef. Chicken stewed in red wine with onions and mushrooms.

Escalope de Veau "Ami Jean." Veal chop in cream sauce *gratinée* (browned on top).

Pot-au-Feu. Boiled beef with vegetables and broth.

Crème Caramel. Vanilla-flavored flan. Reputed to be the best in Paris.

Mousse au Chocolat. Chocolate mousse.

Mystère Flambé à l'Izarra. Ice cream dessert flamed with Izarra, a Chartreuse-like liqueur made in Bayonne.

WINE

Muscadet, Madiran, Cahors, Irouléguy.

LA CIGALE (CHEZ PIERRE ET MICHELINE) ★

M. Pierre Grocat
Mme. Micheline Grocat

ADDRESS: 11 bis, rue Chomel, 75007

CLOSED: Sat., Sun. and August

PRICE RANGE: Moderate

TEL: 45-48-87-87

METRO: Sèvres-Babylone

CREDIT: Visa

You will find simple, quality cuisine with an emphasis on steak and regional sausages in this local bistro practically on the doorsteps of the Bon Marché department store, famous for its housewares and gourmet food departments. This makes a lovely stop for lunch after a morning's shopping.

Pierre and Micheline Grocat opened La Cigale in 1970. After a successful career as a photographer, Pierre was drawn into the restaurant business by his love of food, which is aptly expressed in his down-to-earth cooking. The atmosphere is that of a country farmhouse with two small tables and a bar at the entrance, and, to the right, six or so more tables lining the back wall. Kerosene lanterns, wrought-iron sconces, bunches of dried flowers and food and farm implements decorate the walls. The tables are gaily covered with pink cloths, a nice contrast to the pretty maroon-and-white tile floor. Several *cigales* (cicadas) are in evidence throughout. A simple 150F menu features all the house specialties, such as *rosette* sausage from the forests of the Morvan in Burgundy, pâté with truffles and Armagnac from the Landes in the Southwest, Normandy-style veal in a cream-and-mushroom sauce and lamb with green kidney beans. Steak served tartare, with marrow, shallots or peppercorn sauce are among the other choices. Delicious runny cheeses, Camembert and Brie de Meaux, make a savory dessert, but there is a silky-smooth mousse for chocolate lovers.

RECOMMENDED DISHES

Museau Vinaigrette. Muzzle brawn salad with vinaigrette.
Terrine Landaise de Canard (for two). Duck liver pâté with truffles.
Rosette du Morvan. Large dry pork sausage, sliced and served cold.
Filet de Sandre en Papillotte. Fillet of pike-perch baked in a pouch.
Entrecôte à la Moelle, Pommes Frites. Rib steak with bone marrow served with french fries.
Escalope Normande, Pommes Vapeur. Veal chop in cream sauce with Calvados brandy and apples, served with steamed potatoes.
Steak Tartare. Raw, finely chopped beef mixed with egg, onions and capers.

Pavé de Boeuf au Poivre, Pommes Frites. Thick slice of
beef with peppercorn sauce, served with french fries.
Tartes Maison. Assorted fruit tarts.
Crème Caramel. Vanilla-flavored flan.
Mousse au Chocolat. Chocolate mousse.

WINE

Chinon, Cahors, Sancerre, Beaujolais (by the pitcher).

AUX FINS GOURMETS

Mme. Dupleix

ADDRESS: 213, blvd. Saint-Germain, 75007
CLOSED: Sun. and August
PRICE RANGE: Moderate
TEL: 42-22-06-57
METRO: Rue du Bac
CREDIT: None

*There is a dignified atmosphere in this fine old bistro, where you
will find top-quality food and service. It has a stunning old-
fashioned dining room and a pleasant terrace, bordered by a
hedge, where you can quietly enjoy dinner on a warm evening.*

Michel Dupleix has taken over the running of this outstanding restaurant founded by his parents during the 1950s. Here you will
enjoy solid French cuisine with some Basque and Béarnaise specialties. Nothing has changed on the menu except the prices, and
you will find regional pâtés and sausages, omelettes made with
country ham and fine herbs, *confits* of duck and goose, lightly
salted pork with cabbage, a mutton-and-white-bean stew, leg of
lamb, *piperade,* Basque chicken or veal kidneys and a delicious
house *cassoulet.* The wines are carefully selected to complement the food, with two especially fine Madirans, a white Jurançon, a rosé from Béarn and a Irouléguy from the Basque
country.

Distinguished middle-aged Parisians from the neighboring

ministries frequent this lovely establishment. A magnificent bouquet of fresh flowers, strategically placed on a fine old mahogany bar, greets you as you enter a large, rather austere room where three white-waistcoated waiters move quietly across the tile floor, discreetly taking orders, never disturbing the calm. There are handsome old wall moldings and columns, a countrified wooden ceiling, hanging shaded lights, dark-red-leather banquettes, brass luggage racks, mirrors and a few posters. In every sense this is a place where tradition abounds.

RECOMMENDED DISHES

Jambon du Pays. Cured country ham.

Piperade Basquaise. Basque omelette with tomatoes, peppers and onions.

Pâté du Béarn. Country pâté.

Rillettes Landaises. Cubed and minced pork cooked in its own fat and served as a spread with toast.

Confit de Canard. Grilled preserved duck.

Confit d'Oie (for two). Grilled preserved goose.

Cassoulet Maison au Confit. Languedoc stew with white beans, pork, sausage and preserved duck.

Haricot de Mouton. Mutton stew with potatoes, turnips and onions.

Petit Salé aux Choux. Slightly salted roast pork with cabbage.

Gigot d'Agneau, Flageolets. Roast leg of lamb with small green kidney beans.

Coq-au-Vin. Chicken stewed in red wine with onions and mushrooms.

Prunes à l'Armagnac. Prunes stewed in Armagnac.

Pêches Melba. Vanilla ice cream topped with peaches and cassis.

WINE

Irouléguy, Madiran, Rosé du Béarn, Jurançon Blanc Sec.

LA FONTAINE DE MARS

M. Paul & Mme. Andrée Launay

ADDRESS: 129, rue Saint-Dominique, 75007
CLOSED: Sat. eve., Sun. and August
PRICE RANGE: Inexpensive
TEL: 47-05-46-44
METRO: École-Militaire
CREDIT: Visa and MasterCard

An old neighborhood bistro, convenient to the Eiffel Tower, with checkered tablecloths, nearly illegible menus written in purple ink, generous cuisine, friendly service and moderate prices. Try to eat at one of the windows or on the little terrace facing the fountain constructed by Beauvallet between 1806 and 1809. The bas-relief represents the goddess Hygeia giving drink to the god Mars.

Considering its prime location in the Arcade de la Fontaine, this cozy spot is one of the least touristy restaurants in the area. It is, however, very popular with local residents, making reservations advisable. Owner Paul Launay, who is also the chef, bought the place in 1967 and he and his gracious wife have been serving tasty, homey dishes here ever since. The small dining rooms are simply decorated with lace café curtains, beveled mirrors, long banquettes and little wooden chairs. Most customers drink a full-bodied Cahors to wash down such favorites as *fricassée* of duck, roast leg of lamb, guinea fowl or grandmother's veal cutlets. Indulge in a thick chunk of outstanding fresh foie gras as a start and finish with ice cream *mystére* with rich hot chocolate sauce. This is a good place for an early dinner, as service begins at 7 P.M. and winds down at about 9:30 P.M.

RECOMMENDED DISHES

Foie Gras d'Oie Maison (November–March). Goose-liver foie gras made on the premises.
Poireaux Vinaigrette. Leek salad with vinaigrette.

Filets de Maquereaux au Vin Blanc. Marinated mackerel fillets, served cold.

Daurade à la Provençale. Sea bream cooked Provence-style with tomatoes, garlic, onions, olives and anchovies.

Boeuf Gros Sel (Pot-au-Feu). Boiled beef with vegetables and broth.

Tête de Veau Gribiche. Boiled calf's head in a mustard-mayonnaise sauce with capers, herbs and finely chopped hardboiled eggs.

Cassoulet au Confit du Canard. Languedoc stew with white beans, pork, sausage and preserved duck.

Escalope de Veau Grandmère. Veal chop in cream sauce with onions, mushrooms, bacon and potatoes.

Gigot d'Agneau, Flageolets. Roast leg of lamb with small green kidney beans.

Pintadeau aux Choux. Roast guinea fowl with cabbage.

Compote de Pommes. Stewed apples.

Gâteau au Chocolat. Rich chocolate cake.

Mystère au Chocolat Chaud. Vanilla ice cream in meringue topped with hot chocolate sauce and nuts.

WINE

Cahors.

CHEZ GERMAINE (BABKINE)

M. & Mme. Fernand Babkine

ADDRESS: 30, rue Pierre-Leroux, 75007
CLOSED: Sat. lunch, Sun. and August
PRICE RANGE: Inexpensive
TEL: 42-73-28-34
METRO: Vaneau or Duroc
CREDIT: None

A tiny, very inexpensive and unpretentious place in an upscale neighborhood close to the Bon Marché department store. Freshly made desserts, two or three daily specials, items from the grill, plus a dozen or so entrées are served in a cozy kitchen atmosphere.

For forty years Fernand Babkine and his wife Germaine have run this totally plain bistro to the delight of everyone in the neighborhood. The line starts forming for lunch on the sidewalk in front of Chez Germaine around 11:45 A.M. and by 6:30 P.M. for dinner. Once the clients have squeezed into any available seat at the seven oilcloth-covered tables the doors are shut. If you are one of the lucky ones, prepare for a fine home-style meal at some of the lowest restaurant prices in Paris. No smoking is allowed in the dining room and coffee is not served to discourage lingering, but you will be treated to generous portions of steaming-hot food, always well prepared. Enjoy chicken in cream sauce, mutton stew, steak, pan-fried rabbit or salt pork with lentils or a *gratin* of zucchini. Be sure to save room for the house specialty, *clafoutis* with cream, a nice finale to the meal.

RECOMMENDED DISHES

Croûte du Pêcheur, Sauce Aurore. Seafood puff pastry in a white sauce with tomato purée.

Terrine de Canard. Duck liver pâté.

Hareng de la Baltique Avec Crème. Marinated Baltic herring fillets with cream.

Petits Calamars Braisés aux Olives. Tiny squid braised and served with olives.

Poularde Crème à l'Estragon, Riz. Creamed chicken with tarragon, served with white rice.

Lapin Sautée à la Savoyarde. Sautéed rabbit with cheese and potatoes.

Navarin d'Agneau Gratin de Courgettes. Lamb stew with zucchini cooked *au gratin*.

Petit Salé aux Lentilles. Lightly salted roast pork with lentils.

Boeuf Bourguignon Avec Polenta. Beef stewed in red wine with mushrooms and onions, served with a cornmeal porridge with butter and grated cheese.

Crème Caramel. Vanilla-flavored flan.

Clafoutis aux Fruits du Saison. Custard tart with fresh seasonal fruit. The outstanding specialty of the bistro.

WINE

Côtes-du-Ventoux *en carafe*, Bordeaux *en carafe*.

AU PIED DE FOUET

M. Martial Persoons

ADDRESS: 45, rue de Babylone, 75007
CLOSED: Sat. evening, Sun., August, a week at Easter and a week at Christmas
PRICE RANGE: Inexpensive
TEL: 47-05-12-27
METRO: Sèvres-Babylone, St. François-Xavier or Vaneau
CREDIT: None

Once the best-kept secret in Paris, this minuscule bistro with only four or five tables is now listed in every guide book. First-rate home-style cooking and fine, unpretentious wine are offered at bargain prices. This is an amiable little spot that oozes charm.

No reservations are taken and even if you get here early you will probably have to wait at the tiny, museum-quality zinc bar where your very personable host, Martial Persoons, will pour you a coffee or an aperitif. Formerly a coaching inn, the little dining room is cluttered with wagon wheels, harnesses and other memorabilia. Red-and-white curtains and tablecloths, a moleskin banquette along the wall and tiny bistro chairs, pushed as close together as possible, fill the room. Make sure to ask for *pommes purées,* the meltingly creamy mashed potatoes served with the *faux filet* (sirloin steak), but which may also be ordered à la carte. Other daily favorites are the roast pork, chicken in the pot, rabbit in a lemony sauce, *boudin,* and *tripe à la Provençale.* In addition to the traditional desserts, there is an array of specialties which includes prunes in wine, fresh fruit tarts, rice pudding and chestnut or chocolate *Génoise.* You cannot miss the bright yellow-orange facade on the ancient Rue Babylone, a block or so away from the Swedish embassy.

RECOMMENDED DISHES

Poireaux Vinaigrette. Leek salad with vinaigrette.

Rillettes de la Sarthe. Cubed and pounded pork cooked in its own fat and served as a spread.

Maquereaux au Vin Blanc Maison. Mackerel fillets poached in white wine and served cold.

Lapin aux Citron. Rabbit with lemon sauce.

Filet de Rascasse à la Crème de Poivrons. Grilled fillet of scorpion fish served with creamed sweet peppers.

Langue de Boeuf. Beef tongue with watercress.

Faux Filet Pommes Purées. Grilled beef sirloin with extra-creamy mashed potatoes.

Boudin Noir. Grilled large blood sausage.

Navarin d'Agneau. Lamb stew with potatoes and onions.

Poule-au-Pot. Boiled chicken stew with vegetable broth and stuffing.

Boeuf en Daube. Braised beef stewed in red wine with vegetables in an earthenware pot.

Crème Renversée au Caramel. Vanilla-flavored flan.

Tarte Meringuée à l'Orange. Orange-meringue tart.

WINE

Gamay-de-Touraine, Côtes-du-Rhône.

LA POULE-AU-POT

M. Dumond

ADDRESS: 121, rue de l'Université, 75007
CLOSED: Sat., Sun. and two weeks in August
PRICE RANGE: Inexpensive
TEL: 47-05-16-36
METRO: La Tour-Maubourg or Invalides
CREDIT: Amex, Visa and MasterCard

Movers and shakers from the worlds of politics and television can be found enjoying solid and satisfying "cuisine bourgeois" in this famous turn-of-the-century bistro located near the Invalides. Reserve a day or two in advance and ask to be seated in the lovely dining room to the right of the zinc bar with its rather extraordinary espresso machine.

Owner Jean-Claude Dumond prides himself on a broad choice of classic dishes ranging from omelettes and quiches to more elaborate meat and fish preparations, but the house specialty is the obvious choice. This classic preparation of stewed chicken is served in a clay pot, with steaming broth, several vegetables and a slice of pâté. The best choice for wine is the house Saumur Champigny, an earthy red wine from the Loire Valley and the *oeufs à la neige* (snow eggs) or chocolate mousse, for dessert. The decor is classic bistro with tile floors, dark wood, deep moleskin banquettes, shiny brass rails, beautiful etched-glass panels and potted palms. A delightful sidewalk terrace is a good option on summer days with comfortable bentwood-and-wicker bistro chairs and tables finely set in white linen.

RECOMMENDED DISHES

Maquereaux Frais au Vin Blanc, Pommes à l'Huile. Mackerel fillets poached in white wine served with sliced potatoes in oil.

Soupe à l'Oignon Gratinée. Onion soup, poured over a thick slice of bread, topped with grated cheese, and browned in the oven.

Frisée aux Lardons. Chicory salad with bacon.

Poulourdes Farcies. Stuffed oyster mushrooms.

Brioche à la Moelle. Brioche stuffed with bone marrow.

Poule au Pot Farcie. Chicken stewed in a large clay pot with a rich broth and pâté stuffing. The outstanding specialty of the bistro.

Raie au Beurre Noisette. Skate with black butter.

Andouillette au Chablis, Pommes de Terre au Lard. Pork sausage cooked with Chablis wine and served with potatoes and bacon.

Blanquette de Veau. Veal stew in a white sauce made from cream and egg yolks, served with white rice.

Boeuf Mode. Beef simmered in red wine with vegetables and herbs.

Assiette du Pêcheur. Platter of assorted steamed fish.

Charlotte. Hot fruit pudding lined with buttered bread.

Oeufs à la Neige. Egg whites poached in milk and filled with caramel-covered vanilla custard.

WINE

Côtes-du-Rhône, Saumur Champigny.

THOUMIEUX

M. & Mme. Bassalert

ADDRESS: 79, rue Saint-Dominique, 75007
CLOSED: Monday
PRICE RANGE: Moderate
TEL: 47-05-49-75
METRO: La Tour-Maubourg
CREDIT: Visa

A large and very popular bistro with the ambience and interior of a 1930s-style brasserie. Bright lights, bustling waiters and crowded elbow-to-elbow seating. The menu is extensive, the cooking above average in quality and below average in price. The portions are old-fashioned in their generosity.

A pleasant ten-minute walk from the Invalides brings you to this very popular neighborhood bistro which has an old-time atmosphere and cast of local characters that are hard to beat. The spacious dining room is always packed, so arrive early. Identical tables set in long rows and covered with white linens, bright wall sconces and overhead globe lights are reflected in the mirrored walls. Long banquettes, brass railings, potted palms and communal coatracks are spread throughout the room. Efficient waiters dressed in the traditional bistro uniform of long white apron and black trousers politely take your order.

Unpretentious dishes with a strong Southwestern accent are carefully prepared and tastefully presented. The *cassoulet*, for example, comes to the table in a handsome sealed earthenware casserole pot. There is a long and varied à la carte menu, but if you stick to the *prix-fixe* meals, a luncheon for two may be had for under thirty dollars.

This is a great place to sample the duck specialties from the Southwest and Limousin regions of France: *confit de canard* (preserved duck), *rillettes de canard* (duck pâté), *filet de canard maison* (garlic-enhanced steak of duck breast), *cuisse de canard aux pruneaux et filet d'oie fumé* (duck legs and smoked goose with prunes) and of course the *cassoulet*. The Cahors wine is a good choice to complement these rich dishes. There is additionally a considerably less expensive house *rouge* that is the next best thing. To keep the spirit of the Southwest, finish up with the *clafoutis*, the traditional custard-and-cake dessert from Limousin, made with black cherries and served with vanilla cream.

After your evening meal, work off the calories strolling over to the spectacular illuminated Tour Eiffel.

RECOMMENDED DISHES

Rillettes de Canard Maison. Tiny pieces of duck cooked in its own fat and served as a spread.

Pâté de Campagne. Coarse country pâté.

Charcuteries d'Auvergne. Assorted pork products.

Salade d'Epinards aux Lardons. Spinach salad with bacon.

Raie au Beurre Noir. Skate in black butter.

Cassoulet au Confit de Canard "Maison." Languedoc stew with white beans, pork, sausage and preserved duck served in an earthenware casserole. The outstanding specialty of the bistro.

Tripes à la Mode de Caen. Tripe cooked with cider and Calvados brandy.

Filet de Canard "Maison." Duck breast seasoned with garlic and served with sautéed potatoes.

Gigot d'Agneau aux Flageolets. Roast leg of lamb with small green kidney beans.

Pieds de Porc, Sauce au Vin. Pigs' feet in wine sauce.

Selle d'Agneau. Roast rack of lamb.

Boudin Noir. Large grilled blood sausage.

Flognarde aux Poires. Sweet flan with pears.

Profiteroles au Chocolat. Ice-cream-filled pastry covered with melted chocolate.

WINE

Cahors/Carte Noir.

8^e

CHEZ ANDRÉ

L'ARTOIS (ISIDORE)

CHEZ EDGARD

JEAN DE CHALOSSE

LE MONTALIVET

SAVY

8ᵉ *Arrondissement*

ÉTOILE–CHAMPS-ÉLYSÉES

PLACES OF INTEREST

Arc de Triomphe
Avenue Marigny (the stamp market)
Avenues Montaigne and *Matignon*
Champs-Élysées
Église de la Madeleine
Église St.-Augustin
Gare St.-Lazare
Grand Palais
Musée Cernuschi
Musée de la Découverte (Grand Palais)
Musée Instrumental du Conservatoire National de Musique
Musée Jacquemart-André
Musée Nissim de Camondo
Musée de l'Orangerie
Parc de Monceau
Petit Palais
Place de la Concorde
Pont de l'Alma (Bateaux Mouches and *Vedettes)*
Rond-Point des Champs-Élysées (Théatre du Rond-Point)
Rue du Faubourg–St.-Honoré
Rue Royal

CHEZ ANDRÉ ★ ★

M. Pierre Méthivier

ADDRESS: 12, rue Marbeuf, 75008
CLOSED: Tues. and the first three weeks in August
PRICE RANGE: Moderate
TEL: 47-20-59-57
METRO: Franklin Roosevelt or Alma-Marceau
CREDIT: Visa

Expect solid bistro fare served in traditional style and surroundings frequented by many regulars and tourists. Located in the bustling avenue Montaigne area, near the Champs-Élysées, lunch is always busy but not a madhouse like other restaurants in the district.

Soft lights, flowers and middle-aged waitresses dressed in black lend a sedate atmosphere to this comfortable, unpretentious old dining room where owner Pierre Méthivier, son of André, has presided for over 35 years. The food is not elaborate but it is good and you will find all the bistro classics from eggs in mayonnaise and Bismark herring to leg of lamb, calf's liver, veal stew and a fine table of desserts. The *plat du jour* changes from lunch to dinner. A warm beef and potato salad makes an excellent appetizer or you might choose the soup, a creamy purée of vegetables. Fresh fish, the *choucroute* platter and seasonal game are the most favored specialties. A splendid wine list is well endowed with some excellent crus, but the house red and white wines by the glass or carafe are perfectly acceptable and reasonably priced.

RECOMMENDED DISHES

Terrine de Canard. Duck liver pâté.
Filets de Harengs, Pommes à l'Huile. Marinated herring fillets with sliced potatoes in oil.
Saucisson Chaud, Pommes à l'Huile. Hot Lyon sausage served with sliced potatoes in oil.
Gigot d'Agneau Rôti, Pommes Mousseline. Roast leg of lamb with creamy mashed potatoes.

Navarin d'Agneau. Lamb stew with potatoes and onions.

Sauté d'Agneau aux Haricots Blancs. Pan-fried lamb with white beans.

Merlan Frit. Fried whiting.

Raie Pochée Beurre Noisette. Skate in black butter.

Bouillabaisse. Mediterranean fish soup.

Boudin Noir. Grilled pork blood sausage.

Crème Caramel. Vanilla-flavored flan.

Baba au Rhum. Yeast cake drenched in rum syrup and served with cream.

WINE

Large selection of diverse growths at very reasonable prices, especially Bordeaux crus. Beaujolais-Villages, Macon Rouge.

L'ARTOIS (ISIDORE)

M. Mendiondo

ADDRESS: 13, rue d'Artois, 75008
CLOSED: Sat. lunch, Sun. and August
PRICE RANGE: Moderate
TEL: 42-25-01-10
METRO: St.-Philippe-du-Roule
CREDIT: Visa

A perfect country-style inn with an emphasis on the regional cuisine of central France. The ambience is friendly, informal and the food reasonably priced.

Little tables crowd the corner of Rue Frederic Bastrat and Rue Artois but it is more appealing to eat inside this cozy bistro where a lovely triptych, the *Baie of Anges,* picturing mountains, woods and rolling hills, decorates the back of a handsome bar.

Fresh flowers and a small fireplace, over which hangs the seal of Auvergne, make you forget the honky-tonk of the Champs-Élysées only two blocks away. Here you can relax and enjoy fine country pâtés, hams, sausages, *cassoulet,* duck *confit* with sautéed garlic potatoes, a seafood *pot-au-feu* and, in season, savory *plats du jour* of game and golden french fries or fresh *cèpes.* There are regional cheeses and luscious desserts like a chestnut *charlotte* or lime mousse with raspberry sauce. Wines include some nicely priced Bordeaux, a good Cahors and some little regional crus which the new owner likes to point out. A glass of Armagnac is a splendid finish.

RECOMMENDED DISHES

Cochonnailles Auvergnates (Plat de Charcuteries). Assorted pork products from the Auvergne.

Rillettes d'Oie. Cubed and minced goose cooked in its own fat and served as a spread.

Girolles Sautées Provençale. Sautéed wild mushrooms.

Saucisse Sèche. Large dried sausage sliced thin and served with bread and butter.

Jambon d'Auvergne. Cured Auvergne ham.

Ris de Veau Entier aux Épinards. Whole veal sweetbreads served with spinach.

Coq-au-Vin au Cahors. Chicken stewed in red Cahors wine with tiny onions and mushrooms.

Boudin de Corrèze, Poêlé. Sautéed country sausage.

Tripoux d'Aurillac. Stuffed, heavily seasoned, mutton tripe.

Entrecôte Bercy. Grilled rib steak with shallots, red wine and bone marrow sauce.

Cassoulet. Casserole stew of white beans, sausages, preserved duck and pork.

Confit de Canard "Maison," Pommes Sautées à l'Ail. Grilled preserved duck with sliced pan-fried potatoes and garlic.

Soufflé au Grand-Marnier. Soufflé with orange-flavored cognac.

Charlotte aux Marrons Glacés. Molded lady fingers filled with custard and candied chestnuts.

Tarte aux Framboises. Raspberry tart.

WINE

Excellent selection of little regional wines. Beaujolais, Cahors, Wines of the Auvergne. Extensive collection of first-rate Armagnacs.

CHEZ EDGARD

M. Paul Benmussa
Chef: Moulinier

ADDRESS: 4, rue Marbeuf, 75008
CLOSED: Sun. and holidays
PRICE RANGE: Fairly expensive
TEL: 47-20-51-15
METRO: Franklin Roosevelt or Alma-Marceau
CREDIT: Amex, Visa, Diners and MasterCard

A fashionable, long-established house favored by a select clientele of government officials, media people, "society" and others who make the wheels turn. Newcomers, however, are not neglected and are greeted with equal enthusiasm by "Monsieur Paul," the famous Tunisian-born proprietor who manages to maintain the highest standards in both food and service, running a restaurant of really extraordinary merit.

The bright-red awning with "Chez Edgard" lettered in gold marks a festive corner spot on an otherwise drab street, a short walk from Avenue Georges V and the Champs-Élysées. Sidewalk chairs and tables surrounded by boxes of flowers create a garden setting while inside, red-and-black walls and glass-enclosed booths impart an air of sophistication and intrigue. There are some Southwestern departures from the traditional bistro versions of fish, shellfish and steak in the form of dishes like *salade Niçoise,* a *gratin* of calamaries, a fish-fry of little smelts, grilled red mullet or grouper in a basil-and-tomato sauce and a Provençal beef stew. Delicious ice cream desserts include a banana split, and the house specialty, a *coup du chef:* vanilla ice cream and fruit drizzled with Cointreau.

RECOMMENDED DISHES

Huitres et Coquillages. Fresh oysters and shellfish.
Terrine de Lièvre. Rabbit pâté.
Oeufs Cocotte à la Crème. Lightly baked eggs cooked and
    served in a *cocotte* dish.

Rosette de Lyon. Large dry pork sausage, sliced and served cold.

Daube de Boeuf à la Provençale. Beef braised in red wine with vegetables and herbs, Provence-style, with tomatoes, garlic and onions, served in an earthenware pot.

Palette de Porc aux Haricots Rouges. Roast pork shoulder with red kidney beans.

Navarin d'Agneau aux Fèves Fraîches. Lamb stew with potatoes and onions garnished with fresh broad beans.

Rougets Grillés Nicoise. Grilled red mullet with basil sauce *(pistou).*

Filet de Loup aux Cinq Poivres. Fillet of sea bass with five types of pepper.

Crème Caramel. Vanilla-flavored flan.

Profiteroles Sauce Chocolat. Ice-cream-filled pastry covered with melted chocolate.

Mousse au Chocolat. Chocolate mousse.

WINE

Saint-Pourçain, Côteaux d'Aix, Brouilly.

JEAN DE CHALOSSE ★ ★ ★ ★

M. Jean-Charles Diehl
Chef: M. Alain Mestos

ADDRESS: 10, rue de la Trémoille, 75008
CLOSED: Sat. lunch
PRICE RANGE: Fairly expensive
TEL: 47-23-53-53
METRO: Alma-Marceau
CREDIT: Amex and Visa

A new and elegant gourmet rendezvous, in a smart neighborhood, where the cuisine, the wine and the service are perfection. Unusual Southwestern specialties and refined versions of the classics are stylishly served to an upscale clientele. The proprietor will guide you through the menu suggesting the perfect wine to match the daily specialties.

M. Jean-Charles Diehl is one of the most knowledgeable and charming hosts in Paris. His successes include being *maître d'hôtel* at two of Paris' most prestigious locations, Le Taillevent and Lasserre.

More recently he created a fine bistro, just down the street from Jean de Chalosse, called Jean-Charles et Ses Amis, which is now under the direction of M. Roland Magne. In March of last year he opened another small bistro in the Les Halles quarter called La Belle Corisanole (14, rue Léopold-Bellan, tel. 42-36-78-79) with a scaled-down menu of dishes from Jean de Chalosse. All this experience and energy is what makes dining at this exquisite art nouveau bistro a memorable occasion. Jean-Charles is so enthusiastic about his cuisine and wines you will find yourself eating foods you had never dreamed of, such as cod fish tongues and stuffed pigs' tail. His urgings will turn you toward unusual country wines such as those found in the Jura mountains or in the heart of Gascony. He will explain how perfectly they complement this or that dish, and he will be right.

The decor is enchanting from the glass facade with bright-red awning and gold lettering to the elegant art nouveau salon. The all-mirrored bar is a work of art and invites you to sit down to enjoy a before-meal aperitif. The dining salon has about fifteen tables, many of which are round and well-spaced, surrounded by green-lacquered chairs. Along the walls are comfortable green-corduroy banquettes. Little silver bud vases filled with fresh roses decorate every table. The walls are tastefully accented with mirrors and oil paintings. The most stunning of the appointments are the hanging glass light fixtures, each of which is an original art nouveau design.

The cuisine is every bit as original as the decor, from the daily specials to the ever-present list of ten *entrées*, five fish dishes and ten meat *plats*, all handsomely presented and garnished with just the right vegetables. Desserts, in keeping with the tone of the meal, are unusual and delicious.

Another nice thing about this restaurant is that it stays open all day Sunday and Monday, when many places are closed.

RECOMMENDED DISHES

PLATS DU JOUR
Selle de Agneau Rôtie aux Herbes (Mondays). Roast saddle of lamb.
Estouffade de Sanglier en Veneur (Tuesdays). Wild boar stew.

Pot-au-Feu des Cinq à la Moelle (Wednesdays). Boiled beef with vegetables and bone marrow in broth.

Jeune Lapin au Pistil de Safran (Thursdays). Young rabbit accented with saffron.

Brandade de Morue en Tapenade (Fridays). Creamed salt cod in a thick anchovy paste with capers and olives.

Volaille Fermiere au Vin d'Arbois (Saturdays). Free-range chicken sautéed with vegetables in Jura wine.

Baron d'Agneau Farci (Sundays). Stuffed legs and back of roasted lamb.

Basque Cochonaille aux Petites Vertes. Spicy Pyrénées sausage.

Pot de Saucisse Seche d'Ustaritz Marinée aux Herbs. Poached, marinated sausage, served hot.

Cassolette d'Escargots au Beurre d'Amandes. Snails cooked in a *cassolette* dish with almond butter.

Pimentos de Morue del Piquillo. Spiced codfish tongues in wine sauce.

Poulet Fermier Sauté à la Basquaise. Free-range chicken sautéed with tomatoes, peppers and rice.

Tête de Veau Vinaigrette à l'Ancienne. Boiled calf's head served in a hot vinaigrette.

Tarte Fine Minute (order in advance). Thin apple tart served hot.

Fantasie aux Prunes de la Plume. Prune dessert with Armagnac brandy.

Crème Catalane au Sucre Brûlee. Custard cream topped with brown sugar burned under the grill to form a hard caramel coating.

WINE

Wines are skillfully chosen to complement each dish and are of overall excellent quality and reasonable price. Châteauneuf-du-Pape, Arbois Pinot, Côtes-de-Gascogne, Cahors.

LE MONTALIVET

M. Michel Hersard

ADDRESS: 15, rue Montalivet, 75008
CLOSED: Sat., Sun. and August
PRICE RANGE: Inexpensive
TEL: 42-65-41-98
METRO: Champs-Élysées–Clémenceau
CREDIT: Visa

This picturesque old-style place, small, noisy and animated, is a favorite with a faithful clientele drawn from the business people and government workers in the area. Plain food is admirably cooked and it is fun to watch locals stuffing themselves with such specialties as rabbit with mustard sauce, pan-fried veal and rump steak au poivre.

Rue Montalivet is a tiny street one block north of the Faubourg-St.-Honoré, a few steps away from the Ministry of Interior. A revolving neon beer sign is the first thing you'll see, slowly blinking in front of Le Montalivet's window, indicating what is to be found inside. It is interesting how the *patron* manages to get so many people into such a small space, to feed them and make them satisfied. In addition to the specials mentioned above there are always two *plats du jour,* one fish and one meat. Desserts are limited to ice cream, chocolate mousse, *crème caramel* or an orange flan. The 1950s decor is entirely unpretentious and there is a pleasant atmosphere about the place. At the front is a bar with several marble-and-wood tables tightly squeezed together. There is another small room in the back equally simple. People are here for the fine home cooking and its price, not for the decor.

RECOMMENDED DISHES

Terrine de Canard. Duck liver pâté.
Poireaux Vinaigrette. Leek salad with vinaigrette.
Oeuf Mayonnaise. Hard-boiled eggs with mayonnaise.

Rognons d'Agneau Sautés à la Provençale. Sautéed veal kidneys Provence-style with tomatoes, garlic and onions.

Filet de Merlan à la Dieppoise. Fillet of whiting poached in white wine with mussels, shrimp and mushrooms, served in a cream sauce.

Lapin Chasseur. Rabbit garnished with mushrooms stuffed with onion purée.

Sauté de Veau Marengo. Veal sautéed with onions, garlic, tomatoes, mushrooms, Cognac and croutons.

Andouillette de Troyes, Pommes de Terre Sautées. Grilled pork sausage with pan-fried potatoes.

Pavé de Romsteck au Poivre Flambé aux Pommes. Grilled rump steak flamed with pepper sauce.

Mousse au Chocolat. Chocolate mousse.

Crème Caramel. Vanilla-flavored flan.

WINE

Côtes-du-Rhône, Beaujolais.

SAVY ★ ★ ★

M. Gabriel Savy

ADDRESS: 23, rue Bayard, 75008
CLOSED: Sat., Sun. and August
PRICE RANGE: Fairly expensive
TEL: 47-23-46-98
METRO: Champs-Élysées or Franklin Roosevelt
CREDIT: Visa and MasterCard

A classic regional bistro reflecting the cuisine of the Massif Central. For thirty years chef-owner Gabriel Savy has served his generous Aveyronnais daily specials with the house Cahors, regional cheeses and fine old Armagnacs. Lunchtime is crowded with Parisians who appreciate well-chosen ingredients and flavorful sauces.

This delightful bistro with its comic waiters has long fed the executives from the nearby studios of Radio Luxembourg as well as the models and staff of the famous haute couture houses on Ave. Montaigne and diplomats from the surrounding embassies of Norway, Germany and Brazil.

The front room, which is more like a corridor, has been dubbed *"Le Wagon"* (the Dining Car). The decor, in 1930s bistro style, is set off by marvelous art deco windows. You can eat here or in the paneled, less-congested room in the rear. The "Dining Car" has the atmosphere, though, and it's fun to watch the waiters climb over the tightly packed tables negotiating the narrow room while balancing their platters full of food. Aside from the ever-present daily specials, Savy offers a *petit farçou* (vegetable pancake), ham from the Auvergne and the *épaule d'agneau rôtie* (roast shoulder of lamb), which must be ordered for two. One of the few available seafood dishes is *Saint-Jacques grillées au beurre blanc* (grilled scallops in white-wine butter sauce). The cellar is stocked with good little growers' wines in case the house Cahors doesn't suit you. Finish the meal with the Cantal cheese or with a prune tart and a glass of old Armagnac.

RECOMMENDED DISHES

PLATS DU JOUR
Navarin Agneau (Mondays). Lamb stew with potatoes and onions.
Chou Farci (Tuesdays). Stuffed cabbage.
Jambonneau Lentilles (Wednesdays). Prepared ham with lentils.
Blanquette de Veau (Thursdays). Veal stew in a white sauce of cream and egg yolks.
Pot-au-Feu (Fridays). Boiled beef with vegetables and broth.
Jambon d'Auvergne. Cured, smoked Auvergne ham.
Petit Farcou Aveyronnais. Vegetables-and-herb pancake.
Feuilleté au Roquefort. Puff pastry filled with Roquefort cheese.
Foie de Veau à l'Auvergnate. Grilled calf's liver with mashed peas.
Épaule d'Agneau Rotie (for two). Roast shoulder of lamb.
Poule Farcie Aveyronnaise (Poule-au-Pot). Stuffed chicken poached with vegetables.
Coquilles Saint-Jacques Grillées au Beurre Blanc. Grilled scallops in a white-wine butter sauce.

Tarte au Prunes. Prune tart.

Glace Noix et Miel. Walnut ice cream with honey.

Charlotte au Chocolat. Baked custard pudding in molded ladyfingers, filled with chocolate.

WINE

Cahors, Morgon.

9e

LES BACCHANTES
AU PETIT RICHE
LE ROI DU POT-AU-FEU

9e *Arrondissement*

OPÉRA–TRINITE–PIGALLE

PLACES OF INTEREST

Boulevard Haussmann (Au Printemps and
Galléries Lafayette)
Boulevards de la Madeleine, des Capucines and *des Italiens*
Églises Sainte-Trinité and *Notre-Dame-de-Lorette*
Hôtel Drouot (largest auction house in Paris)
Musée Cognacq-Jay
Musée Grévin (wax museum)
Musée Gustave Moreau
"La Nouvelle Athens" (bordered by *Rues Saint Georges* and
Notre-Dame-de-Lorette)
Passages Verdeau, Jouffroy and *du Havre*
Place Pigalle
Théâtre des Folies-Bergère
Théâtre National de l'Opera

LES BACCHANTES

M. Raymond Pocous
Chef: M. Laurent Trouve

ADDRESS: 21, rue Caumartin, 75009
OPEN: Daily
CLOSED: One week middle of August
PRICE RANGE: Inexpensive
TEL: 42-65-25-35
METRO: Havre–Caumartin
CREDIT: Amex and Visa

A new but very authentic wine bistro attracting a chic clientele. This is a good place to acquaint yourself with unfamiliar wines from Anjou, the Ardèche, the Pyrénées and Provence along with tasty slices of sausage, bread and cheese.

Les Bacchantes, recently opened by the affable Raymond Pocous, an expert in the wine and food business, has already established itself as one of the premier *bistros à vin* in the city. The decor, style and menu are classic wine bar offering plates of country *terrines,* sausages, *rillettes,* hams, omelettes and salads. It is worth coming here for the judicious selection of country wines, the bread and the garlic sausage alone, but chef Trouve's first-quality *plats du jour* greatly enhance the restaurant's attractiveness. Extremely good *coq-au-vin,* lamb with white beans, tripe in Calvados, and lightly salted pork with lentils nicely complement the house selections of *charcuterie.* The atmosphere is relaxed and the room gaily decorated with posters, mirrors, brass rails, banquettes and marble tables. A young staff in firemen's aprons provides fast and pleasant service.

RECOMMENDED DISHES

Plats du Jour. Depend on the availability of meats and vegetables in the produce markets.
Coq-au-Vin (Plat du Jour). Chicken stewed in red wine with onions and mushrooms.

Petit Salé au Lentilles (Plat du Jour). Lightly salted cooked pork with lentils.

Gigot d'Agneau Haricots Frais (Plat du Jour). Roast leg of lamb with fresh beans.

Coquelet Grillé au Beurre d'Estragon (Plat du Jour). Grilled cockerel in tarragon butter served with a *gratin* of cockerel livers.

Andouillette de Chez Duval. Grilled pork sausage supplied by the top-rated House of Duval.

Jambon de Bayonne. Smoked regional ham.

Brochettes de Coeurs de Canard en Persillade. Skewered parslied duck hearts.

Salade de Chèvres Chauds Sur Toasts. Hot goat-cheese salad with toast.

Tartine Chaude au Bleu des Causses et Jambon Cru. Sliced bread with blue cheese and smoked ham.

Tabliers de Sapeur. Ox tripe coated with egg and bread crumbs grilled and served with garlic butter.

Mousse au Chocolat. Chocolate mousse.

Pêches au Vin. Peaches stewed in red wine.

Tarte au Citron. Lemon tart.

WINE

Fine selection of diverse wines available by the glass or bottle. Madiran, Cahors, Saint-Joseph, Chinon.

AU PETIT RICHE

M. Christian Schmidt

ADDRESS: 25, rue Le Peletier, 75009
OPEN: Daily all year
CLOSED: Sun. and holidays
PRICE RANGE: Moderate
TEL: 47-70-68-68
METRO: Le Peletier and Richelieu-Drouot
CREDIT: Amex, Visa, Diners and MasterCard

An historic old bistro with authentic turn-of-the-century decor, serving classic fish and meat preparations with some specialties and wines from the Touraine and Anjou regions.

The Café Riche was opened as a *Grand Café* around 1865 but disappeared by 1873, leaving the "little Riche" to carry on alone. There is no main dining room; rather, there are a series of little dark-wood-paneled salons linked by corridors and kitchens. Painted ceilings, frosted glass, tall mirrors, brass overhead luggage racks, red upholstery and formally dressed waiters create a gracious atmosphere. The daily specials remain consistent with a few *plats du marché* prepared each day. The extensive wine list still specializes in wines from the Loire but no longer contains a portrait of Rabelais with the verse he put in Gargantua's mouth: "Refill your empty glass, empty your full glass; I cannot bear to see in thy hand thy glass neither empty nor full."

RECOMMENDED DISHES

Rillettes de Saumon à l'Aneth et Son Coulis de Concombre et Tomate. Preserved, mashed salmon pieces served as a spread with a purée of cucumbers and tomatoes.

Rillons de Vouvray en Gelée. Preserved potted pork cubes in aspic.

Pâté de Lapereau en Gelée aux Pruneaux. Rabbit pâté in aspic with prunes.

Assiette de Pecheur au Beurre Blanc. Assortment of poached fish in a white-wine butter sauce.

Filet de Turbotin à la Ciboulette. Grilled fillet of small turbot with chives.

Brandade de Morue. Creamed salt cod.

Magret de Canard Rôti au Poivre Vert. Fattened duck breast roasted with green peppercorns.

Boeuf Miroton. Slices of boiled beef simmered in a rich brown onion sauce.

Andouillette Grillée au Vouvray. Grilled pork sausage in Loire wine, served with a seasonal salad.

Petit Salé aux Lentilles. Lightly salted cooked pork with lentils.

Râble de Lapereau Farci aux Pruneaux. Saddle of hare roasted with a prune stuffing.

Tarte Fine aux Pommes Chaudes (order in advance). Thin, hot apple tart.

Crème Caramel. Vanilla-flavored flan.

WINE

Very large selection of first-quality wines from the Loire. Sauvignon de Cheverny *(en carafe)*, Gamay-de-Touraine *(en carafe)*, Vouvray Tranquille ou Pétillant *(en carafe)*.

LE ROI DU POT-AU-FEU ★ ★

M. Daniel Anée

ADDRESS: 34, rue Vignon, 75009
CLOSED: Sun. and July
PRICE RANGE: Moderate
TEL: 47-42-37-10
METRO: Madeleine
CREDIT: Amex, Visa, Diners and MasterCard

Old musical instruments and cartoon-covered walls are part of the decor in this offbeat little spot specializing in a classic pot-au-feu. *A steaming bowl of golden bouillon is followed by a platter of tender cuts of boiled beef, vegetables and bone marrow. Crusty bread, a fresh Gamay d'Anjou and* crème caramel *complete the meal.*

Located in the busy shopping district off the Place de la Madaleine, this intimate art deco bistro with zinc bar and red-checkered tablecloths serves hearty plates of carefully chosen cuts of meat. Almost everyone orders the *pot-au-feu*, which comes with spicy Dijon mustard, coarse salt, *cornichons* and delicious bread freshly baked across the street at Fournil de Pierre. A branch of Le Roi du Pot-au-Feu (40 rue de Ponthieu, tel. 43-59-41-62), in the 8ᵉ near the Champs-Élysées, also serves a generous *pot-au-feu* along with other specialties such as a fine calf's head in vinaigrette and a tasty *hachis parmentier* (hash made from boiled beef leftovers and potatoes, served in a sauce). Reservations are not necessary, but both places are often crowded with well-heeled shoppers and their companions.

RECOMMENDED DISHES

Bol de Bouillon. Bowl of beef broth.
Terrine de Foies de Volaille. Chicken liver pâté.
Poireau Vinaigrette. Leeks in vinaigrette.
Pot-au-Feu. Enormous plate of boiled beef rib and shoulder
   with turnips, carrots, cabbage and bone marrow cooked in

a rich broth accompanied by *cornichons,* Dijon mustard, coarse salt and crunchy bread.

Crème Caramel. Vanilla-flavored flan.
Mousse au Chocolat. Chocolate mousse.
Tarte-Tatin. Upside-down apple pie.

WINE

Gamay d'Anjou, Côtes-du-Rhône.

10e

CHEZ CASIMIR
LA GRILLE

10e Arrondissement

GARE-DU-NORD–GARE-DE-L'EST

PLACES OF INTEREST

Canal Saint-Martin
Gare du Nord, Gare de l'Est
Musée de l'Affiche et de la Publicité
Place de la République (3e, 10e, 11e)
Porte Saint-Denis
Porte Saint-Martin
Rue de Paradis

CHEZ CASIMIR

M. Maurice Beringer

ADDRESS: 6, rue de Belzunce, 75010
CLOSED: Sat. lunch and Sunday
PRICE RANGE: Fairly expensive
TEL: 48-78-32-53
METRO: Gare du Nord or Poissonnière
CREDIT: Amex, Visa, Diners and MasterCard

A snug little bistro in an obscure neighborhood frequented by a knowledgeable Parisian clientele who flock here for exquisite fresh foie gras, sumptous cassoulet, and imaginative fresh fish dishes. The tiny terrace is very popular in good weather.

Chez Casimir, which must be reached on foot, is located on a narrow street behind the church of Saint-Vincent de Paul. There is nothing to bring you to this corner of Paris except fine food, which you will find both here and down the block at the Michelin-starred restaurant Chez Michel. When Casimir opened in the 1960s it enjoyed much success and now has risen to even greater heights under the energetic direction of the new owner and chef, Maurice Beringer. There is a certain charm to the decor, enhanced by the wine labels which paper the walls. The front room is more spacious than the rear, but you will prefer the back for its intimate atmosphere. Lunch is busy but dinner is quiet and you can relax as you enjoy a glass of *sauternes* with the house *foie gras*. Fish is a specialty, but you might also consider the fillet of beef "Boston," which is served in a delicious oyster sauce. The *prix-fixe* menu at 170F includes a choice of three *entrées*, three *plats*, brie and *pâtisserie*. A small group of unusual house wines are bottled exclusively for Beringer.

RECOMMENDED DISHES

Foie Gras de Canard Frais Maison et Bon Verre de Sauternes. Fresh made duck liver foie gras served with a glass of sauterne wine.
Soupe de Poissons "Maison." House fish soup.

Rillettes de Lapereau. Coarse rabbit spread.

Salade de Mesclun au Noix. Mixed green salad with walnuts.

La Bourride de l'Atlantique. Fish and shellfish stew.

Cassoulet Landais à ma Façon. White bean stew with a choice of duck or goose confit.

Brochettes de St. Jacques Pannées "Beurre Blanc." Skewered scallops served with white wine butter sauce.

Lotte du Vendangeur Bordelais. Monkfish with grapes.

Filet de Boeuf "Boston." Broiled fillet of beef with a sauce of cooked oysters.

Foie de Veau au Vinaigre de Framboise. Grilled calf's liver with raspberry vinegar sauce.

L'Andouillette Diplomée à la Moutarde de Meaux. Grilled pork sausages in a mustard and mushroom sauce.

Brie de Meaux. Finest quality brie.

Sorbets Maison. Homemade assorted sherbets.

WINE

Extensive selection of Burgundies (an especially fine Meursault), Bordeaux and Loire wines. A small group of Trouvailles (discoveries) are always available.

LA GRILLE ★ ★ ★

M. Yves Cullère
Mme. Geneviève Cullère

ADDRESS: 80, rue du Faubourg-Poissonière at the Intersection of rue de Montholon and rue des Méssageries, 75010

CLOSED: Sat., Sun., August and one week in February

PRICE RANGE: Fairly expensive

TEL: 47-70-89-73

METRO: Poissonière

CREDIT: Diners

One of the last old-time family bistros, where everything is carefully prepared and well looked-after. The setting is cozy with lots of lace, embroidery and damask, and the cuisine is fresh and of very good quality.

Mme. Geneviève Cullère puts as much into welcoming her guests and overseeing the dining room as her husband does into the superb specialties which have won him a glowing reputation. Perfectly grilled turbot, served for two, accompanied by a bowl of exquisite, tangy *beurre blanc* and a side of fabulous sliced potatoes baked in butter, is what brings people here, but the menu includes many other tempting choices. Excellent cuts of steak and little *andouillettes* (pork sausages) in mustard sauce, luscious scallops and salmon served with *beurre blanc* and a sumptuous *boeuf bourguignon* are all worthwhile. A crisp-white or fruity-red wine grown around the village of Ménétou Salon in the Loire Valley are fine choices with the food.

RECOMMENDED DISHES

Maquereau Frais au Vin Blanc. Whole fresh mackerel in white wine.

Filets de Sardine Marinés. Marinated sardine fillets.

Terrine de Canard aux Noisettes. Duck liver pâté with hazelnuts.

Terrine de Gibier. Various game pâtés in season.

Terrine de Fruits de Mer. Seafood terrine.

Saint-Jacques au Beurre Blanc. Pan-fried scallops in a white-wine butter sauce.

Turbot Grillé Beurre Blanc Avec un Gateau de Pommes de Terre au Lard (for two). Grilled turbot in a white-wine butter sauce. The outstanding specialty of the bistro. Served with a potato loaf cooked with bacon.

Boeuf Bourguignon à l'Ancienne. Beef stewed in red wine with mushrooms and onions.

Pavé de Boeuf à la Moutarde. Thick slice of broiled beef steak in mustard sauce.

Tête de Veau, Sauce Gribiche. Calf's head served hot with a mustard-mayonnaise sauce.

Poulet aux Écrevisses. Young chicken cooked with crayfish tails in cream sauce.

Mousse au Chocolat. Chocolate mousse.

Crème Caramel. Vanilla-flavored flan.

Oeufs à la Neige. Whipped, sweetened egg whites, poached in milk and served with a vanilla custard sauce.

WINE

Ménétou-Salon (white, rosé or red), Muscadet, Côtes-du-Rhône, Beaujolais.

11ᵉ

À SOUSCEYRAC

ASTIER

AUBERGE PYRÉNÉES CÉVENNES

(CHEZ PHILIPPE)

CARTET

LE CHARDENOUX

CHEZ FERNAND (LES FERNANDISES)

11ᵉ Arrondissement

RÉPUBLIQUE–NATION

PLACES OF INTEREST

Cirque d'Hiver
L'Église de Sainte-Marguerite
Hôtel Tubeuf
Place de la Bastille (Opéra de la Bastille)
Place de la République
Rue du Faubourg St.-Antoine
Rue de Lappe
Rue Roquette

À SOUSCEYRAC

M. Gabriel Asfaux
M. Patrick Asfaux

ADDRESS: 35, rue Faidherbe, 75011
CLOSED: Sat., Sun. and August
PRICE RANGE: Expensive
TEL: 43-71-65-30
METRO: Faidherbe–Chaligny
CREDIT: Amex, Visa, Diners and MasterCard

First-rate ingredients and careful preparation, with an emphasis on intensely rich specialties from the Quercy and Lot regions of Southwestern France, are the mainstays of this distinguished old bistro located in a remote corner of the 11ᵉ.

Sousceyrac is the name of a small village in the Quercy, and the cuisine here reflects the heartiness of old-fashioned Gascon cookery: delicious pâtés and *terrines* of foie gras, truffle salad, truffles and morels, sausages with morels in cream sauce, lamb sweetbreads, slices of duck breast, liver and kidneys in cream sauce with wild mushrooms and copious peasant stews. The house specialty is a wild hare preparation, *lièvre à la royale*, served on Fridays from mid-October to late December. This famous dish requires the hare to be marinated for several hours in red wine, herbs and onions then stewed for more hours with its liver, vegetables, herbs and seasonings all of which are finally blended with foie gras and truffles into a coarse mixture with a fine gamey flavor and rich texture. The small wine list includes some excellent choices including a fine Cahors by the pitcher and some old Armagnacs.

Opened in 1923 by Adolphe and Ida Asfaux, the restaurant is now run by grandsons Luc and Patrick. The decor is old-fashioned but comfortable and the paneled dining room is decorated with pictures and a collection of attractive country crockery.

RECOMMENDED DISHES

Foie Gras Frais de Canard. Fresh duck foie gras with truffles.

Foie Gras Frais d'Oie. Fresh goose foie gras.

Timbal Chaude de Lapereau aux Écrevisses. Hot rabbit *mousseline* with crayfish tails.

Tourte aux Cailles. Hot quail pie.

Pavé de Saumon Sauvage Rôti au Coulis de Poivron Rouge. Thick slice of wild salmon roasted with a purée of sweet red peppers.

Andouillette au Four. Roast pork sausage.

Civet de Canard. Rich duck stew.

Cassoulet Comme à Sousceyrac (Wednesdays and Fridays). Languedoc stew with mutton, preserved duck and goose, sausage and white beans. A great favorite of this bistro.

Ris de Veau Entier Étuvé. Whole braised sweetbreads with mushrooms.

Pieds de Porc Grillé Saint-Antoine. Grilled breaded pigs' feet.

Angus d'Ecosse à la Forestière. Grilled beef steak with mushrooms, bacon and potatoes.

Saucisson Chaud Pistaché. Hot pork sausage studded with pistachio nuts and served in a cream sauce with morel mushrooms.

Lièvre à la Royale (Friday nights from early October through Christmas). Stewed red hare. The outstanding specialty of the bistro when available.

Profiteroles au Chocolat. Ice-cream-filled pastries covered with melted chocolate.

Tarte Tiède aux Poires. Warm pear tart.

Pruneaux à l'Armagnac. Prunes stewed in Armagnac brandy.

Glace aux Marrons Confits. Vanilla ice cream with candied chestnuts.

WINE

Cahors (in the pitcher).

ASTIER

M. Michel Picquart

ADDRESS: 44, rue Jean-Pierre-Timbaud, 75011
CLOSED: Sat., Sun. and August
PRICE RANGE: Inexpensive
TEL: 43-57-16-35
METRO: Parmentier
CREDIT: Visa

Superior home cooking at bargain prices brings a young, well-heeled, exclusively Parisian clientele to the heart of the 11e. Reservations are an absolute must, as this bustling place turns away as many people each night as it serves.

Decor is nonexistent and the elbow-to-elbow tables make service a bit strained, but no one seems to mind as they dig into heaping plates of shrimp, *terrines,* oysters, herring, foie gras, marinated leeks, salmon, sausages, turbot, veal stew, rabbit in mustard sauce, fillets of beef and pigeon *confit.* The astounding menu at 110F offers no less than nine *entrées,* ten *plats,* cheese and a half-dozen desserts, including a rich bittersweet chocolate cake and *fromage blanc.* There are two dining rooms and a constant flow of customers heading up the narrow stairs to the first floor. Downstairs, a tiny bar in the back serves as a waiters' station. The ambience is young, the room noisy and smoky, but everyone seems to enjoy themselves.

RECOMMENDED DISHES

Terrine de Lapin Maison. Rabbit pâté.
Terrine aux Foies de Volaille Maison. Chicken liver pâté.
Friture de Céteaux. Tiny fried sole.
Cassoulette d'Escargots aux Girolles. Cassoulette dish of snails and mushrooms.
Mousseline de Haddock, Beurre Blanc. Puréed haddock beaten with egg yolks and cream, poached and served with a white-wine butter sauce.
Brandade de Morue aux Brocolis. Creamed salt cod with broccoli.

Tête de Veau Ravigote. Calf's head served hot in a vinaigrette with capers, parsley and tarragon.

Brochette de Lotte aux Lard. Skewered monkfish wrapped in bacon and grilled.

Andouillette (A.A.A.A.) Grillée. Grilled pork sausage.

Magret de Canard à la Crème de Foie Gras. Fattened duck breast grilled and served with a creamy foie gras sauce.

Lapin à la Moutarde Pâtes Fraîches. Rabbit in mustard sauce, served with fresh pasta.

Fricassée de Rognons et Ris de Veau au Poivre Vert. Light stew of veal kidneys and sweetbreads with green peppercorns.

Plateau de Fromages. Exceptional-quality cheese platter.

Gâteau au Chocolat. Chocolate cake.

Clafoutis. Baked custard fruit tart.

Crème Caramel. Vanilla-flavored flan.

WINE

Excellent selection of Burgundy and Bordeaux wines at bargain prices. Beaujolais (by the pitcher), Chinon Blanc, Mersault, Cabernet-de-Touraine, Saint-Nicolas-de-Bourgueil.

AUBERGE PYRÉNÉES-CÉVENNES (CHEZ PHILIPPE)

M. Philippe Serbource

ADDRESS: 106, rue de la Folie-Méricourt, 75011
CLOSED: Sat., Sun. and August
PRICE RANGE: Fairly expensive
TEL: 43-57-33-78
METRO: République
CREDIT: None

A Pyrénéan-style auberge *where the atmosphere is intimate and gay. The menu offers superb Gascon food and spicy Basque specialties. These, accompanied by marvelous country wines, make this one of the most delightful and best regional bistros in the city.*

Owner Philippe Serbource, who bought the restaurant 25 years ago, added his own name to the old one but never changed the unpretentious exterior of this 60-year-old country-style inn located across the St. Martin Canal from the Place de la République. Beamed ceiling, ochre walls, red-tile floors, hanging sausages, hams and garlic, copper pots, shields and bull-fight posters make for cozy surroundings. The meal begins with a *Kir* offered by Mme. Serbource and a choice between generous portions of rich creamy pâté, a huge basket of assorted sausages or a deep tureen of herring fillets floating in vinegar brine with slices of pickles and onions, served with a crock full of fresh cream. Many order the *entrecôte*, in a rich sauce made with Burgundy and poached marrow served with crisp potatoes, or the lobster, served in two parts, the claws after the body, but one really ought to try the regional food. The *cassoulet* Toulousian-style, the *piperade Basquaise* and the paella *Valenciana* are as authentic as the country wines included on the excellent *carte des vins*.

RECOMMENDED DISHES

Foie Gras de Canard Naturel. Block of fresh duck foie gras.

Caille Confite au Foie Gras. Potted quail perserves with foie gras.

Cochonnailles de Pays. Large basket of assorted pork sausages.

Piperade Basquaise. Basque omelette with tomatoes, peppers and onions, served with sliced Bayonne ham.

Harengs Bismark. Marinated herring fillets brought to the table in a tureen with cream on the side.

Jambon Persillé de Bourgogne. Parslied ham molded in its own aspic.

Rougets Grillés au Beurre d'Anchois. Grilled red mullet with anchovy butter.

Sole Belle Meunière. Fillet of sole coated with flour, sautéed in butter and served with brown butter.

Homard Grillé à l'Estragon. Whole grilled lobster with tarragon.

Jambon Braisé au Gratin de Macaroni. Braised ham served with a *gratin* of macaroni.

Chou Farci. Stuffed cabbage.

Coq-au-Vin Bourguignon. Chicken stewed in Burgundy wine with mushrooms and onions.

Paella "Valenciana." Spanish dish of chicken, hot sausage

and seafood with green and red peppers mixed with saffron rice. Extraordinary.

Cassoulet d'Oie Toulousain. Languedoc stew of white beans, pork, preserved goose, sausage and a generous addition of garlic and bread crumbs. An outstanding specialty of this bistro.

Confit d'Oie "Auberge." Preserved goose with white beans.

Petit Salé en Potée. Lightly salted pork stewed with vegetables.

Rognon de Veau en Cocotte. Veal kidneys served in a casserole.

Entrecôte à la Moelle. Sautéed ribsteak with bone marrow.

Profiteroles Glacées Sauce Chocolat. Ice-cream-filled pastry shells covered with melted chocolate.

Crème Caramel. Vanilla-flavored flan.

Vacherin Praliné. Baked meringue with almond flavoring.

WINE

Excellent selection of red Bordeaux and Burgundy wines. Cahors, Beaujolais Villages, Madiran, Aligoté de Bourgogne.

CARTET

M. Raymond & Mme. Marie-Thérèse Nouaille

ADDRESS: 62, rue de Malte, 75011
CLOSED: Sat., Sun. and August
PRICE RANGE: Fairly expensive
TEL: 48-05-17-65
METRO: République
CREDIT: None

A small, unpretentious place made famous by Mme. Marie Antoinette Cartet. The kitchen is now in the capable hands of owners Raymond and Marie-Thérèse Nouaille, who carry on the traditions of fine, wholesome home-cooked cuisine.

You must reserve a few days in advance as there is only room for 25 or 30 people at the six or so little tables in the 1930s-style dining room. Vinyl banquettes, mirrors, wooden walls and pink damask linens add a quaint touch, evoking an intimate homey atmosphere. When Mme. Cartet arrived in Paris from Bourgen-Bresse she wanted a place where people could come to eat simply but well. She opened in 1936 and within a few years transformed an old *bougnat* (café), which also sold wood and charcoal, into a renowned bistro. She retired in 1980, but the Nouailles continue to serve abundant portions of meaty *terrines,* creamed pike dumplings, *boeuf à la ficelle* and a delicious lemon tart which Marie-Thérèse prepares twice daily.

RECOMMENDED DISHES

Charcuteries Maison (Cochonnailles). Assorted pork products.

Maquereau Marinés au Vin Blanc. Fresh marinated mackerel in white wine.

Jambon Persillé. Parslied ham in aspic.

Saucisson Chaud de Lyon. Large pork slicing sausage, served hot.

Frisée aux Lardons. Chicory salad with bacon.

Croûte aux Morilles. Puff pastry filled with wild mushrooms.

Quenelles de Brochet Sauce Nantua. Pike dumplings in a crayfish purée.

Baudroie Sauce Nantua. Monkfish in a crayfish purée.

Brandade de Morue. Creamed salt cod.

Pieds de Mouton, Sauce Poulette. Sheep's feet in a mushroom-flavored white sauce with lemon juice.

Palette de Porc à la Bourguignonne. Pork bladebone in a red-wine sauce with mushrooms and onions.

Gigot d'Agneau, Gratin Dauphinois. Roast leg of lamb with sliced potatoes baked in cream and browned on top.

Boeuf à la Ficelle. Slightly roasted fillet of beef tied and lowered into simmering broth. Served with *gratin dauphinois.*

Gras-Double. Scalded ox tripe cooked for hours in bouillon then sliced and sautéed with minced onions, vinegar and chopped parsley.

Tarte au Citron. Lemon tart.

Profiteroles aux Fraises. Chocolate covered ice-cream-filled pastry shells with strawberries.

Bugnes. Sweet pastry fritters.

Gâteau au Chocolat. Chocolate cake.

WINE

Vin du Bugey (red, white and rosé), Morgon, Brouilly.

LE CHARDENOUX ★ ★ ★

Mme. Anne Krajewski

ADDRESS: 1, rue Jules-Vallès, 75011
CLOSED: Sat. lunch, Sun. and August
PRICE RANGE: Fairly expensive
TEL: 43-71-49-52
METRO: Charonne
CREDIT: Amex and Visa

Subtle and simple food in a Belle-Époque working-class café
du coin, *where the new owner contines to offer unpretentious,
good-quality cuisine.*

All the original fixtures are beautifully preserved in this charming corner bistro located in an up-and-coming, but out-of-the-
way, part of town. An unrestored marble entrance leads into a
small room divided by etched-glass and wood panels dating
from the 1880s. Original paintings, mirrors, gilt ceiling appli-
qués and tulip lamps also remain untouched, but the bar, which
is made of 17 different marbles, is the room's masterpiece.
Even the original horse rings and polished brass spigot where
customers used to water their horses are still at its front end.
You don't come to Chardenoux by chance, but it is worth the
trip for the authentic decor and cuisine lightened by modern
touches.

RECOMMENDED DISHES

Oeufs en Meurette. Poached eggs in red-wine sauce.
Poireaux "Vigneronne." Leeks "wine-grower style" with
    grapes and *marc.*
Foie Gras de Canard "Maison." Fresh duck foie gras.
Salade Frisée aux Lardons, Avec Son Oeuf Mollet.
    Chicory salad with bacon and a soft-boiled egg.

Saumon à l'Unilatéral. Salmon grilled on one side.

Andouillette Grillée (A.A.A.A.A.). Grilled pork sausage.

Confit de Canard, Pommes Anna. Preserved duck, served with a baked potato cake.

Boudin Noir aux Deux Pommes. Grilled blood sausage with fried potatoes and apples.

Cassoulet au Confit de Canard. Languedoc stew with preserved duck, sausage and white beans, cooked and served in a casserole.

Magret de Cannard Grillée. Grilled fattened duck breast.

Tripes aux Calvados. Braised ox tripe cooked with carrots, onions, garlic, tarragon, cider and Calvados brandy.

Sorbet Pommes Vertes, Calvados. Green apple sherbet laced with Calvados brandy.

Fondant de Chocolat aux Marrons de l'Ardèche, Crème Anglaise. Cake with chocolate icing and chestnuts in a light egg custard.

WINE

Côtes-du-Rhône (Chez Sinard), Gamay (Chez Marrionnet), Loire.

CHEZ FERNAND (LES FERNANDISES)　★ ★

M. Fernand Asseline

ADDRESS: 17, rue de la Fontaine-au-Roi, 75011

CLOSED: Sat. lunch, Sun. and August

PRICE RANGE: Moderate

TEL: 43-57-46-25

METRO: Goncourt or République

CREDIT: Visa

One of the only restaurants in Paris where you will find true Norman cooking. Each day owner-chef Fernand Asseline prepares crusty multigrain bread, his famous skate with Camembert, tripe with cider, crêpes, and an apple tart flamed with Calvados. Fernandise, next door, is a less expensive version of Fernand, but the two places share the same menu on Fridays and Saturdays.

Fernand moved to this location close to the Canal St. Martin, just off the Place de la République, in 1986. The little bistro-yellow dining room is scattered with a few paintings and pieces of copper. There is a bar along one side of the room and the ten tables are finely set with pink cloths and napkins. There is a *prix-fixe* menu at 110F, but the most outstanding dishes of the house, such as the grilled foie gras, the golden roast baby pig with garlic cream or the *emincé* of duck, Rouen-style, in a rich blood-thickened sauce, are listed à la carte. The only cheese is Camembert, but it is ripe and delicious served five ways: plain, or with pink peppercorns, hay, caraway or chopped walnuts. There are some fine crus from the Loire, including a red Valencay which is light in alcohol and fruity in flavor.

RECOMMENDED DISHES

Rillettes de Maquereaux. Cooked mackerel bits preserved in a jar, pounded to a pâté-like consistency and served as a spread.

Salade de Moules Fraîches aux Fines Herbes. Fresh mussel salad.

Foie Gras Frais de Canard. Fresh duck foie gras grilled and served with country bread.

Salade de Foies de Canard au Vinaigre de Cidre. Green salad with duck livers in a cider vinaigrette.

Raie au Camembert. Skate cooked with Camembert cheese.

Filets de Rascasse Vallée d'Auge. Scorpion fish fillets cooked with Calvados brandy and cream.

Porcelet Rôti à la Crème d'Ail. Roast baby pig with garlic cream.

Confit de Canard Pommes à l'Ail. Preserved duck, served with potatoes sautéed with garlic.

Emincé de Canard (Grillé, Cidre et Pomme, Rouennaise, au Foie Gras). Four distinct preparations of sliced duck, including the famous *"Rouennaise"* with its blood-thickened red-wine-and-duck-liver sauce.

Tripes au Calvados. Braised ox tripe, cooked with carrots, onions, garlic, tarragon, cider and Calvados brandy.

Plateau de Camemberts Affinés Par Fernand. Five versions of Camembert cheese (plain, pink peppercorns, hay, caraway, chopped walnuts) prepared by the chef.

Tarte aux Pommes. Hot apple tart.

Crêpes aux Pommes Flambée Calvados. Thin pancakes stuffed with apples and flamed with Calvados brandy.

WINE

Well-chosen selection of country wines at attractive prices. Most from the Touraine, Auvergne and Bordeaux regions. Madiran, Sancerre, Côtes-de-Blaye, Valencay.

12^e

CHEZ MARCEL (ANTOINE)

12ᵉ *Arrondissement*

GARE-DE-LYON–DAUMESNIL–REUILLY DIDEROT

PLACES OF INTEREST

Place de la Bastille
Place de la Nation
Gare de Lyon (Restaurant Le Train Bleu)
Bois de Vincennes (Château de Vincennes,
Parc Zoologique, Parc Floral)
Musée National des Arts Africains et Océaniens
Cimetière de Picpus
Place d'Aligre (flea market)

CHEZ MARCEL (ANTOINE)

★ ★ ★

M. Trottet

ADDRESS: 7, rue Saint-Nicolas, 75012
CLOSED: Sat., Sun., August and holidays
PRICE RANGE: Fairly expensive
TEL: 43-43-49-40
METRO: Ledru-Rollin
CREDIT: Visa

If you are looking for authenticity you will find it in this won-derful old-fashioned bistro where the decor, the atmosphere, the service, the portions and the cuisine are absolutely tradi-tional. A clientele of serious eaters is drawn here by the aro-mas of yesteryear.

In Chez Marcel there is a nice custom. As soon as you sit down three bottles are placed on your table: a Beaujolais Vil-lages, a Muscadet, and a Crème de Cassis, the last two for making yourself a *Kir*. The red and the white remain through-out the meal, and are replaced if necessary; you pay for only what you drink. Located in a quiet neighborhood, the restau-rant consists of a long room divided into two sections by beau-tiful etched glass. At the front is a bar, in the back red moleskin banquettes, large wall mirrors, a lovely tile floor and tables covered in white damask. Everything gives the impres-sion that here good cooking will be found.

Appetizers come to the table in large bowls from which you can help yourself. *Cochonnailles* are brought back several times because the table is not big enough to hold them. Next, there are generous servings of beef, tripe and pork in old-fashioned sauces, quail with Chartreuse, grilled pigs' feet, Morteau sausage with lentils and delicious house desserts. The service is provided by the *patronne* and another woman dressed in cardigan sweaters and skirts. The bill will be expensive, but you will have received much more than you paid for.

RECOMMENDED DISHES

Terrines. Assorted pâtés (duck with hazelnuts, quail with raisins, thrush, rabbit with prunes, chicken liver, country style).

Cochonnailles. First-quality pork products.

Salade de Lentilles. Lentil salad with onion rings.

Pissenlits Blancs aux Oeufs Durs. Dandelion-leaf salad served with hard-boiled eggs.

Maquereaux Frais au Vin Blanc. Fresh mackerel fillets poached in white-wine bouillon, served chilled.

Harengs de la Baltique à la Crème. Terrine of marinated herring fillets, served with cream on the side.

Saumon Frais, Sauce Tartare (Froid). Thick slice of fresh salmon served cold with tartar sauce.

Selle d'Agneau à l'Aillade. Roast saddle of lamb served with a garlic-mayonnaise-herb sauce similar to *aïoli.*

Estouffade de Boeuf. Beef stewed in a sealed pot with vegetables and a remarkable wine sauce.

Boudin, Pommes en l'Air. Large pork blood sausage grilled and served with fried apples.

Deux Cailles Fraîches Perigourdine. Quails browned in sauce and garnished with sliced potatoes, onions and truffles.

Pieds de Porc. Pigs' feet served roasted (*au four*) or stuffed and grilled (*farci aux herbes*).

Tripes Maison, au Sancerre. Ox tripe cooked in white Loire wine.

Andouillette. Pork sausage, served poached (*à la ficelle*) or grilled with green peppercorns (*au poivre vert*).

Coq-au-Beaujolais. Chicken stewed in Beaujolais wine with onions and mushrooms.

Saucisson Chaud Poivre Vert Pommes à l'Huile. Large slicing sausage accompanied by hot potato salad.

Civet de Porcelet. Piglet stew.

Civet de Lièvre. Stewed hare with red wine and vegetables.

Poire au Vin. Poached pears in wine.

Pruneaux au Vin. Prunes in wine.

Glace Miel et Noix. Honey ice cream with walnuts.

WINE

Muscadet (Sèvres et Maine), Beaujolais Villages.

13*e*

LE BOEUF BISTROT
CHEZ GRAND-MÈRE
LE PETIT MARGUERY

13e Arrondissement

PLACE D'ITALIE

PLACES OF INTEREST

La Bièvre (small river which flows into the Seine)
La Butte-aux-Cailles
La Cité Floréale (artists' colony)
La Cité Verte
Gare d'Austerlitz
Manufacture des Gobelins
Les Olympiades
Place d'Italie
Le Quartier Chinois

LE BOEUF BISTROT ★ ★

M. Jean Claude Amice
Mme. Isabelle Garnia

ADDRESS: 4, place des Alpes, 75013
CLOSED: Sat. lunch, Sun. and August 10–20
PRICE RANGE: Moderate
TEL: 45-82-08-09
METRO: Place d'Italie
CREDIT: Amex, Visa, Diners and MasterCard

Superior cuts of beef and farm-fresh vegetables are the mainstays of the imaginative cuisine in this neighborhood spot filled with young habitués. Wonderful grilled steak, delicious potatoes and Beaujolais by the glass make a satisfying and moderately-priced meal.

One block east of the immense Place d'Italie, Le Boeuf Bistro is far from the bustling Latin Quarter yet manages to capture a Left-Bank ambience with little sidewalk tables and a dining room tastefully decorated with posters and drawings. By day the room is sunny and bright with cream-colored walls and clear light fixtures. In the evening it becomes romantic with its burgundy velour curtains, candles on each table and pleasant background music. The cooking is simple, blending classics with some more original creations. Beef is a specialty and is served several different ways: cured with marrow bones and vegetables, braised, grilled or tartare. Salmon, tuna and pike dumplings are light and very good. Fresh *entrées,* cheese and enticing desserts complete the menu.

RECOMMENDED DISHES

Gros Escargots de Bourgogne. Large vineyard snails in garlic butter.
Salade Melée aux Gésiers Confits et Magret Fumé. Mixed salad of preserved gizzards and smoked duck breast.
Truite Fumée Sauce Raifort. Smoked trout with creamy horseradish sauce.

Rognons de Veau Entiers au Vinaigre de Xérès. Whole veal kidneys braised with sherry vinegar from Jerez.

Coeur de Rumsteak à la Moutarde Fine. Heart of the rump steak grilled with mustard sauce.

Côte de Boeuf à la Moëlle (for two). Roast ribs of beef with bone marrow.

Entrecôte aux Échalotes. Rib steak sautéed with shallots.

Emincé de Volaille à l'Estragon Frais. Thinly sliced chicken creamed with fresh tarragon.

Magret de Canard Aigre-Doux. Fattened duck breast in a sweet-and-sour sauce.

Mousse au Chocolat. Chocolate mousse.

Tarte Chaude aux Pommes. Hot apple tart.

Fraises à la Grenadine. Strawberries in Grenadine.

WINE

Saumur Champigny, Chinon, Sancerre, Saint-Amour, Brouilly, Croze-Hermitage.

CHEZ GRAND-MÈRE ★

MM. Rouvre

ADDRESS: 92, rue Broca, 75013
CLOSED: Sunday
PRICE RANGE: Moderate
TEL: 47-07-13-65
METRO: Gobelins
CREDIT: Visa

The decor is a bit precious; otherwise everything is nicely presented in this intimate place popular with an upscale clientele. The cooking is classically based, but light and very good.

Nothing has changed in grandmother's lace-curtained bistro, although it was bought in 1987 by the Rouvre brothers. Located beneath the Boulevard Porte Royal, just off the Boulevard Arago in a totally uninteresting part of town, this tiny place is well known to Parisians. The restaurant looks more like an antique shop painted pink, with Victorian bric-a-brac in the front windows and on display inside. A tiny bar, large lace doilies draped over hanging lights, and a wonderful old hutch grace the aqua-carpeted dining room. Tempting pastries and cakes are spread in a glass-enclosed bakery case along one wall. For luncheon a *prix-fixe* menu at 62F is limited to steak or the *plat du jour,* one or two simple hors d'oeuvres and three or four desserts. À la carte specialties are the *pot-au-feu,* trout with vegetables and rabbit with mustard sauce and *tagliatelles.* After dinner you can relax with an Armagnac, Calvados or an excellent Cognac, all offered at bargain prices.

RECOMMENDED DISHES

Terrine de Lapin au Vouvray. Rabbit pâté made with white Vouvray wine.

Escargots Farcis au Beurre d'Ail. Stuffed snails with garlic butter.

Crottins Rôtis à la Fleur de Thym. Grilled goat cheese accented with thyme.

Soupe de Poissons et sa Rouille. Rich fish soup served with a spicy sauce made from tomatoes, olive oil, peppers and garlic.

Lapin à la Moutarde aux Tagliatelles. Rabbit with mustard sauce, served with noodles.

Pot-au-Feu à l'Ancienne. Boiled beef with vegetables, broth and bone marrow.

Tête de Veau Gribiche. Boiled calf's head in a mustard-mayonnaise sauce with capers, herbs and finely chopped hard-boiled eggs.

Bavette à l'Echalote. Beef skirt sautéed with shallots.

Carré d'Agneau Rôti (for two). Roast rack of lamb.

Filet de Rascasse à l'Oseille. Fillet of scorpion fish with sorrel.

Suprême de Truite Rose à l'Etuvée de Légumes. Trout served in a thick, floured cream sauce with steamed vegetables.

Saint-Jacques à la Provençale. Pan-fried scallops served Provence-style with tomatoes, garlic and onions.

Tarte-Tatin Chaude. Hot upside-down apple pie.

Mousse au Chocolat. Chocolate mousse.

WINE

Sauvignon Blanc (in the pitcher), Côtes-du-Rhône (in the pitcher), Sancerre, Cahors, Brouilly, Saint-Amour, Saumur-Champigny.

LE PETIT MARGUERY

M. Alain, Jacques & Michel Cousin

ADDRESS: 9. blvd de Port-Royal, 75013
CLOSED: Sun., Mon., August and December 24–January 3
PRICE RANGE: Fairly expensive
TEL: 43-31-58-59
METRO: Gobelins
CREDIT: Amex, Visa, Diners and MasterCard

The Cousin brothers are perfect hosts, and you will enjoy delicious seasonal seafood and game in a gay and very stylish bistro atmosphere. Many of the dishes are changed daily and prepared with great imagination by chefs Michel and Jacques.

Marvelous tile floors, old-fashioned sconces and matching chandeliers, mirrors and terra-cotta-colored walls are part of the delightful turn-of-the-century decor in the two dining rooms charmingly accented by shades of red, pink and blue. Hand-painted frescoes create a festive backdrop within but, weather permitting, the outside terrace is most attractive. The mood is high-spirited, fostered by the amiability of the proprietor, Alain, and friendly waiters who bustle about in black waistcoats, their white shirt sleeves rolled to the elbow. You will want to begin with an aperitif as you sit trying to decipher the extensive handwritten menu. A special *degustation* menu of four varied *plats,* lime sherbert in a Gewurtztraminer *marc,* cheese and a choice of desserts must be ordered by the entire table. Enticing fish specialties are carefully prepared and served in combinations to enhance their natural flavors: turbot with lobster sauce, fresh cod with crayfish and asparagus, little red mullets garnished with tiny vegetables and fillet of sole with fine herbs and light pasta. During the fall and winter there are succulent *"specialités de chasse"* such as wild boar prepared in pâté, grilled with pepper sauce or stewed and served with fresh noodles. Slices of wild duck or pigeon on a bed of green cabbage and foie gras, superb cuts of beef and veal in rich wine or cream sauces, wild mushrooms, *tagliatelle,* truffles and marvelous lightly salted duck with cabbage leaves are also delicious. A distinguished and expensive list of Burgundy wines includes a Hospices-de-Beaune, Chambolle-Musigny "Les Charmes," Charmes-Chambertin and many others imported by the famous houses of Louis Latour and Jaboulet.

RECOMMENDED DISHES

Cochonnailles. Assorted pork products, especially *fromage de tête* (headcheese) and *saucisse sèche* (dry sausage).

Maquereau Marinés au Poivre Vert. Mackerel marinated with green peppercorns.

Foie Gras Frais de Canard "Maison." Fresh duck foie gras.

Salade Maraîchere Embaumée de Truffes Fraîches. Mixed vegetable salad scented with fresh truffles.

Cassolette d'Escargots de Bourgogne aux Champignons. *Cassolette* dish of sautéed vineyard snails with mushrooms.

Terrines. Exceptional *terrines: de canard au foie gras* (wild duck with foie gras), *de faisan au foie gras* (pheasant with foie gras), *de lièvre* (hare), *de volaille au foie gras* (fowl with foie gras).

Spécialités de Chasse. Large selection of outstanding game dishes available seasonally.

Petit Salé de Canard à la Poitevine. Duck cured in salt brine then poached and served in the style of Poitou with lentils.

Pintadeau Fermier aux Champignons Sauvages Suivant Season. Young farm fresh guinea fowl, roasted with wild mushrooms.

Quartier d'Agneau de Lait des Pyrénées au jus de Persil. Roast suckling Pyrénées lamb, served with parsley juice and garlic.

Civet de Lièvre "Vielle France" aux Pâtes Fraîches. Rich hare stew with red wine, served in a thickened sauce with fresh pasta. *Civet de marcassin* (wild boar) is also available in season.

Bourride de Coquilles Saint-Jacques au Fenouil. Scallop-and-fish stew flavored with fennel and served with a garlic-mayonnaise sauce (aïoli).

Blanc de Turbot au Coulis de Homard. Large grilled, white turbot served with a purée of lobster.

Raie Rôtie au Gingembre et à la Menthe Fraîche. Roast skate with ginger and fresh mint.

Tarte Amandine aux Poires. Almond-flavored pear tart.

Gâteau Chocolat à l'Alcool de Framboise. Chocolate cake infused with raspberry-flavored *eau-de-vie.*

Île Flottante. Poached meringue floating in vanilla custard sauce.

WINE

Very strong list of Burgundy wines fairly priced. Quincy, Bourgueil, Cornas, Saint Joseph, Sancerre.

14^e

L'AUBERGE DU CENTRE
LA CAGOUILLE
LES PETITES SORCIÈRES
RESTAURANT BLEU

14ᵉ Arrondissement

MAINE–MONTPARNASSE

PLACES OF INTEREST

Alésia
Boulevard du Montparnasse
(la Coupole, le Dôme, le Sélect, la Rotonde)
Les Catacombes
*(*tours leave from 1, pl. Denfert-Rochereau*)*
Cimetière du Montparnasse
Cité Universitaire
Parc de Montsouris, l'Observatoire
*Place Denfert-Rochereau (*Lion of Belfort by Bartholdi*)*
*Puces de la Porte de Vanves (*flea market*)*
*Rue Daguerre (*open-air market*)*
Les Villas (Léone, Camélias)

L'AUBERGE DU CENTRE ★

M. Pierre Berthier

ADDRESS: 10, rue Delambre, 75014
CLOSED: Sat. lunch, Sun. and August
PRICE RANGE: Fairly expensive
TEL: 43-35-43-09
METRO: Edgar-Quinet or Vavin
CREDIT: Amex, Visa and MasterCard

Known in literary history as The Dingo (the crazy one), a favorite hangout of Hemingway and Fitzgerald, this picturesque bistro now reflects the robust cuisine of Central France.

You can still have a drink at the bar and sit on one of the six original stools where Picasso drank with Jean Cocteau. The present owners have been in charge for about twenty years and have developed a nice restaurant business. There are two *prix-fixe* menus: one at 98F, which includes cheese and dessert, and one at 160F with a better selection including the *plat du jour* which might be *coq-au-vin, tournedos* with Roquefort sauce, turbot or salmon. The *tourte Bourbonnaise* (a potato tart) and *oeufs en meurette* (eggs in a red-wine sauce) are specialties, and you might like to try the *"vin de notre pays,"* a Saint-Pourcain which complements the food.

RECOMMENDED DISHES

Tourte Bourbonnaise. Covered tart filled with veal in a cream sauce.
Soupe à l'Oignon Gratinée. Onion soup poured over a thick slice of bread then topped with grated cheese and browned.
Oeufs en Meurette. Poached eggs in a red-wine sauce.
Truite à la Crème et à l'Estragon. Broiled trout in a cream sauce flavored with tarragon.
Pavé Flambé au Poivre (Gris ou Vert). Thick beef steak flamed with a choice of two peppers (gray or green).
Magret de Canard au Poivre Vert. Fattened duck breast with green peppercorns.

Brandade de Morue. Creamed salt cod.

Coq-au-Vin. Chicken stewed in red wine with onions and mushrooms.

Crêpes Flambées au Grand-Marnier (for two). Thin pancakes filled with fruit and flamed with Grand Marnier Cognac.

Sorbet. Selection of six fresh-fruit sherbets.

WINE

Saint-Pourcain/Berthier (Cuvée de L'Auberge).

LA CAGOUILLE

M. Gerard Allemandou

ADDRESS: 10, place Brancusi (25, rue de L'Ouest), 75014
CLOSED: Sun., Mon., the week between Christmas and New Years and the first two weeks in August
PRICE RANGE: Expensive
TEL: 43-22-09-01
METRO: Gaité
CREDIT: Visa

Delicious ultra-fresh seafood is simply prepared with no heavy sauces or garnishes to spoil its natural flavor. The shrimp are cooked live, the salmon grilled on one side and the steamed mussels lightly sprinkled with pepper. Reservations are essential as this is the best seafood bistro in Paris.

Gerard Allemandou, the chef-patron, comes from the Charentes, a region of France's Atlantic coast north of Bordeaux. He attaches as much importance to wine and rare cheeses as he does to fresh seafood and has amassed one of the finest collections of Cognacs in Paris. The menu inscribed on a large slate offers a list of dishes which change daily according to what is available that morning at the Rungis market. Though the *cagouille* is a little snail from Charente, no snails are served here. Instead there are delicate dishes of fish seasoned with simple herbs, salt or pepper and garnished with steamed or lightly sautéed vegetables; baby squid roasted in hot oil; skate in mustard sauce; a stewed assortment of *fruits de mer* and pan-fried scallops with garlic. The desserts are sophisticated treats and there are over eighty Cognacs with which to complete your meal. The decor is clean and modern with stone floors, marble-topped tables, natural wood and a wall divider filled with bottles of Cognac. Bread and salted Charentais butter are on each table. The room can become a bit noisy and crowded, but there is a large terrace facing the Place Brancusi.

RECOMMENDED DISHES

Céteau Poêlés. Tiny pan-fried sole.

Coques Vapeur. Steamed cockles.

Pétoncle Nature. Queen (tiny) scallops cooked without seasoning.

Crevettes Roses Poêlées Vivantes. Pink shrimp pan-fried while alive.

Flan de Brocheton au Beurre Blanc. Pike dumplings served in a white-wine butter sauce.

Turbotin Grillé. Small grilled turbot.

Raie Sauce Gribiche. Skate grilled and served with a spicy mayonnaise sauce with capers, cornichons and herbs.

Saint-Jacques Poêlées à l'Ail. Scallops pan-fried with garlic and butter.

Rouget Barbet à l'Huile d'Olive. Grilled red mullet in olive oil.

Poire Super. Fresh pear served on pear sherbet.

Profiteroles au Chocolat. Ice-cream-filled pastries covered with a glaze of melted chocolate.

Tarte Maison au Citron. Lemon tart.

WINE

Well-chosen wine list of mostly whites from all the great areas, including many small-vineyard Champagnes. Quincy, Sancerre, Chablis.

LES PETITES SORCIÈRES ★ ★

M. Christian Teule
Mme. Carole Teule

ADDRESS: 12, rue Liancourt, 75014
CLOSED: Sat. lunch and Sun.
PRICE RANGE: Moderate
TEL: 43-21-95-68
METRO: Denfert-Rochereau or Mouton-Duvernet
CREDIT: Visa

A new and pretty little place where everything is neat and care-fully looked after, including the simple but finely executed cuisine. The prices are very modest and there is a nice dining terrace.

Mme. Carole Teule is a charming hostess and her husband, Christian, a talented chef who prepares exquisite bistro food in modern style. The dining room is tastefully done-up in dark wood and rose tones with dried flowers and simple bistro chairs and tables. On the small à la carte menu you will find *entrées* like cold tomato soup, zucchini flan with tarragon and a rabbit *terrine* with bacon. The main courses are also executed with imagination such as a tempting grilled salmon in vin-aigrette, a fish *blanquette* with lime, *entrecôte* with Roquefort and a bewitching rabbit with rosemary. Enticing homemade desserts include a coffee mousse and a *marquise au chocolate.* There is a *prix-fixe* menu at 120F for lunch and a copious din-ner menu which includes wine at 180F.

RECOMMENDED DISHES

Moules Marinière. Mussels cooked with shallots, white
    wine and herbs.
Filets de Maquereaux Frais au Vin Blanc. Mackerel fil-
    lets marinated in white wine, served cold.
Terrine de Lapin au Bacon. Rabbit pâté with bacon.
Flan de Lentilles aux Saucissons de Morteaux. Lentil
    tart with Jésus sausage.

Marmite de Poissons au Curry. Fish-and-shellfish stew flavored with curry.

Blanquette de Sole au Citron Vert. Fillet of sole in a white cream-and-egg-yolk sauce with lime juice.

Ragoût de Travers de Porc. Light pork stew.

Gras-Double à la Lyonnaise Avec Gratin de Macaroni. Ox tripe sliced and fried with onions, vinegar and parsley, served with macaroni sprinkled with cheese then browned on top.

Blanquette de Veau aux Petits Légumes. Veal stew in a white sauce with baby vegetables.

Râble de Lapin au Romarin. Roast saddle of rabbit with rosemary.

Marquise au Chocolat et Noisettes. Chocolate mousse cake with hazelnuts.

Profiteroles au Chocolat. Ice-cream-filled pastries covered with melted chocolate.

Tarte aux Pommes Parfumée à la Cannelle (must be ordered in advance). Hot apple tart with cinnamon.

WINE

Wines of the Loire Valley. Anjou Rouge, Chinon, Gamay-de-Touraine.

RESTAURANT BLEU

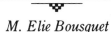

M. Elie Bousquet

ADDRESS: 46, rue Didot, 75014
CLOSED: Sat., Sun. and August
PRICE RANGE: Moderate
TEL: 45-43-70-56
METRO: Pernety
CREDIT: None

A simple but wonderful neighborhood bistro frequented mainly by Parisians who come for the hearty Auvergnat food and wine. Don't be misled by the casual appearance. The quality of the produce and cooking is first rate.

Owner-chef M. Elie Bousquet is an Auvergnat who insists on using only quality ingredients in his preparations. A meal here might begin with a glass of Sauternes and some fine regional pâté or ham, *andouillettes* from Vive or Guéméné or *cou d'oie farci* (the neck skin of goose stuffed as a sausage with meat and spices). Recommended main courses include a crispy grilled *boudin* (blood sausage), grilled Charolais beef, veal braised with *cèpes, tripoux* (mutton tripe) and a delicious *truffade* made with sautéed potatoes, tomatoes, herbs and garlic. The setting, entirely decorated in blue, is simple, with lace curtains, a beautiful zinc bar and old engravings on the wall.

RECOMMENDED DISHES

Plat de Cochonnailles. Platter of assorted pork products.
Jambon d'Auvergne. Smoked ham from the Auvergne region.
Terrine Rouergate. Country pâté.
Salade Frisée aux Lardons. Chicory salad with bacon.
Truffade Auvergnate. Potato cake with Cantal cheese and bacon.
Chou Farci. Stuffed cabbage.
Pièce de Charollais Grillée (for two). Finest-quality grilled beef.
Tripoux Auvergnats. Stuffed and heavily seasoned mutton tripe.
Rouelle de Veau Braisée aux Cépes. Boned fillet of veal braised and served with wild mushrooms.
Confits de Canard et Oie. Grilled preserved duck or goose.
Boudin de Campagne Grillé. Large grilled blood sausage.
Charlotte au Chocolat. Molded lady fingers filled with custard and covered with chocolate.
Tarte aux Prunes. Prune tart.

WINE

Saint-Pourcain, Cahors, Marcillac.

15^e

LE BISTROT D'ANDRÉ
LA GITANE
AU PASSÉ RETROUVÉ
LE PETIT MÂCHON
PIERRE VEDEL
CHEZ YVETTE

15ᵉ *Arrondissement*

PORTE DE VERSAILLES

PLACES OF INTEREST

Gare Montparnasse
Heliport de Paris
Institut Pasteur
Musée Antoine Bourdelle
Musée Postal
Palais des Sports, Parc des Expositions
Parc Georges Brassens
La Ruche (The Beehive, an artists' colony
built by Gustave Eiffel)
Square Saint-Lambert
Statue de la Liberté
Tour Montparnasse
Le Village Suisse (antiques market)

LE BISTROT D'ANDRÉ

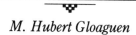

M. Hubert Gloaguen

ADDRESS: 232, rue Saint-Charles at the corner of Rue
Leblanc, 75015
CLOSED: Sunday
PRICE RANGE: Inexpensive
TEL: 45-57-89-14
METRO: Balard
CREDIT: Visa

A simple place offering good home cooking in a relaxed atmosphere. The low prices and generously served plats du jour *draw a middle-class crowd to throng here for lunch and dinner.*

Hubert Gloaguen, the energetic owner of Bistro d'André,
named his restaurant after André Citroën, the Henry Ford of
the French automobile industry. This bustling spot is located in
a 100-year-old building, the only original structure left standing
on the Citröen property, which is undergoing total reconstruction. Two rather plain dining areas are decorated with posters
and old photographs commemorating the days when the factories flourished here. Food is served by the owner and one or
two others on small tables, covered with paper and tightly
packed together. *Entreés* from 16F to 22F include a nice country pâté, ham and a half-dozen tasty Burgundy snails. The main
courses of duck *confit,* lamb with *dauphinois* potatoes, steak
and *andouillettes* are offered at pre-World-War-II prices. A
small selection of cheeses and desserts completes the menu.

RECOMMENDED DISHES

Terrine de Càmpagne et Cornichons. Coarse country pâté
    served with tart gherkins.
Céleri Rémoulade. Shredded celery root in spicy mayonnaise.
Escargots de Bourgogne. Vineyard snails in garlic butter.
Gigot d'Agneau et Gratin Dauphinois. Roast leg of lamb,
    served with sliced potatoes baked in cream and browned
    on top.

Boeuf Bourguignon. Beef cooked in red wine with onions and mushrooms.

Andouillette de Vouvray, Sauce Moutarde et Pommes Boulangères. Pork sausage cooked in white wine, served in a mustard sauce with potatoes with onions.

Confit de Canard et Pommes Rissolées. Grilled preserved duck, served with fried potatoes.

Pintade Rôtie et Choux de Bruxelles. Roast guinea hen with brussels sprouts.

Brochette d'Agneau au Riz. Lamb grilled on a skewer, served on a bed of rice.

Crème Caramel Maison. Vanilla-flavored flan.

Tarte-Tatin Maison. Upside-down apple pie.

WINE

Brouilly, Juliénas, Beaumes de Venise, Cahors, Sauvignon Blanc, St.-Nicolas-de-Bourgueil.

LA GITANE ★

M. Francis Mouchet

ADDRESS: 53 bis, ave. de la Motte-Piquet, 75015
CLOSED: Sat. and Sun.
PRICE RANGE: Moderate
TEL: 47-34-62-92
METRO: Motte-Piquet or École-Militaire
CREDIT: Visa and MasterCard

A popular bistro of this quarter, serving solid bourgeois dishes in an unpretentious setting. There is a pretty, secluded, plant-bordered summer terrace, a nice alternative to the rather large, impersonal dining room.

Located across from the Village Suisse, an antiques-dealers' mart, this neighborhood spot is busy for lunch and dinner. Since there is no written *carte*, the menu is handwritten on wall tiles and often changed according to market produce. There are no unusual specialties, but the standard fare is well handled and nicely priced. Simmered *pot-au-feu, confit de canard,* calf's head in vinaigrette and stuffed cabbage are some of the favorites. Service is a bit slow, but it is worth a luncheon if you happen to be in the area.

RECOMMENDED DISHES

Moules de Bouchot à la Normande. Tiny mussels served in cream and cider.
Filets de Hareng Cotonneaux. Herring fillets in oil.
Fromage de Tête, Sauce Ravigote. Headcheese in a spicy vinaigrette with mustard, *cornichons* and capers.
Escargots de Bourgogne. Vineyard snails in garlic butter.
Pot-au-Feu. Boiled beef with vegetables and broth.
Chou Farci Paysanne. Stuffed cabbage with onions and carrots.
Manchons de Canard Confit. Small cakes of preserved duck.
Tête de Veau, Sauce Ravigote. Calf's head in a spicy vinaigrette with mustard, *cornichons* and capers.
Fricassée de Canard aux Pâtes Fraîches. Light duck stew served with fresh pasta.
Cassoulet Toulousain. White-bean stew cooked in an earthenware pot with pork, sausage and duck.
Mousse au Chocolat. Chocolate mousse.
Profiteroles au Chocolat. Small ice-cream-filled pastries, covered with chocolate.

WINE

Côtes-de-Saint-Mont (Gascogne).

AU PASSÉ RETROUVÉ ★ ★

M. Daniel Haumont
Mme. Dominique Haumont

ADDRESS: 13, rue Mademoiselle, 75015
CLOSED: Sun., Mon. and two weeks in May
PRICE RANGE: Moderate
TEL: 42-50-35-29
METRO: Commerce
CREDIT: Amex, Visa

It is essential to reserve in this Auvergnat bistro, which is full of character and characters. The theatrical decor and animated ambience make for an entertaining evening.

The imaginative decor here can only be described as Auvergnat kitsch and nostalgia. An incredible hodgepodge of bric-a-brac, dolls, pots, bottles, beamed ceilings, Victorian chairs, draped-velvet curtains and huge dried flower arrangements clutters the dining room, which is nevertheless comfortable. The *Plats du Marché,* changed daily, are decided upon each morning at the market and listed separately from the à la carte menu. A nice touch is the *Kir* offered by the house, and there are interesting regional wines to accompany the hearty cuisine which features air-dried sausages, country hams, fresh trout, duck *confit* with sweet garlic and leg of lamb with cherries. A second restaurant, Au Refuge du Passé (32, rue du Fer à Moulin, tel. 47-07-29-91), serves similar food in the 5e.

RECOMMENDED DISHES

Planchette Bougnate (Assortment de Charcuterie). Platter of pork sausages and pork products.

Jambon d'Auvergne. Country ham platter.

Salade de Sarlat. Salad with baked, sliced potatoes and truffles.

Assiette de Tartine au Foie Confit (for two). Liver preserves served on slices of buttered country bread.

Magret de Canard au Miel. Fattened duck breast grilled with honey.

Choux Farci. Stuffed cabbage.

Tripoux d'Auvergne. Stuffed, heavily seasoned veal tripe.

Jambonneau au Four Maison. Small roasted ham.

Coquelet aux Cèpes du Sud-Ouest. Young cockerel garnished with wild mushrooms cooked in oil, garlic and parsley.

Cassoulet au Confit de Canard. Meat-and-white-bean stew with preserved duck.

Truite au Champagne. Trout served in Champagne sauce.

Pied de Porc Farci de Rocamadour. Grilled, stuffed pigs' feet.

Civet de Lièvre aux Airelles du Chef. Rabbit stew with berries.

Tourte aux Poires. Pear tart.

Dôme Glacé Sauce Caramel. Mound of ice cream topped with a caramel sauce.

Crème Brûlée aux Pruneaux. Cream custard garnished with prunes, topped with brown sugar and burned under the grill to form a hard coating.

WINE

Côtes-du-Rhône, Bergerac, Saint-Pourcain.

LE PETIT MÂCHON ★ ★

Mme. J. Moussié
Chef: Alain Besnard

ADDRESS: 123, rue de la Convention, 75015
CLOSED: Sun., Mon. and July 25–August 20
PRICE RANGE: Moderate
TEL: 45-54-08-62
METRO: Boucicaut or Félix-Faure
CREDIT: Visa

You will need to reserve in this splendid bistro elegantly decorated in faux *marble, leather and mirrors. This is the annex to the prestigious Bistro 121 and here, as next door, you will find typical Lyonnais food and wine served in high style.*

The Petit Mâchon has been described as the most Parisian of the Lyonnais *bouchons*. A Lyonnais *bouchon,* by the way, is a delicatessen-type restaurant serving hearty food at all hours. The Lyonnais are traditionalists and the menu is an anthology of classic regional dishes including *rosettes, andouillettes, cervelas* served with buttery hot potatoes, steaming tripe prepared in various ways and dishes of mutton, veal or pigs' trotters. The wines naturally come from Lyon's backyard, the Beaujolais.

RECOMMENDED DISHES

Pâté de Canard Maison. Duck liver pâté.
Petits-Gris en Cassolette. Cassolette dish of tiny gray snails in cream sauce.

Salade de Pieds de Mouton, Foies de Volaille et Oeuf Dur. Salad of pigs' feet, chicken livers and a hard-boiled egg.

Caviar Lyonnais. Warm lentils with shallots.

Andouillette Sauce Moutarde. Pork sausage in mustard sauce.

Tripoux. Heavily seasoned stuffed tripe.

Gras-Double à la Lyonnais. Ox tripe sliced and fried with onions, vinegar and parsley.

Tablier de Sapeur. Ox tripe grilled with egg and bread crumbs.

Confit de Canard. Grilled preserved duck.

L'Onglet de Boeuf à l'Échalotes. Beef flank grilled with shallots.

Pieds de Porc Farci. Stuffed pigs' feet.

Jambonneaux aux Lentilles. Small roast ham knuckle with lentil garnish.

Gâteau de Riz Crème Anglaise. Rice pudding with fruit *confit* in a light egg custard.

Tarte-Tatin. Upside-down apple pie.

WINE

Cahors, Côteaux Lyonnais, Saumur-Champigny, Beaujolais.

PIERRE VEDEL ★ ★ ★

M. Pierre Vedel

ADDRESS: 19, rue Duranton, 75015

CLOSED: Sat., Sun., last two weeks in July and Christmas week

PRICE RANGE: Fairly expensive

TEL: 45-58-43-17

METRO: Boucicaut

CREDIT: Visa

The atmosphere is intimate, the decor elegant and the cuisine astonishingly good in this classic bistro very popular with French gourmets. Both traditional and regional dishes are exquisitely prepared and the prices are well below what you might expect for such food and lovely surroundings. Reservations are essential.

Intense Mediterranean flavors highlight the imaginative cuisine of *patron* Pierre Vedel, a most creative chef and generous personality. The *carte* retains the specialties that have kept his customers returning year after year. Among them are duck with turnips, a *bourride* of white fish with creamed vegetables and *aïoli* (garlic mayonnaise) and *tête de veau* with capers, which is superb in its simplicity. The foie gras is among the best in the city, and a bittersweet chocolate *charlotte* is only one of the splendid desserts. High ceilings create a spacious atmosphere in the two dining rooms with comfortable chairs and large, well-spaced tables. Red-striped velvet curtains, a red-leaf-motif carpet, mirrors, potted plants, and cream-colored walls enhanced by painted anaglyphic wallpaper complete the lovely decor.

RECOMMENDED DISHES

Foie de Canard Frais Maison. Fresh duck foie gras.
Fricassée d'Escargots à l'Oseille Beurre de Cerfeuil. Light snail stew in sorrel butter and chervil.
Terrine de Lentilles au Museau de Cochon. Terrine of lentils with pork brawn in a sherry vinegar dressing.
Civet de Porcelet aux Airelles et Croutons. Piglet stew with berries and croutons.
Filet de Rascasse au Safran en Bouillabaisse. Scorpion fish in a Mediterranean fish soup seasoned with saffron.
Bourride de Lotte à l'Ailloli Comme à Sête. Authentic fish stew with garlic-flavored mayonnaise.
Rable de Lapin à l'Ail et au Miel. Saddle of rabbit with garlic and honey.
Tête de Veau en Vinaigrette et Câpres. Calf's head in a spicy vinaigrette with capers.
Côte de Boeuf Poêlée Legumes du Marché (for two). Ribs of beef pot-roasted on a bed of garden-fresh vegetables.
Brandade de Morue Chaude au Céleri. Creamed salt cod.
Oeufs à la Neige au Caramel. Egg whites poached in milk and served with vanilla custard.
Charlotte au Chocolat Sauce Vanille. Baked bread filled with chocolate pudding, covered with vanilla sauce.
Crème Brûlée. Cream custard topped with brown sugar and burned under the grill to form a hard coating.

WINE

In-depth selection of moderately priced Bordeaux. Languedoc/Cuvée P. Vedel, Saumur-Champigny, Chinon, Sancerre de Bué/Maison Pinard.

CHEZ YVETTE ★

M. Christian Pineau

ADDRESS: 1, rue d'Alençon, 75015
CLOSED: Sat., Sun. and August
PRICE RANGE: Moderate
TEL: 42-22-45-54
METRO: Montparnasse or Falguière
CREDIT: Visa

Nothing is missing in this neighborhood family bistro on the outskirts of Montparnasse. The patron is warmhearted, the chef friendly, the waiters solicitous, the food tasty, the portions generous and the prices right.

Chez Yvette is one of those rare little finds frequented by regulars who come here for the marvelous old-fashioned atmosphere, the hospitality and the simple but delicious classic cuisine. The decor is a little elaborate, with crimson velour and walls decorated with old hunting trophies. A huge basket of bread is served with large crocks of *terrines,* pâtés, herring or sardines. You can help yourself at your own discretion but save room for the other good things to follow. *Boudin* grilled and served with potatoes, savory game in season, even the common steak *au poivre* or sole *meunière* are excellent. There are light and flaky house fruit tarts for dessert. The wine to drink is the Beaujolais.

RECOMMENDED DISHES

Terrine de Foie de Volaille. Chicken liver pâté.
Terrine de Lapin en Gelée. Rabbit pâté in aspic.
Filets de Hareng Pommes à l'Huile. Herring fillets with
  potatoes in oil.
Boudin Pommes en l'Air. Large sausage served with fried
  apples, onions and bacon.
Gibiers en Saison. Game served in the fall and winter
  months.
Andouillette Délice. Pork sausage.

Sole Meunière. Fillet of sole coated in flour and sautéed in butter.

Ris de Veau aux Champignons. Sweetbreads grilled with mushrooms.

Magret de Canard au Poivre Vert. Fattened duck breast with green peppercorns.

Lapin Sauté aux Herbes. Rabbit sautéed with herbs.

Mousse au Chocolat. Chocolate mousse.

Tartelettes aux Quetsches. Savory little plum tarts.

WINE

Côtes-du-Rhône, Beaujolais.

16ᵉ

PIERRE LE LYONNAIS
LE SCHEFFER

16ᵉ Arrondissement

AUTEUIL–PASSY–MUETTE–TROCADÉRO

PLACES OF INTEREST

Bois de Boulogne (Longchamp and *Auteuil* racetracks,
Jardin d'Acclimatation children's park, *Fleuriste d'Auteuil*
gardens, hothouses and arboretum, *Jardins de Bagatelle)*
Cimetière de Passy
Maison de la Radio France
Musée d'Art Moderne
Musée de la Mode du Costume
Musée des Arts et Traditions Populaires
Musée Balzac
Musée Guimet
Musée Marmottan (Jardins du Ranelagh)
Musée du Vin
*Palais de Chaillot (Musées de la Marine, de l'Homme, des
Monuments Français, du Cinéma Henri Langlois)*
Palais de Tokyo (Musée d'Art Essai)
Place du Trocadéro (gardens and aquarium)
Rue la Fontaine (buildings by *Henri Guimard*)

PIERRE LE LYONNAIS ★ ★

M. Gérard Léonetti

ADDRESS: 10, rue Géricault, 75016
CLOSED: Sat. lunch, Sun. and August
PRICE RANGE: Moderate
TEL: 45-27-20-36
METRO: Michel-Ange–Auteuil
CREDIT: None

Hearty and generous plates of very good bistro food with some Lyonnais specialties are served in cozy provincial surroundings. There is great activity at lunch, but the evening quiets down making this a most agreeable place for dinner.

The countrified look of the entrance with its honey-colored canopy and light-oak facade is extended into the pretty little pine-paneled dining room cheerfully decorated with prints and earthenware plates. There is a small bar in the corner and straight, high-backed wooden chairs with wicker seats clustered around nine or ten little tables covered in white linen. A cream-colored tile floor and café curtains complete the picture. Delectable Lyonnais sausages, snails and *quenelles de brochet* (pike dumplings) are real winners among the *entrées*, and the *plats du jour* often include tender *gras-double* (tripe), a succulent guinea fowl with cabbage and frogs' legs *Provençale*. Côtes-du-Rhône or Beaujolais are the best wines to accompany this appetizing regional fare.

RECOMMENDED DISHES

Saucisson Chaud Lyonnais, Pommes à l'Huile. Large slicing sausage with potatoes in oil.
Rosette de Lyon. Large dry pork sausage sliced and served cold.
Oef en Gelée Maison. Egg in aspic.
Foie Gras de Canard Maison. Fresh duck foie gras.
Terrine de Canard. Duck liver pâté.
Cuisses de Grenouilles à la Provençale. Frogs' legs with tomatoes and garlic.

Saumon Poché à l'Oseille. Poached salmon with sorrel.

Pintade aux Choux. Guinea fowl with cabbage.

Tête et Langue de Veau Vinaigrette. Calf's head and tongue in vinaigrette.

Quenelles de Brochet à la Lyonnais. Pike dumplings in a rich cream sauce.

St.-Jacques Frâiches Beurre Blanc. Scallops in a white-wine butter sauce.

Rognons de Veau, Morilles. Veal kidneys cooked with mountain mushrooms.

Gras-Double à la Lyonnaise. Ox tripe, sliced and fried with onions, vinegar and parsley.

Confit de Canard. Grilled preserved duck.

Crème Caramel. Vanilla-flavored flan.

Mousse au Chocolat. Chocolate mousse.

WINE

Beaujolais-Villages, Côtes-du-Rhône.

LE SCHEFFER   ★

M. Chauvia

ADDRESS: 22, rue Scheffer, 75016
CLOSED: Sun.
PRICE RANGE: Moderate
TEL: 47-27-81-11
METRO: Pompe or Trocadero
CREDIT: Visa

An animated neighborhood bistro popular with a smart set of Passy regulars. The food is typical bistro with some regional dishes thrown in for good measure.

A red-lacquered facade and awning decked with colored lights are a gay welcome to this friendly spot a few blocks from the Trocadéro Gardens. There is a nice wooden bar at the front of a large dining room lined with several rows of little tables covered with red-and-white-checkered cloths protected by paper. A pretty floral-patterned white-tile floor is a nice contrast to the dark red ceiling. Lace curtains, old posters and photos scattered about the walls add a pleasant touch to the room. If you choose the *plat du jour,* posted on the window, with a pitcher of the Côtes-du-Rhone you will have eaten well for the price. The service is friendly but may be a little slow if it's crowded.

RECOMMENDED DISHES

Frisée aux Lardons. Chicory salad with bacon.
Poêlon d'Escargots. Casserole of snails served with garlic butter.
Rosette de Lyon. Large dry pork sausage, sliced and served cold.
Filet de Boeuf à la Ficelle. Poached fillet of beef with vegetables.
Haricot de Mouton. Mutton stew with white beans.
Andouillette à la Moutarde de Meaux. Pork sausage in mustard sauce.
Noisette de Porc au Porto. Round center-cut of pork cooked with Port wine.
Escalope de Saumon à l'Oseille. Salmon steak cooked with sorrel.
Profiteroles au Chocolat. Ice-cream-filled pastry shells topped with chocolate.
Mont-Blanc. Puréed chestnut dessert with whipped cream.

WINE

Muscadet, Sancerre, Cahors, Chinon.

17^e

LE BISTROT D' À CÔTÉ "FLAUBERT"
LE BISTROT DE L'ÉTOILE
CHEZ FRED
CHEZ GEORGES
CHEZ GORISSE
LES GOURMETS DES TERNES
L'OEUF À LA NEIGE
LE PETIT SALÉ

17e Arrondissement

BATIGNOLLES–TERNES

PLACES OF INTEREST

Avenue de la Grande Armée
Musée de l'Air
Palais des Congrès
Parc Monceau
Place des Ternes
Sainte-Marie-des-Batignolles
Square des Batignolles

LE BISTROT D' À CÔTÉ "FLAUBERT"

M. Michel Rostang

ADDRESS: 10, rue Gustave-Flaubert, 75017
CLOSED: Sat. lunch, Sun. and one week in August
PRICE RANGE: Moderate
TEL: 42-67-05-81
METRO: Ternes
CREDIT: Visa and MasterCard

Flea market bric-a-brac decorate the walls of M. Rostang's "Bistro Next Door," the first of three new establishments operating under the same name. The menu includes traditional bourgeois fare with some interesting Lyonnais and modern specialties.

You will feel instantly at home in this small, colorful bistro installed on the premises of an old 1900s grocery store. The original shelves, tin ceiling and tile floor provide a perfect backdrop for the many interesting pictures and antiques used as decoration. Ten or so marble-top bistro tables fill the cozy room inside and several more crowd the sidewalk out front.

The waiters are young and attentive and will guide you through the menu and daily specials, which are chalked on a centrally located blackboard. Included on the list is a nicely prepared salad of warm lentils with sausages, a *carpaccio* of fresh tuna and basil in olive oil, and a tasty chicken liver *terrine*. The main courses include chicken in red-wine sauce and Lyonnais sausage with ravioli. A warm *clafoutis* is a good choice for dessert. The wine list is strongly oriented toward the Bordeaux and Rhone, and some of the less-expensive crus are very good. Only one of the other two branches has already opened (16, ave. de Villiers, tel. 47-63-25-61).

RECOMMENDED DISHES

Boudin Noir aux Pommes Fruits. Blood sausage and apples served with a buckwheat flat cake.

Terrine de Foie de Volaille Campagnarde. Country-style duck-liver pâté.

Salade Tiède de Lentilles et Cervelas de Lyon. Warm lentil salad with smooth pork sausage.

Andouillette Tirée à la Ficelle. Poached pork sausage cut into long strips.

Gratin de Gras-Double "Léon de Lyon." Oven-browned tripe served in a *gratin* dish.

Sabodet Lyonnais aux Ravioles de Romans, Crème Vinaigrée. Hot pigs'-head sausage served in thick slices with tiny ravioli.

Poulet à la Fermière Rôti (for two). Roast chicken "farmhouse"-style.

Joues de Cochon Confites au Vin Rouge. Pigs' cheeks preserved in red wine.

Fricassée de Volaille au Curry, Riz Blanc et Riz Sauvage. Curried chicken stew served with white and wild rice.

Gratin de Pommes aux Amandes et Calvados (must be ordered at start of meal). Browned apple dish with almonds and apple brandy.

Clafoutis Chaud aux Framboises (must be ordered at start of meal). Custard tart with raspberries.

Crème Brûlée à la Vanille. Custard, topped with brown sugar caramelized under the grill.

WINE

Crozes-Hermitage, Sancerre, Saint-Nicolas-de-Bourgueil, Brouilly, various Bordeaux.

LE BISTROT DE L'ETOILE ★ ★ ★

M. & Mme. Guy Savoy

ADDRESS: 13, rue Troyon, 75017
CLOSED: Sat. lunch and Sun.
PRICE RANGE: Moderate
TEL: 42-67-25-95
METRO: Charles-De-Gaulle–Étoile
CREDIT: Visa

*M. Savoy's first Bistrot de l'Étoile skillfully updates tradi-
tional cuisine to match the sophisticated, uncluttered decor of
his contemporary new restaurant. His second Bistrot de
l'Étoile-Neil (also in the 17e) wisely offers a different, but
equally enticing, menu so one can dine happily in both.*

Everything is clean, simple and in good taste in this tiny modern bistro. The decor is a bit austere with blond ash-paneled
walls, a spider-web-motif ceiling and little *coude-à-coude* tables
seating about 25. Soft lights and mirrors give an illusion of
more space than there is. Chef William Ledeuil turns out well-
prepared plates of sausage, steak and fish. There is a good *tête
de veau* simmered with olives and an interesting *gras-double*
(tripe) with macaroni. Not far away, in the Neil establishment
(75, ave. Neil, tel. 42-27-88-44), a traditional bistro atmosphere is enhanced by large mirrors and a nice bar. Here, chef
Bruno Gensdarmes offers *andouillettes* (pork sausages) in a
buttery mustard sauce and a wonderful rabbit flavored with
sage and served with little ravioli.

RECOMMENDED DISHES

The following are specialties from both establishments
Soupe de Moules et Potiron. Mussel-and-pumpkin soup.
Haddock Pommes à l'Huile. Smoked haddock with potatoes
   in oil.
Salade Tiède de Petits Gris aux Pommes de Terre (Neil).
   Chanterelle mushroom salad with potatoes.
Saucisson Chaud en Brioche. Hot Lyonnais sausage in a
   rich bun.
Morue à la Crème d'Ail, Pommes de Terre Écrasées
   (Neil). Garlic-creamed salt cod with potatoes.
Sabodet aux Ravioles, Vinaigrette Émulsionnée. Pork
   sausage studded with pieces of rind, served in hot, thick
   slices with tiny raviolis.
Tête de Veau Croustillante. Crunchy calf's head.
Entrecôte Poêlée au Gratin de Macaronis. Rib steak sau-
   téed with bone marrow, served with macaroni.
Gras-double à la Lyonnaise et Gratin de Macaronis.
   Sliced ox tripe fried with onions, vinegar and parsley,
   served in a *gratin* of macaroni.
Andouillette au Beurre de Moutarde (Neil). Pork sausage
   in mustard butter.
Gâteau de Pain Perdu. French toast.

Crème Brûlee. Custard topped with brown sugar browned to a hard coating under the grill.

Clafoutis aux Framboises avec Crème Anglaise. Custard tart with raspberries and whipped cream.

WINE

Modest selection of little wines by the bottle or carafe. Pot Du Bistrot/Bordeaux.

CHEZ FRED

M. Robert Marc

ADDRESS: 190 bis, blvd. Pereire, 75017
CLOSED: Sat. lunch, Sun. and two weeks in August
PRICE RANGE: Moderate
TEL: 45-74-20-48
METRO: Ternes, Porte-Maillot or Pereire
CREDIT: Amex, Visa, Diners and MasterCard

One of the most convivial neighborhood bistros, with all the trappings of a Lyonnais bouchon *(tap room). The* plats du jour *are always traditional meat preparations complemented by a few Lyonnais bistro offerings.*

Fred, short for Alfred Peyraud, was the original owner of this famous bistro containing the actual table where fictional detective Inspector Maigret sat for lunch with his cronies from the Sûreté. The new *patron,* M. Marc, has not missed a beat since taking over in 1985. He kept the old 1930s decor and traditional *plats du jour* to the delight of regulars. An hors d'oeuvre table at the entrance displays tempting *terrines,* sausages, salads, beef headcheese and herring fillets. The *carte* is a roster of true bistro dishes featuring the specialties which for years have made this place popular. This is a good place to try the pork sausages *(andouillettes A.A.A.A.A.)* or the *tête de veau.* Freshly made *tartes,* chocolate cake and the candied chestnuts with *crème fraîche* are the most notable desserts. There is a nicely varied wine list.

RECOMMENDED DISHES

PLATS DU JOUR

Gigot d'Agneau Rôti aux Flageolets (Mondays). Roast leg of lamb with small green kidney beans.

Petit Salé (Tuesdays). Lightly salted cooked pork.

Tête de Veau (Wednesdays). Calf's head.

Pot-au-Feu (Thursdays). Boiled beef with vegetables and broth.

Boeuf à la Mode (Fridays). Braised pot roast with vegetables.

Sauté d'Agneau (Saturdays). Sautéed lamb.

Cochonnailles (Assiette de Saucisson Ailles). Assorted pork products.

Jambon de Campagne. Smoked country ham.

Saucisson Chaud Pommes à l'Huile. Hot Lyonnais sausage with potatoes in oil.

Andouillettes Grillées de l'A.A.A.A.A. Grilled pork sausages.

Pavé de Rumsteak "Fred" (for two). Thick beef steak.

Confit de Canard. Broiled preserved duck.

Marrons Confits à la Crème Fraîche. Preserved chestnuts with slightly soured cream.

Tarte-Tatin. Upside-down apple pie.

WINE

Muscadet-Sur-Lie, Gamay-de-Touraine, Chénas.

CHEZ GEORGES ★ ★ ★ ★

M. Roger Mazarcuil
Chef: Jean Merle

ADDRESS: 273, blvd. Pereire, 75017
CLOSED: August
PRICE RANGE: Fairly expensive
TEL: 45-74-31-00
METRO: Porte-Maillot
CREDIT: Visa and MasterCard

A famous old bistro that has remained unchanged for half a century. It lacks charm but has plenty of character. Here is an opportunity to enjoy old-fashioned cooking at its best.

Chez George, which was opened by the Mazarcuil family in 1926, has since been filled with members of a loyal following who come to this out-of-the-way spot in droves. This is one place that is absolutely worth the trip, but don't go without a reservation or a hearty appetite. The scene you'll enter is classic bistro: crowded tables, banquettes, etched glass, mirrors and lace curtains. Jostling waiters, balancing huge heavily laden trays over their heads, push through the line of customers waiting to be seated. Most come for one of the three famous specialties. Most sought after is the leg of lamb with *flageolets,* small tender green kidney-shaped beans. The second favorite choice is the ribs of beef with sliced potatoes, and the third is *petit salé* (salt-cured pork) with cabbage. Daily specials and a variety of tempting hors d'oeuvres add diversity to the menu. The most popular desserts are the giant eclair and the *tarte-Tatin.* There are several wine options but the best is a Cahors.

RECOMMENDED DISHES

Salade de Museau de Boeuf. Headcheese salad served in vinaigrette.

Tête de Veau, Sauce Vinaigrette. Calf's head served in a cold oil-and-vinegar sauce.

Saucisson Chaud Pistaché à la Lyonnaise. Large slicing sausage studded with pistachio nuts, served warm.

Soupe au Chou. Cabbage soup.

Pied de Veau Vinaigrette. Veal foot in a cold oil-and-vinegar dressing.

Escargots Bourgogne. Vineyard snails served in garlic butter.

Baltique Hareng à la Crème. Marinated herring fillets served with thick sour cream.

Cochonnailles (Andouilles de Vire et de Guéméné). Two varieties of large, smoked pork sausage.

Saumon Cru Mariné à l'Aneth. Cured, marinated salmon with dill.

Gigot Rôti aux Flageolets Fins. Roast leg of lamb with small green kidney beans.

Petit Salé au Chou. Lightly salted pork with cabbage.

Train de Côtes de Boeuf, Gratin Dauphinois. Ribs of
beef, served with sliced potatoes baked in cream and
browned.

Plat de Côtes Gros Sel en Pot-au-Feu (Wednesdays).
Boiled beef ribs with vegetables and broth.

Hachis Parmentier (Plat du Jour). Minced-meat-and-potato casserole (shepherd's pie).

Haricot de Mouton (Plat du Jour). Mutton stew with potatoes, turnips and onions.

Glace Café, Sauce Caramel. Coffee ice cream with caramel
sauce.

Eclair Géant. Large cream-filled pastry with choice of chocolate or coffee topping.

WINE

Côte-de-Brouilly, Quincy, Cahors.

CHEZ GORISSE ★ ★ ★

M. & Mme. Dominique Terrasson
Chef: Serge Lebrec

ADDRESS: 84, rue Nollet, 75017
CLOSED: Sunday
PRICE RANGE: Moderate
TEL: 46-27-43-05
METRO: Brochant
CREDIT: Visa and MasterCard

A sumptuous pot-au-feu, coq-au-vin *and* navarin *(veal stew)
are among the "traditions" of the day in this old-time bistro
with a countrified atmosphere. At dinner the tables are filled
with a mixture of smart-looking sophisticates, yuppies and a
few interesting trendy types.*

You will definitely need to reserve in this popular restaurant
situated in an out-of-the-way neighborhood near the Square
des Batignolles. The *faux* half-timbered exterior is a bit passé,

but the dining room is pleasantly decorated with high-backed benches, copper pots, pink tablecloths and fresh flowers. Copious portions of bourgeois classics are served alongside more modern seafood preparations like a stew of fish, leeks and shellfish or a mélange of steamed fish and seafood sausages on a bed of cabbage. There is a fine *terrine,* good crus from the Loire and classic desserts. Guests are warmly welcomed and looked after by the charming *patrons,* continuing the tradition established in 1936 by the original owner, Madame Gorisse.

RECOMMENDED DISHES

Terrine Maison. Country pâté.

Frisée aux Lardons. Chicory with bacon bits.

Rillettes de Saumon. Preserved, minced salmon spread.

Beurre d'Échiré. Famous Poitou butter served with freshly made bread.

Tête de Veau Ravigote. Calf's head in a spicy vinaigrette with mustard, *cornichons* and capers.

Sandre au Beurre Blanc Nantaise. Pike-perch in a white-wine butter sauce.

Coquilles Saint-Jacques au Noilly. Broiled scallops in Vermouth.

Marmite de Poissons. Fish-and-shellfish stew.

Choucroute de Poissons. Steamed seafood sausages served on a bed of cooked cabbage.

Pot-au-Feu Ménagère. Boiled beef with vegetables served "housewife-style" with onions.

Vol-au-Vent à l'Ancienne. Puff pastry filled with chicken in cream sauce.

Filet à la Ficelle. Poached fillet of beef.

Tournedos à la Moelle. Beef fillet in bone-marrow sauce.

Oeufs à la Neige. Egg whites poached in milk and served in vanilla custard.

Marquise au Chocolat. Chocolate mousse cake.

WINE

Saumur-Champigny, Sancerre, Chinon.

LES GOURMETS DES TERNES

M. Francis Marie

ADDRESS: 87, blvd. de Courcelles, 75017
CLOSED: Sat., Sun. and August
PRICE RANGE: Moderate
TEL: 42-27-43-04
METRO: Ternes
CREDIT: Visa

This celebrated old bistro, with a reputation for serving excellent, no-nonsense food made from the finest ingredients, is always crowded and full of life. The owner selects the products, oversees the cooking and welcomes and seats the guests. For summer dining there are sidewalk tables just around the corner from the Place des Ternes.

It is almost impossible to get a reservation in this unpretentious establishment, soon to celebrate its centennial year, where yuppies, sophisticates, businessmen, tourists, professionals and interesting trendy types sit elbow-to-elbow at little paper-covered tables. Artificial flowers, aging wall mirrors, worn leather banquettes, old light fixtures and other relics of the past are part of the outdated 50's decor. Meats are exceptional, bought and aged by the owner who was once a butcher, and while you wait for a steak grilled exactly to your order you might try the celery root salad, the artichoke bottoms or the Burgundy snails. Salmon and sole are the only alternatives to meat and the *pêche melba* or *baba* with rum the best desserts. The service is professional but often brusque.

RECOMMENDED DISHES

Céleri Rémoulade. Raw shredded celery root in a spicy mayonnaise dressing.
Rosette du Beaujolais. Large dry pork sausage, sliced and served cold.

Museau de Porc Vinaigrette. Salad of pork brawn in a spicy vinaigrette.

Saint-Jacques à la Provençale. Pan-fried scallops served Provence-style with tomatoes, garlic and onions.

Boeuf Bourguignon au Vieux Vin. Beef stewed in vintage wine with tiny onions and mushrooms.

Andouillette de Campagne Grillée. Grilled country pork sausage.

Entrecôte à la Moelle avec Frites. Broiled rib steak with bone-marrow sauce, served with french fries.

Côte de Boeuf. Roast ribs of beef.

Crème Caramel. Vanilla-flavored flan.

Pêche Melba. Vanilla ice cream with sliced peaches covered in a black currant sauce (*cassis*).

Baba au Rhum. Yeast cake drenched in rum syrup and served with cream. A bottle of rum accompanies this dish and is at your disposal.

WINE

Côtes-du-Rhône, Beaujolais.

L'OEUF À LA NEIGE

Mme. Anne Gérard and M. Michel Gérard
Chef: Jean-Luc Bergerot

ADDRESS: 16, rue Salneuve, 75017
CLOSED: Sat. lunch, Sun. and August
PRICE RANGE: Moderate
TEL: 47-63-45-43
METRO: Malesherbes or Villiers
CREDIT: Amex, Visa, Diners and MasterCard

A wonderful new address where chef Jean-Luc Bergerot prepares tempting specialties from the Alsace and Lorraine regions of Northeastern France.

Patron M. Gerard, who is originally from Nancy, has found some interesting regional wines including a superb sparkling Moselle and a Gris de Toul (a very pale light rosé with slight acidity) to accompany his fresh and robust fare. There is a bar on the right as you enter the bright but modest little dining room decorated with an old armoire and antique furniture. The ten tables can become a bit cramped when filled, but the room is never stuffy. Flavorful food from a short but select *carte* includes such specialties as rabbit *terrine* in a white-wine aspic, pigs' feet St.-Menehould-style, a delicious fish stew and veal kidneys in *vin jaune* (a deep-yellow-colored, strongly flavored wine from the Jura) served with mushrooms of the season. On Tuesdays you can try the *hachis parmentier* (a meat-and-potato casserole) and on Thursdays the *tête de veau*. There are home-made *patisseries*, sherbets and naturally *oeufs à la neige* for dessert.

RECOMMENDED DISHES

Terrine de Lapin à la Gelée de Gewürtztraminer. Rabbit pâté in a white-wine aspic.

Terrine Maison de Foies de Volaille. Chicken liver pâté.

Tarte Flambée Comme à Strasbourg. Large open fruit tart flamed with Kirsch.

Moules aux Petits Légumes. Mussels in broth.

Pot-au-Feu du Patron. Boiled beef with vegetables and broth.

Rognon de Veau au Vin Jaune et aux Champignons de Saison. Veal kidneys in white Jura wine with wild mushrooms.

Bäckoffe. A *ragoût* of beef, mutton and pork cooked and served in a sealed casserole.

Brandade Nîmoise. Creamed salt cod.

Pieds de Porc à la Mode de Saint-Menehould. Grilled pigs' feet rolled in bread crumbs and served with a spicy white-wine sauce.

Hachis Parmentier (Tuesdays). Minced-meat-and-potato casserole (shepherd's pie).

Tête de Veau (Thursdays). Calf's head served in a cold vinaigrette.

Oeufs à la Neige. Egg whites poached in milk and served with a vanilla custard sauce.

Sorbet aux Mirabelles. Plum sherbet.

WINE

Well chosen selection of wines of the Moselle, Alsace and Jura. Gris-du-Toul, Côte-Roannaise, Sparkling Moselle.

LE PETIT SALÉ

Mme. Laraki

ADDRESS: 99, ave. des Ternes, 75017
CLOSED: Sunday
PRICE RANGE: Moderate
TEL: 45-74-10-57
METRO: Porte-Maillot
CREDIT: Amex, Visa, Diners and MasterCard

A minuscule bistro with a charming patronne where you can choose a robust Gamay or Côtes-du-Rhone to accompany a heaping plate of salt pork, vegetables and lentils served with crusty slices of bread. A selection of cheese and a tarte-Tatin complete this very substantial meal.

Petit salé is one of the old-time favorite bistro specialties. Various cuts of pork, usually the shoulder, shank or breast, are pickled in brine for three to six days. The meat is then boiled and served with an aromatic vegetable garnish. In the classic preparation the lentils are served separately. In a restaurant so named, this is of course the specialty, but there are other good main-course choices on the menu such as leg of lamb, steak and Kakos, *jarret* of pork with potatoes. The house foie gras, marinated leeks, and herring with hot potatoes are tasty additions to this limited menu and you will be pleased with the liter of Gamay d'Anjou placed on your table.

RECOMMENDED DISHES

Foie Gras Frais Maison. Fresh duck liver.
Salade aux Lardons. Chicory salad with bacon.

Poireaux Vinaigrette. Leeks in vinaigrette.

Entrecôte. Grilled rib steak.

Selle d'Agneau. Roast saddle of lamb.

Petit Salé aux Lentilles et aux Carottes. Lightly salted cooked pork with lentils and carrots.

Tarte-Tatin. Upside-down apple pie.

Mousse au Chocolat. Chocolate mousse.

Crème Caramel. Vanilla-flavored flan.

WINE

Gamay d'Anjou, Sauvignon Blanc, Côtes-du-Rhône.

18^e

À LA POMPONNETTE

18e Arrondissement

MONTMARTRE–CLICHY

PLACES OF INTEREST

Basilique de Sacré-Coeur
Cimetière St.-Vincent
Marché aux Puces (Porte de Clignancourt)
Moulin de la Galette
Moulin Rouge, Lapin Agile
Musée d'Art Juif (Jewish Art Museum)
Musée du Vieux Montmartre
Place du Tertre
La Vigne (Vineyard)

À LA POMPONNETTE ★ ★ ★

Mme. Paulette Carteron

ADDRESS: 42, rue Lepic, 75018
CLOSED: Sun. evening, Mon. and August
PRICE RANGE: Fairly expensive
TEL: 46-06-08-36
METRO: Blanche
CREDIT: None

The old-fashioned entrées and generous home-style cuisine may be expensive but you will spend an unforgettable evening surrounded by fascinating photographs and a cast of colorful characters. Reservations are recommended.

It is a scene out of the past as you make your way through the colorful bar, crowded with habitués smoking hand-rolled cigarettes and kibitzing with the bartender, to the dining room where Mme. Carteron is dishing out copious portions of fresh greens from a display table covered in oilcloth. The walls are filled with old prints, paintings and photographs, all having some connection with the family.

The large handwritten menu is supplemented by a list of daily specials and cautions a 5F charge for any change. The mackerel marinated in Muscadet is the thing to begin with, but the herring and the Burgundy snails are also good choices. Any of the poultry dishes will be well done, including perfectly roasted quail with cherries. If you feel in an adventurous mood, try the *tête de veau*. It is served here with enormous slices of tongue and brains. There are some fine desserts, including a selection of cakes, sherbets and ice cream.

RECOMMENDED DISHES

Lapin en Gelée aux Fèuilles d'Estragon. Rabbit *terrine* cooked with tarragon leaves.
Maquereau Mariñé aux Aromates et Muscadet. Superb version of mackerel fillets poached in white wine and served cold as a first course.

Escargots de Bourgogne. Vineyard snails served in garlic butter.

Crudités. Varied and copious selection of raw vegetables served with a cold sauce.

Tête de Veau, Langue et Cervelle Sauce Ravigote. Calf's head, tongue and brains in a spicy vinaigrette with mustard, *cornichons* and capers.

Magret de Canard Sauce Moutarde au Poivre Vert. Fattened duck breast grilled in a mustard sauce with green peppercorns.

Confit de Canard Maison. Preserved duck grilled and served with sautéed potatoes in oil.

Blanquette de Veau à l'Ancienne. Veal stew in white sauce made from cream and egg yolks.

Charlotte au Fromage Blanc au Coulis de Framboise. Fruit custard mold with cream cheese and raspberries.

Vacherin. Baked meringue filled with ice cream, whipped cream and fruit.

WINE

Adequate selection of fairly uninteresting wines not up to the quality of the cuisine.

19e

LE POUILLY-REUILLY (PRÉ-ST.-GERVAIS)
LE SANCERRE

19ᵉ *Arrondissement*

Buttes-Chaumont

PLACES OF INTEREST

Bassin de la Villette
Canal de l'Ourcq, Canal St.-Denis
La Cité des Sciences et de l'Industrie
Parc de la Villette (Inventorium)
Parc des Buttes-Chaumont
Le Pont de Crimée (last surviving drawbridge in Paris)

LE POUILLY-REUILLY (PRÉ-ST.-GERVAIS)

★ ★ ★

M. Jean Thibault

ADDRESS: 68, rue André-Joineau, 93310
CLOSED: August through September 7
PRICE RANGE: Moderate
TEL: 48-45-14-59
METRO: Hoche
CREDIT: Amex, Visa, Diners and MasterCard

High-quality cuisine, half-bistro and half-regional, with specialties from the Berry, Auvergne, Nivernais and Solonge regions, is served in a warm and provincial atmosphere. Located on the outskirts of town, at the Porte de Pantin. Reservations are suggested.

A heavy, wooden, zinc-top bar, little tables covered in yellow cloths, fresh flowers, paintings and various other bric-a-brac brighten the decor of this famous old-time bistro which attracts a fanatically loyal, upscale clientele. Mme. and M. Thibault began the business many years ago, he in the kitchen and she in the dining room. Everyone receives a warm welcome and a taste of the very good freshly made foie gras to start, but after that one is on one's own in choosing from an extensive menu. All the down-to-earth basics are excellent: *boudin, andouillettes* in Pouilly wine, calf's sweetbreads, knuckle of ham with cabbage, chicken with crayfish, a stew of freshwater eel, veal kidneys in mustard sauce and *confit* of duck with small green kidney beans. The portions are enough to satisfy any appetite and may be accompanied by "little" wines from Berry, grand crus from Bordeaux or the outstanding Pouilly Fumé for which the house is famous.

RECOMMENDED DISHES

Oeufs en Meurette. Poached eggs in a red-wine sauce.
Pâté de Grenouilles Chaud. Pâté made from frogs' legs and
    served hot.

Andouillette Grillée au Pouilly. Grilled pork sausage cooked in Pouilly wine.

Escargots en Coquilles. Snails with garlic butter served in shells.

Ris de Veau aux Morilles. Calf's sweetbreads in mushroom sauce.

Boudin Noir. Grilled blood sausage.

Rognon de Veau Dijonnaise. Veal kidneys in mustard sauce.

Paupiettes à la Morvandelle. Thin slices of beef, rolled and braised.

Queue de Boeuf Vinaigrette. Oxtail braised and served in vinaigrette.

Raie Beurre Noisette. Skate in brown butter sauce.

Éclair Géant Café. Eclair with coffee-cream filling, topped with coffee icing.

Gâteau de Riz au Coulis d'Abricots. Rice pudding filled with an apricot mixture.

WINE

Especially fine selection of small young growths from Bordeaux and Beaujolais. Excellent Pouilly-Fumé. Also a few great old vintage bottles of Burgundy and Bordeaux.

LE SANCERRE

Mme. Elisabeth Poignant
Chef: M. Patrice Verge

ADDRESS: 13, ave. Corentin-Cariou, 75019
CLOSED: Sat., Sun. and August
PRICE RANGE: Moderate
TEL: 46-07-80-44
METRO: Corentin-Cariou or Porte de la Villette
CREDIT: Visa

A very old-fashioned bistro without much charm but serving marvelous cuts of meat from some of the best butchers in the city. There is a fabulous pot-au-feu *served on Wednesday and a juicy plate of cuts of boiled beef also served on Wednesday or on request.*

If you're visiting the new museum of Science and Industry, Le Sancerre is a nostalgic detour for lunch or dinner. There are exceptional Auvergnat *charcuteries,* beef headcheese and wonderful *côtes* (ribs) of beef and lamb. ·The Beaujolais is a good alternative to the Sancerre, which is a bit expensive.

The Villette area, once the central meat market of Paris, is rapidly being developed as a cultural center with large museums and futuristic buildings. This simple and sincere bistro stands as a reminder of the days when such places were thronged with cattle merchants and lusty eaters who knew their meats and came to this area from all parts of the city to enjoy the best.

RECOMMENDED DISHES

Charcuteries d'Auvergne. Pork cold cuts from the Auvergne.

Saucisson Chaud Pommes a l'Huile. Large slicing sausage served hot with potatoes in oil.

Andouillette au Sancerre. Pork sausage cooked with Sancerre wine.

Tripoux d'Auvergne. Small, strongly seasoned, stuffed pieces of veal tripe.

Pieds de Porc Grillé. Grilled pigs' feet.

Steak au Poivre Vert. Broiled steak with green peppercorns.

Pot-au-Feu (Wednesday). Boiled beef with vegetables and broth.

Plat de Côtes (Wednesdays or on request). Beef ribs like those in *pot-au-feu.*

Côte de Boeuf Villette. Ribs of beef.

Carré d'Agneau (for two). Rack of lamb.

Crème Caramel. Vanilla-flavored flan.

Tarte Feuilleteé aux Pommes. Puff-pastry tart made with apples.

WINE

Beaujolais and Sancerre.

20ᵉ

AUX BEC FINS
LE BISTROT DU XXᵉ
BOEUF GROS SEL
CHEZ ROGER

20ᵉ *Arrondissement*

MÉNILMONTANT

PLACES OF INTEREST

Carrefour de Belleville—Café la Veielleuse
Cimetière de Belleville
Cimetière du Père Lachaise
L'Eglise de Saint-Germain-de-Charonne
Villa d'Ermitage
Villa Faucher

AUX BECS FINS

Mme. Édith Lefebvre

ADDRESS: 44, blvd. de Ménilmontant, 75020
CLOSED: Sun. lunch, Sept. 10–26
PRICE RANGE: Moderate
TEL: 47-97-51-52
METRO: Père-Lachaise
CREDIT: Amex, Visa, Diners and MasterCard

*Delectable cuisine with the taste of the Perigord region is skill-
fully prepared by Mme. Lefebvre and served in a friendly
rustic atmosphere. Fish appears daily on the menu but cassoulet or gras-double (tripe) are the dishes to order.*

Wooden rakes hang from the ceiling in this well-known old
auberge near the Père Lachaise cemetery. A pretty striped awning covers a little closed outdoor terrace. Inside, a long row
of small tables faces the bar and an iron spiral staircase leads to
another room above. The whole feeling is one of a country
cottage. Copious house *terrines* and delicious foie gras are
among the notable starters to be followed by either fish stew
or tripe. Almost everything on the menu, though, is excellent
and the helpings are generous.

RECOMMENDED DISHES

Foie Gras Maison. Exceptional, fresh duck liver.
Terrine de Foie de Canard. Duck liver pâté.
Terrine de Campagne. Coarse country pâté.
Truffade Perigourdine. Potato cake with Cantal cheese.
Gras-Double Lyonnais. Ox tripe sliced and fried with
    onions, vinegar and parsley.
Cassoulet à l'Oie Perigourdin. Goose-and-white-bean stew
    cooked in an earthenware pot.
Rognons de Veau en Cassolette. Veal kidneys served in a
    small casserole dish.
Ragoût de Poisson Mère Edith. Light fish stew.
Pavé au Poivre. Thick slice of beef steak with pepper sauce.

WINE

Muscadet, Burgundy, Beaujolais.

LE BISTROT DU XXe ★

M. Bilhoues-Le Chevallier

ADDRESS: 44, rue du Surmelin, 75020
CLOSED: Sat., Sun. and August
PRICE RANGE: Moderate
TEL: 48-97-20-30
METRO: Saint-Fargeau
CREDIT: Amex, Visa

An excellent and, considering the quality of the food, relatively inexpensive little place. Patron-chef, *M. Bihoues-Le Chevallier, makes everything himself and proposes two remarkable menus which at dinner include an apéritif, wine and coffee.*

This perfect bistro is installed in an old *charcuterie* whose original decorations, a bit worn, are still intact. There are two rooms, seating about 50 people, covered by an especially lovely old glass ceiling. The *carte* is small but there is a splendid choice including some fine *terrines,* delicious sausages and wonderful fish. Lunch can be hectic, crowded with regulars who know they can enjoy a well-prepared meal, made with fine ingredients, for under 100F with wine. At dinner, a chef's choice of the "Halles" might include hot Lyonnais sausage, duck *salé,* cheese and dessert for around 150F. The atmosphere is lively, the service attentive and the wine list adequate.

RECOMMENDED DISHES

Cochonnailles. Assorted pork dishes served with mustard and pickles.
Pâté de Canard. Duck pâté.
Maquereaux au Vinaigre. Mackerel fillets poached in vinegar, served cold.

Saumon Frais à l'Avocat. Fresh salmon steak with avocado.

Saucisson Chaud Lyonnaise. Large slicing sausage served warm with hot potato salad.

Aiguillettes de Canette au Citron Vert. Thin slices of duckling breast cooked with fresh lime.

Petit Salé de Canard. Lightly salted duck.

Lotte au Four Niçoise. Baked monkfish with tomato, garlic, anchovies, olives and capers.

Île Flottante. Poached meringue floating in vanilla custard sauce.

WINE

Careful selection of good "little" wines.

BOEUF GROS SEL

M. Gilbert Brett

ADDRESS: 120, rue des Grands-Champs, 75020
CLOSED: Sat lunch, Sun., July 15–Aug. 24
PRICE RANGE: Moderate
TEL: 43-73-96-58
METRO: Maraîchers
CREDIT: None

A unique menu, a congenial, countrified atmosphere and a mixed clientele with a common appreciation for hearty, rib-sticking food.

You'll know you are on the right block when you see the welcoming little red facade of Boeuf Gros Sel. Inside, the feeling extends to two rustic rooms, simply decorated with lace curtains and red-and-white cloths, an amiable *patron* and happy customers who know how to live. There is only one menu which lists ten appetizers including a choice of pâtés, salads, *boudins* and herring. You should go easy here because there is a gigantic *pot-au-feu* to follow—boiled beef with vegetables, marrow bones, coarse salt and *cornichons*. If you still have room there are cheese and dessert. If beef *gros sel* doesn't strike your fancy, *petit salé* is offered as an alternative.

RECOMMENDED DISHES

Des Saladiers et des Terrines. Abundant and varied selection of salads and pâtés served as hors d'oeuvres.

Petit Salé aux Lentilles. Lightly salted cooked pork served with lentil beans.

Boeuf Gros Sel (Pot-au-Feu). Boiled beef with vegetables and broth.

Brie de Meaux. Exceptionally good cheese cut from the center portion of the brie.

Tarte aux Pommes Maison. Apple tart.

WINE

Beaujolais or Côtes-du-Rhône.

CHEZ ROGER ★

M. George Gilly

ADDRESS: 145, rue d'Avron, 75020
CLOSED: Wed. evening, Thurs., August, Dec. 20–Jan. 5
PRICE: Moderate
TEL: 43-73-55-47
METRO: Porte-de-Montreuil
CREDIT: None

Everything here is what you would expect from an old neighborhood bistro: red-checkered cloths, an old-fashioned menu, warm and friendly service, and good little wines at reasonable prices.

Far from the center of the city, Chez Roger is located in the vicinity of a spectacular new sports center near the Porte de Montreuil. Should you plan to be in this area, this is a good find.

There is a formica bar, and an old gas stove stands in the center of the bourgeois dining room. Although the old *patron* Roger has left, habitués remain—a testament to how good an old-fashioned restaurant can be. Among the well-executed classics are grilled wild salmon and calf's kidneys sautéed in wine. All the lamb dishes are fine and there is a tasty chocolate eclair for dessert.

RECOMMENDED DISHES

Céleri Rémoulade. Raw celery root shredded and served in a spicy mayonnaise.

Haddock Avec Salade de Trévise. Smoked haddock in a salad of red chicory.

Saucisson de Lyon Pommes à l'Huile. Large slicing sausage with potatoes and oil.

Lapin Sauté Sauvignon. Rabbit browned in white wine.

Saumon Sauvage Grillé Sauce Choron. Wild salmon grilled with a béarnaise sauce and tomato purée.

Andouillette. Grilled pork sausage served hot with mustard and vegetables.

Gigot d'Agneau aux Flageolets. Leg of lamb with small green kidney beans.

Rognons de Génisse Sautés au Vin. Calf kidneys browned in wine.

Lapin Sauté Sauvignon. Rabbit browned in white Bordeaux wine.

Éclair Geant. Cream-filled pastry topped with chocolate.

WINE

Especially fine "little" wines of the Bordeaux region.

PART II

Bistro Cuisine

Bistro cuisine is traditional French home cooking, the kind that is found in the memories and long-established traditions of French grandmothers. It is uncomplicated, yet full-flavored and richly satisfying, food made from the finest farm-fresh ingredients: a big pot filled with chunks of beef, vegetables, a sausage or two and just the right seasoning simmered all morning in broth; a creamy veal stew; a fat hen stuffed and poached in bouillon or roasted, unstuffed, to a golden brown and served with pan juices deglazed with fruity wine; tender sausages, poached or grilled, accompanied by sliced potatoes sprinkled with vinegar and parsley; wild mushrooms, turnips, carrots, cabbage, leeks or lentils buttered and salted.

One of the wonderful aspects of bistro cuisine is its extraordinary diversity. There are hundreds of dishes that are considered authentic bistro fare, and of these, standard classics such as *pot-au-feu* and *boeuf bourguignon* are prepared in dozens of different ways as each cook adds to them his or her own personal touch. There is much room for improvisation and no two recipes are exactly the same. Menus change from season to season, reflecting the freshest products available at the market. Most chefs offer daily specials, many with a regional inspiration. Others create new dishes, rendering old favorites in lighter, simpler ways to give them a more contemporary taste. It is well worth some time to become acquainted with the menu items described in this section, as many are virtually unknown outside of France. *Tête de veau sauce ravigote, blanquette, boudin, gratin dauphinois, gigot, onglet, fricassée de poulet, gras-double, boeuf môde,* and *petit salé aux choux* are the sort of lusty foods appreciated by those who love to eat. As French law requires that the menu and prices be posted on the door or window of every restaurant, you will have an idea of what you will encounter before entering.

You will not be surprised to find there is nothing more satisfying than a well-prepared bistro meal. A bottle of crisp white wine with thick slices of sturdy duck pâté, or silvery fish marinated in brine with chunks of pickles and onions whet your appetite for roast leg of lamb seasoned with garlic and served with tiny green kidney beans or grilled duck breast, tender and rare, accompanied by turnips no bigger than spring onions, and washed down with hearty red wine. Farm-fresh goat cheese or a fruit tart may follow, along with strong coffee and perhaps an Armagnac. "The truth is," wrote Brillant-Savarin in *The Physiology of Taste,* "that at the end of a well-savored meal, both soul and body enjoy an especial well being."

LA CARTE

La Carte. The menu.

Prix-Fixe. A set meal at a fixed price, including a choice for each of several courses (*au choix*). Sometimes a drink is included (*boisson compris*).

Menu Dégustation. A tasting menu. Usually a small sampling of the restaurant's specialties.

Apéritif. A before-dinner drink.

Kir. An apéritif made by adding Crème de Cassis (black currant) or Framboise (raspberry) liqueur to a glass of dry white wine or champagne (Kir Royal).

Pousse-Rapière. An apéritif made by adding Armagnac brandy to sparkling white wine; served with a slice of orange. A specialty of Gascogny in Southwest France.

Hors d'Oeuvres. Appetizers.

Potages. Soups.

Sur Commande. Available by request though possibly not on the menu.

Marée. Seafood (all kinds).

Coquillages/Crustacés. Shellfish.

Fruits de Mer. Seafood. Usually shellfish and crustaceans.

Poissons. Fish.

Entrées. May or may not mean the main course. Usually the *entrées* refer to "appetizer" courses, before the main course.

Chaud(e). Hot.

Froid(e). Cold.

Un Plat. A course.

Plats du Jour. Specials of the day.

Maison (à la). A specialty of the chef or restaurant.

Viandes. Meats (*bleu:* very rare; *saignant:* rare; *à point:* medium; *bien cuit:* well done).

Grillades. Grilled meats.

Volailles. Fowl.

Légumes. Vegetables.

Garnitures. Garnishes (additional vegetables or sauces may be offered at an extra charge).

Salade. Salad.

Fromages. Cheeses.

Le Plateau de Fromages (Variés). A cheese platter. Usually a large selection of assorted cheeses.

Assiette de Fromages. A small plate of three or four cheeses.

Desserts. Desserts.

Desserts (à commander au debut du repas). Desserts (must be ordered at the beginning of the meal).

Délices. All sorts of pastries and sweet desserts.

Entremets. Sweet or cooked desserts, usually served after the cheese course.

CARTE DES VINS

Carte des Vins. Wine list.

Sommelier. Wine steward.

Doux. Sweet.

Mousseaux. Sparkling wine.

Sec. Dry.

Vins Blancs White wines.

Vins Rouges. Red wines.

Vins Rosés. Rosé wines.

Vin de la Maison. House wine.

Vin Ordinaire. Non-vintage table wine.

Vins du pays. Local wines: fresh and palatable. Usually a local luxury, must be drunk at an early age.

Alcools. A general term for spirits, after-dinner drinks and digestives.

Alcools Blancs. White alcohols. Clear brandies that are colorless because they are distilled in glass, not wood. They are not sweetened, so the flavor is very strong.

Eaux-de-vie. Fruit brandies. White alcohols distilled from fruit, e.g. raspberry (*framboise*), pear (*poire*), or plum (*mirabelle*).

Marcs. Brandies distilled from the skins, stems, pips and liquid not drained off after the wine has been pressed. They are colorless, dry and very strong, e.g. Marc de Bourgogne or Marc de Champagne.

HORS D'OEUVRES/ENTRÉES

Anchois. Anchovy, usually preserved fillets.

Andouille. A type of smoked sausage generally containing pork tripe, although there are good veal, mutton and beef versions. They are ready-cooked, highly seasoned and served cold as any salami-type sausage or saveloy. The best come from Normandy and Brittany.

> **de vire.** A smoked pork-tripe sausage from Normandy which is well-seasoned and marbled. It is tender and has a mild flavor.

Andouillettes. A smaller version of the above, but which must be cooked before eating and is generally grilled or fried. Usually served hot with mustard and vegetables such as potatoes, cabbage or white beans. There are different varieties, distinguished by their seasonings. Most are rich, pungent and have an overripe sweet flavor which may not appeal to all tastes. The best come from Caen and Cambrai in Flanders and from Troyes in Champagne.

> **A.A.A.A.A..** The *Association Amicale des Amateurs d'Authentique Andouilletes* (The Amicable Association of Appreciators of Authentic Pork Tripe Sausages). An exclusive gourmet group who award their diploma to a few restaurants serving what they consider to be the best tripe sausages. The ideal is made of pig's intestines filled with strips of choice innards mixed with pork fat and seasonings. It is fleshy without too much fat.

> **À la Ficille.** Steeped *à point* in a light broth or wine, giving them a subtle and aromatic flavor.

> **Au vin blanc.** Grilled in butter and garnished with pan juices de-glazed with white wine.

Artichaut. Artichoke.

Asperges. Asparagus.

Assiette. Plate.

Anglaise. A plate of cold meats, e.g. veal, roast beef, ham, etc.

Assorti(e)s. Assorted.

Avocat. Avocado.

Belons. A white-fleshed oyster from Brittany (see *Huîtres*).

Betteraves. Beets/Beetroot.

Boeuf en Salade. Slices of cold beef served on lettuce. Sometimes other items are added, such as hard-boiled eggs, tomatoes and potatoes.

> **Salade tiède de boeuf.** Warm beef salad.

Bouquet. Large reddish shrimp, prawn (see *Crevettes*).

Carottes Rapées. Grated carrot salad. Finely grated carrots in a vinaigrette dressing.

Céleri Rémoulade. Celery root salad. Grated raw celery root garnished with tangy mayonnaise or creamy vinaigrette dressing. (*Céleri-rave* is a type of celery cultivated for the root.)

Cervelas. A closely textured, lightly smoked pork sausage with a smooth skin and mild garlic flavor; usually poached in a light broth and served either cold in slices with a vinaigrette, *tartare* or *rémoulade* dressing, or hot with sliced potatoes or lentils. The best come from Lyon, Nancy and Paris.

> **Aux Pistaches.** Stuffed with pistachio nuts and whole spices.

> **Aux Truffles.** Stuffed with truffles.

Champignons à la Grècque. Mushrooms marinated "Greek style" in olive oil, lemon juice and spices. Served cold in the marinade.

Chou(x). Cabbage.

Chou-fleur. Cauliflower.

Chou Rouge. Red cabbage.

Cochonnailles. Assorted pork products such as sausages, hams, *terrines, rillettes,* headcheese, etc. Served with mustard and *cornichons*.

Concombres. Cucumbers.

Cornichons. Tart gherkins.

Crevette(s). Shrimp.

> **Grises.** Small shrimp, grayish in color. They can be eaten whole with the shell.

> **Roses.** Medium-sized pink shrimp; served cold. The larger ones are called *bouquets*.

Crudités. Assorted raw vegetables.

Écrevisse. Crayfish.

Endives: Endives.

Épinards. Spinach.

Escargots. Snails.

> **De Bourgogne.** With garlic butter and parsley.
>
> **Petits Gris.** Small gray garden snails.

Foie Gras. Lit. "Fat Liver." Liver of a goose or duck which has been force-fed with maize. Cooked either whole or in slices and served hot in a sauce, or cold. (See *Pâté*.)

Frisée aux Lardons. A salad of chicory garnished with crisp bacon bits in a vinegar, hot bacon-fat and garlic dressing. Sometimes pieces of fried bread are added.

Fritons. Leftover pieces of pork, duck, or goose skin slowly cooked in fat until their own fat is rendered and they are tender. They are then quickly fried until they bubble and become crisp, drained and pressed to extract all the fat, then salted and left to cool. They may also be pressed into a mold turning them into a kind of coarse pâté. They should not be confused with *rillettes*, which are made differently. (See *Rillettes*.)

Fromage de Tête. Headcheese, usually pork. (See *Hure de porc*.)

Grillettes. Pieces of fatty meat, usually goose, pork or duck, grilled until crisp.

Hareng. Herring. Usually herring fillets marinated with herbs and seasonings and served with cream.

Huîtres. Oysters.

> **Belons.** From Brittany; round and flat with white flesh.
>
> **Marennes.** From near Bordeaux; long and naturally colored green from algae.
>
> **Fines de Claires.** A designation of oyster indicating they are raised in *"Claires"*—oyster beds in salt marshes rich in seaweed, where they are fattened up for a few months before going to market. Usually from Brittany and Arcachon.
>
> **Spéciales.** These are the largest. They are immersed in the *claire* basins for six to eighteen months before harvesting.

Hure de Porc. Headcheese. This is usually sold in butcher shops ready to eat. The entire head of a pig or boar is steeped in brine for several days, drained, then braised for several hours. The best parts of the skin are removed and spread out. The head, ears, tongue and brains are cut into pieces and seasoned with spices and shallots. They are arranged in such a way as to mix the various meats, folded into the skin and replaced in the braising liquid (wrapped in a napkin) to cook. The contents are then removed from the napkin, put into a brawn mold, pressed and left to cool in their own aspic.

Jambon. Ham.

    Blanc. A boiling or cooking ham. The meat is lightly salted and unsmoked, or only lightly smoked. This ham is also called *jambon demi-sel, jambon glacé* and *jambon de Paris.*

    De Campagne/Du Pays. Country ham. These hams carry the name of the place of origin such as those from the Auvergne, Brittany, Burgundy, Bayonne, the Vosges, Alsace-Lorraine, Touraine, etc. They are cured (salted and smoked, or salted and dried) according to local methods. They are eaten raw or used in cooking, but not boiled.

    Cru. Raw. Ham that has been cured but not cooked, such as Jambon de Bayonne. This is a famous raw ham that is cured in a pickling mixture that includes wine, and is delicious eaten raw in postcard-thin slices or fried with tomatoes and pimientos.

    Cuit. Cooked. *Jambon cuit à l'os* is a country ham cooked on the bone. Served in slices with bread, butter, mustard and pickles.

    Fumé. Smoked. *Jambon fumé de Savoie* is a particularly fine raw smoked ham from the Savoy region. Eaten alone in thin slices.

    de Montagne. Mountain ham (see *Jambon de Campagne*).

    Persillé/De Bourgogne. Parslied ham. A specialty of the Morvan in Burgundy. The ham is shredded into large chunks and cooked in heavily seasoned and parslied aspic and wine. It is then placed in a mold, chilled and pressed. Sliced and served cold in its own aspic.

    Sec. Dried ham. Raw ham, salted and dried.

Jésus (Gésu) de Morteau. This smoked sausage comes from the Franche-Comté. It is made of coarsely chopped pork and fat, flavored with cumin. It has a mild, sweet flavor and is generally poached in wine with shallots and served with hot potatoes in oil or buttered string beans. (See *Plats.*)

Maquereaux au Vin Blanc (au Cidre). Mackerel fillets poached in white wine, cider, or cider vinegar and marinated with herbs. Served chilled with a sauce, or mustard, and chopped parsley. (Sometimes the entire mackerel is served.)

Mâche. Lamb's lettuce.

Moules. Mussels.

> **Farcies.** Mussels stuffed with a mixture of chopped garlic, shallots and parsley, butter and sometimes bread crumbs. Browned in the oven and served on the half-shell.
>
> **Marinières.** Mussels steamed in white wine, shallots, parsley-butter and herbs. Served in the shell.

Museau de Boeuf (de Porc). Beef (or pork) headcheese/ muzzle brawn, vinegared ox muzzle (pig's snout). These brawns are usually sold ready-made in a *charcuterie*. The meat is cut into thin slices seasoned with a vinaigrette, chopped herbs, onions, pickles and parsley, and served cold.

Oeuf Dur Mayonnaise. Cold hard-boiled eggs, sliced in half lengthwise and often served on a bed of lettuce, garnished with fresh mayonnaise and a sprinkling of finely chopped parsley.

> **Oeuf Meurette.*** Eggs poached in red wine seasoned with onions, garlic and herbs. Served on fried toast, covered with a sauce made from the poaching liquid, enriched and thickened with flour and butter, then garnished with bacon bits.

Pamplemousse. Grapefruit.

Pâté. Minced meat (poultry, game or fish) and spices molded and baked in a *terrine* or pastry shell. Usually eaten cold in thick slices.

> **De Campagne.** Country pâté; often made with pork, liver and veal.
>
> **De Fois Gras.** Goose liver pâté.

Pissenlits. Dandelion greens.

> **Aux Lardons.** With bacon bits.

Poireaux Vinaigrettes. Leeks vinaigrette. The whites of leeks are poached in salted water and marinated in an oil-and-vinegar dressing.

Potage. A thick soup.

Radis Beurre. Red radishes served with fresh butter and salt.

Rillettes. A spread of minced pork. (Some varieties can be greasy, bland and stringy.) Pieces of fat and lean pork are cooked slowly with lard and herbs, cooled,

---

*Meurettes. A general term used for all the wine sauces used in Burgundian cooking. They are usually red-wine sauces, well spiced and thickened with flour and butter. They appear in various forms, depending on the foods they accompany (e.g., meat, fish or eggs).

pounded together in a mortar to form a paste, then preserved in jars. *Rillettes* may also be made with goose, duck, fish or rabbit. They are served cold with rolls, bread or toast.

De Tours. A finer variety than most others.

Rillons. A variation of *rillettes*. Pork belly is cut into chunks and cooked in seasoned lard until crisp, then drained of fat and preserved. Rillons can also be made of duck, goose or rabbit.

Rollmops. Herring fillets prepared in a highly seasoned white-wine based marinade, rolled around *cornichons,* and pinned with a wooden skewer. Sometimes served with cream.

Rosette. Dry pork sausage. Pork is soaked in a *marc* and seasoned with pepper and herbs, then chopped and stuffed into a pig's large intestines. During the curing process, the thick, fat skin nourishes the meat and gives it a rich, moist quality. Served in thin slices with butter. The best come from Lyon, the Ardéche, Beaujolais and the Morvan.

Salade. Salad.

> **Blettes.** Leaves of the beet-root plant (similar to Swiss chard).
>
> **Cervelas.** Sausage salad.
>
> **D'Epinards.** Spinach salad.
>
> **De Foies de Volaille.** Chicken-liver salad.
>
> **Marche—Betteraves.** Lamb's lettuce and shredded beets.
>
> **Panachée.** Mixed salad.
>
> **Verte.** Green salad.

Sardines à l'Huile. Sardines in a vinaigrette dressing.

Saucisse. Usually refers to a small sausage that must be cooked before eating. The majority of fresh or partly cured sausages are made of pork and carry the name of the place where they are made.

> **D'Alsace Chaudes au Raifort.** Hot Alsatian sausage with horseradish.
>
> **De Campagne.** Small country sausages.
>
> **Sèche de Vans.** A small dry sausage from Vans, well seasoned with a firm texture. Served in thin slices with bread and butter.
>
> **Sèches à Vouvray.** Small, dry red sausages. The pork is mixed with Vouvray, a dry, rich, slightly crisp wine from the Loire Valley.

De Strasbourg. Smoked beef-and-pork sausage usually eaten with *choucroute.*

De Toulouse. A fresh pure-pork and garlic sausage coarsely cut with a good deal of fat. It is poached to stiffen it, then grilled or fried in butter and placed in the oven to finish. Served with mashed potatoes, stewed white beans, or cabbage. In another preparation it is sautéed in garlic and butter and served with tomatoes, parsley and capers.

Saucisson. Usually refers to an air-dried sausage, sliced and eaten cold as a first course, but others are cooked and served hot (see below).

À l'Ail. Garlic sausage. Large saveloy-type sausage, cooked and served warm with hot potato salad.

De Campagne (Fumé). Thick (smoked) country sausage. Served hot with fried potatoes or cold.

Chaud. Hot garlic sausage poached in water and served plain with hot potato salad.

Chaud à l'Huile. (See *Pommes à l'Huile,* below.)

Chaud à la Lyonnaise. Sausage from Lyon, usually poached and served with hot sliced potatoes. (See *Cervelas.*) Also called *Saucisson Chaud de Lyon.*

Chaud au Macon. Hot sausage simmered in white Macon wine.

En Croûte. Any cooking sausage, coarsely cut and interlaced with cubes of fat, may be used. It is first poached in water and skinned. Then it is encased in brioche dough, glazed with cream, baked to a golden brown and served in thick slices.

Cru. Raw.

Pommes à l'Huile. Sliced hot sausage tossed in oil with warm potatoes.

Sec. An air-dried sausage which is hung to ripen naturally. The composition and seasoning vary according to region. The coarser the grain, the milder the flavor. The best known come from Arles (made of pork and beef and mildly seasoned with pepper, garlic and paprika), Lyon (a cured salami-type sausage—which tastes nothing like salami—flavored with garlic and pepper and studded with cubes of fat), the Ardèche (see *Rosette*) and the Morvan.

Terrine. Usually refers to a meat, game or fish mixture cooked in a rectangular earthenware dish and eaten cold in thick slices. (See *Pâté.*)

De Foie de Volaille. A coarse pâté made with chicken livers.

De Lapereau en Gellée. Rabbit potted in aspic.

Tomate. Tomato.

Thon. Tuna, eaten fresh or canned.

À l'Huile. Chunks of canned tuna in olive oil. Served with lemon, bread and butter.

LES PLATS

Agneau. Lamb. The principal cuts of lamb are: *Baron:* Saddle and both legs. *Carré:* Rack. *Côte:* Chop. *Côtelette:* Cutlet, lamb chop. *Épaule:* Shoulder. *Gigot:* Leg. *Médaillon/ Mignonette:* (See *Noisette.*) *Noisette:* Small round boned cutlet. *Poitrine:* Breast. *Selle:* Saddle.

Aiglefin (Églefin). Haddock.

Aiguillette. Usually refers to long, thin slices cut from the breast of game or poultry. (See *Boeuf.*)

Ail. Garlic.

Aile. Wing (of poultry or game birds).

Aïoli. Garlic-flavored mayonnaise. (See *Bourride.*)

Aligot. Puréed potatoes with cheese, usually fresh Cantal cheese from Auvergne.

Alose. Shad.

Alouette. Lark.

Anguille. Eel. Freshwater eel as opposed to *Congre* sea eel. (See *Matelote.*)

Anis. Aniseed.

Anisé. Flavored with aniseed or caraway.

Aromates. Herbs and spices.

Aubergine. Eggplant.

Bar. Sea bass.

Barbue. Brill, a sea fish similar to turbot.

Basilic. Sweet basil.

Bavette. Flank steak.

 Aux Echalotes. With shallots.

 Poêlée. Pan fried.

Béarnaise. A butter sauce made with egg yolks, white wine, sometimes vinegar, tarragon and minced shallots which melt into the sauce as they are cooked.

Bécasse. Woodcock.

Beurre. Butter.

 Blanc. White butter. A thick creamy sauce of butter, white wine, "melted" shallots and vinegar. The making of this sauce is an art, depending as much on the hand of the chef as on the ingredients.

Meunière. Melted herb-butter flavored with lemon juice and parsley.

Noir. Black butter. Melted butter blackened with vinegar and flavored with lemon juice, parsley and sometimes capers. (See *Raie.*)

Noisette. Brown butter. Melted butter, lightly browned with lemon juice and parsley.

Bifteck. Steak. An inexpensive cut which is often made into hamburger.

Blanquette de Veau (d'Agneau). Veal (lamb) stewed in a white cream sauce with mushrooms and onions. The sauce is enriched with egg yolks and flour. *Blanquettes* are also made with chicken and seafood.

Boeuf. Beef. The principal cuts of beef are: *Aiguillette:* A thin steak from the end of the loin (rump), also called *pièce de boeuf* or *culotte. Aloyau:* Tenderloin, the long strip around the loin. *Bavette:* Flank steak. (See *Bavette.*) *Bifteck:* Steak. (See *Bifteck.*) *Châteaubriand:* Steak cut from the fillet. *Contre Filet:* Sirloin steak, also called *faux-filet. Côte:* Rib. *Entrecôte:* Rib steak, from between the ribs and loin. (See *Entrecôte.*) *Faux Filet:* Sirloin steak. (See *Faux-filet.*) *Filet:* Fillet steak. Filet de Boeuf Poêle. Sautéed beef tenderloin. *Onglet:* Mitre-joint, a cut similar to flank steak. (See *Onglet.*) *Pavé:* A thick slice of beef steak. *Romsteck/Rumsteak.* Rumpsteak. *Tournedos*: Steak from the best part of the fillet. (See *Tournedos Rossini.*)

Boeuf Bourguignon. Beef stewed in red wine, bacon, onions, mushrooms and herbs.

Boeuf Carotte. Pot roast with carrots.

Boeuf en Daube. Chunks of marinated beef braised in red wine with aromatic vegetables.

Daube. A method of braising meat, poultry, game or fish in wine, stock, herbs and vegetables. The exact mixture is a matter of choice. A special earthenware pot called a *daubière* is often used. In some *daubes* the meat is cut up; in others it is cooked whole.

Boeuf à la Ficelle. A fillet of beef is wrapped tightly with string, quickly browned in a hot oven, then placed, suspended, into an herbal bouillon made from aromatic vegetables. The meat is then poached for several minutes until tender and served rare in slices with or without vegetables.

Boeuf Gros Sel. Chunks of boiled beef in the stockpot broth, with vegetables. Served with coarse salt and other condiments such as mustard, *cornichons,* horseradish, etc.

Boeuf Miroton. Left-over *pot-au-feu* meat that has been chilled, sliced and reheated by simmering in a sweet brown sauce made with butter, flour, onions, seasonings and a dash of vinegar.

Boeuf Mode (á la mode). Pot roast marinated in herbs and brandy, larded, then braised with red wine, carrots and onions. Sometimes other vegetables such as mushrooms and turnips are included. Served hot from the pot or cold, when it becomes a sort of jellied meat dish.

Boudin. A type of soft sausage.

> **Blanc.** White pudding. Today this sausage is stuffed largely with bread, eggs, onions, fat and herbs, and can be poached, grilled or fried. In some areas the bread is replaced by veal, chicken (*Boudin Blanc Touraine*), or pork (*Boudin Blanc Lyonnais*).

> **Noir.** Blood sausage/black pudding. A soft sausage made with pork, pig's blood, fat, herbs and garlic. It is usually grilled and served with roasted potatoes and sautéed apples. When well prepared, it is crisp on the outside and moist on the inside.

Bouillabaisse. Mediterranean fish stew traditionally made with *rascasse, congre* and *grondin* plus other fish, shellfish, onions, tomatoes, garlic, saffron and herbs. Served with *rouille,* a hot pepper mayonnaise.

Bourride. Mediterranean fish stew traditionally made with white fish only. Served with *aïoli,* a garlic flavored mayonnaise.

Brandade. A mousse-like blend of fish, garlic and oil.

> **De Morue.** Purée of desalted salt cod, cut into pieces and mixed with cream, olive oil and garlic. The mixture is pounded in a mortar while a thin thread of olive oil is poured in, transforming it into a purée with the consistency of cream cheese. Sometimes mashed potatoes are added. Served warm with fried bread.

Brochet. Pike. (See *Quenelles.*)

> **Au Beurre Blanc.** Poached and served with white-wine butter sauce.

Burbot. (See *Lotte.*)

Cabillaud. Fresh codfish.

Caille. Quail.

Calamars. Cuttlefish, squid.

Canard. Duck.

Aux Choux. With cabbage.

Aux Navets. Braised and served with small turnips in a brown butter sauce.

Au Poivre Vert. Roasted, and served in a sauce made with green peppercorns.

Sauvage. Wild duck, mallard.

Caneton. Duckling (male).

Canette. Duckling (female).

Carré. Rack (Lit. "square"). Usually rack of lamb, but also pork or veal.

Cassoulet. A casserole of white beans and varying fresh or preserved meats such as sausage, pork, mutton, lamb, *confit* of duck, goose, etc. The ingredients are different in each region.

Cèpes. Wild flat mushrooms.

Cervelles. Brains. Usually calf or lamb brains, sautéed and served in a butter sauce.

Meuniere. Floured and fried in butter. Served with a sauce of brown butter, lemon and parsley.

Champignon. Mushroom.

Chanterelle. A yellow, trumpet-shaped mushroom with a fragrant flavor. Also known as *Girolle*.

Chapon. Capon.

Charolais. A region in Burgundy whose breed of light-colored cattle produces high-quality beef.

Cheveuil. Venison.

Choucroute (Garnie). Sauerkraut (garnished) with an assortment of sausages, bacon, pork, ham and served with boiled potatoes.

Chou Farci. Leaves or small heads of cabbage, scalded then stuffed and cooked in various ways. A common preparation stuffs scalded cabbage leaves with minced pork or beef, bacon, onions, herb, cream, and eggs, then bakes or boils them in bouillon with onions, cloves and parsley. In another variation, small cabbage heads are stuffed with minced pork, veal and mushrooms then simmered for several hours in white wine.

Civet. In the past, a *civet* was simply a stew with onions (*cives*). Today, it usually refers to a game stew (unless otherwise indicated) in a rich red wine sauce made with onions, mushrooms, spices and thickened with the animal's blood.

Cochon. Pig.

De Lait. Suckling pig.

Colin. Hake, a kind of codfish. (See *Merlin.*)

Colombe. Dove.

Congre. Sea eel, an ocean fish resembling eel.

Confit. Meat that has been salted to draw out the moisture then cooked and preserved in its own fat.

> **De Canard.** Preserved duck, usually grilled and served in large pieces.

Contre Filet. Sirloin steak.

Coq. Cock, cockerel.

Coq-au-Vin. Chicken braised in red wine with onions, pork, mushrooms, herbs and sometimes tomato paste.

Coquelet. Young (male) chicken.

Coquilles Saint-Jacques. Sea scallops.

Côte. Rib, chop.

Cotriade. Brittany fish stew.

Cou d'Oie. Stuffed neck of goose. A goose neck skin is marinated in brandy and spices, stuffed with force meat, duck liver or foie gras, chopped truffles, spices, tied-up and cooked. Served like a sausage.

Coulis. A general term for a thick sauce or purée, often of vegetables or fruit.

Cru. Raw, uncooked.

Cuisse. Leg, thigh.

> **De Grenouilles à la Provençale.** Frogs' legs in garlic and oil.

> **De Poulet.** Chicken drumstick.

Daube. (See *Boeuf en Daube.*)

Daurade. Sea bream, a gilt-head fish similar to porgy. Not to be confused with *dorade* or red sea bream which is not as good.

Dauphinois. Layers of thin sliced potatoes, baked in milk with grated cheese and nutmeg. (*Gratin Dauphinois.*)

Dinde. Turkey (hen).

Dindon. Turkey (cock).

Dodine. A preparation of poultry (or meat) boned, stuffed and braised; often refers to duck.

Dorade. Red sea bream. (See *Daurade.*)

Échalote. Shallot.

Échine. Lit. "spine." Backbone of loin of pork, pork shoulder.

Écrevisse. Freshwater crayfish.

Entrecôte. Steak from between the ribs and loin.

> **Bercy.** Pan-fried or grilled steak served with chopped shallots, marrow, lemon juice, parsley and butter creamed with a reduction of white wine.

> **Marchand de Vin.** Steak grilled or pan-fried and served in

a reduction of red wine with brown sauce (*demi-glace*), butter, chopped shallots and parsley.

À la Moelle. Steak grilled or pan-fried with bone marrow. Served in a sauce of wine, pan juices, marrow and herbs and garnished with poached marrow.

Épaule. Shoulder. Refers to lamb, pork, or veal. Beef shoulder is called *paleron*.

Éperlan. Smelt. Usually fried, as in *Friture d'Eperlans.*

Escalope. A thin slice of meat.

Escalope Panée. Breaded veal cutlet.

Espadon. Swordfish.

Estragon. Tarragon.

Faisan. Pheasant.

Faisandeau. Young pheasant.

Faisane. Pheasant (hen).

Farci. Stuffed. (See *Chou Farci.*)

Faux-filet. Steak sirloin, lit. "false fillet."

Fenouil. Fennel.

Foie. Liver.

>   **De Veau (Rôti).** Calf's liver (roasted).

>   **De Veau au Vinaigre de Xérès.** Calf's liver with sherry vinegar from Jerez, Spain.

Flageolet. A small, tender pale-green kidney-shaped bean (baby lima bean).

Flétan. Halibut.

Fricandeau.* Thinly sliced veal or rump roast larded with bacon and braised with white wine and vegetables. Served on a bed of braised vegetables such as chicory and sorrel or celery, lettuce and spinach.

Fricassée. A light stew usually consisting of meat in a cream sauce. The meat is first sautéed which distinguishes it from a *blanquette.*

>   **De Poulet aux Morilles.** Chicken sautéed, then braised in a sauce containing crinkled black wood-mushrooms, and thickened with egg yolks and cream.

>   **De Veau à l'Oseille.** A stew of veal with mushrooms and onions in cream sauce seasoned with sorrel.

Frites. French fries. (Short for *Pommes Frites.*)

Friture. Fried food. Usually refers to tiny deep-fried fish. (See *Éperlan.*)

Gibier. Game.

>   **À Plume.** Refers to game birds. (Lit. "with feather.")

---

*Fricandeau also applies to pork-liver pâté cooked in a casing made with the lining of a sheep's stomach.

À Poile. Refers to deer, rabbit, hare, wild boar, etc. (Lit. "with fur.")

Gibelotte de Lapin. Rabbit stewed with onions, garlic, herbs and white wine; served on fried toast.

Gigot. Leg (usually) of lamb or mutton.

    Aux Flageolets. Roast leg of lamb seasoned with garlic, served with pan juices and tomato purée and accompanied by small, pale-green kidney-shaped beans.

    De Pré-Salé. Salt-marsh mutton, often served with white beans. (See *Pré-Salé.*)

Girolles. Wild curly mushrooms. (See *Chanterelle.*)

Gras-Double. Ox tripe. (Refers to 3 stomachs of ox as opposed to *tripe,* which includes all four.) Tripe (from the inner belly; tender and juicy) is scalded, cooked for several hours in bouillon, drained, braised with lard then sautéed with white wine, minced onions and butter. Served sprinkled with vinegar or lemon and chopped parsley.

    À la Lyonnaise. Poached tripe, sliced, breaded and fried. Served with snail butter or a sharp sauce.

    Aux Haricots Blancs. Tripe with white beans.

Gribiche. A thick creamy vinaigrette made with oil, vinegar, hard-boiled-egg yolks and chopped pickles, capers and herbs.

Gros Sel. Coarse salt. (See *Boeuf Gros Sel.*)

Hachis Parmentier. Mincemeat hash with potatoes. Best when made with leftovers from a good *pot-au-feu* and quality potatoes. Ground beef (or pork) and puréed potatoes are sprinkled with bread crumbs and grated cheese then browned in an oven. Sometimes served in potato jackets.

Haddock. Haddock, a sea fish of the cod family but smaller than cod.

    À l'Anglais. Haddock sautéed English-style with egg and breadcrumbs.

    Au Beurre Blanc. Haddock poached in water or milk and served in a white-wine butter sauce.

    Emincée à la Crème de Raifort. Haddock with horseradish cream.

Hake. A sea fish of the cod family. It is called *merlin* in Provence and *colin* in Paris, and sometimes referred to as *saumon blanc* (white salmon).

Haricot. Bean.

    Blanc. White bean.

    Vert. String bean.

Haricot de Mouton. A stew of white beans and lamb. Today the word *haricot* replaces the obsolete word *halicot* (meaning stew). The latter traditionally included mutton, turnips, potatoes and onions but no beans. The former contains white beans as well, and is seasoned with garlic and herbs.

Hochepot (le). A northern version of *pot-au-feu* with a variety of meats and vegetables. The famous version is *Queue de Boeuf en Hochepot,* made with oxtail, pig's trotters, ears, cabbage, carrots, onions and turnips.

Homard. Lobster.

Jambon. Ham. (See *Hors d'Oeuvres.*)

Jarret. Shin, knuckle of veal, beef, etc.

> **De Porc aux Lentilles.** Pork shank with lentils.
> **De Veau.** Veal shank (stew).

Jambonneau. Pork knuckle/shoulder of pork.

Jésus Lyonnais. A small dried sausage.

Jésus (Gésu) de Morteau. A smoked pork-sausage from the Franche-Comté.

> **Au Vin Blanc.** Smoked pork-sausage sautéed in butter until brown then simmered with small whole potatoes, onions, garlic, parsley, tomato paste and white wine. The sausage is sliced and served with the potatoes and reduced pan juices, then garnished with parsley.

Langouste. Spiny lobster.

Langoustine. A delicate pink crustacean (scampi) resembling a small lobster.

Langue. Tongue. Usually beef (*langue de boeuf*) unless otherwise designated. Served in a sauce of butter, minced *cornichons,* white wine, vinegar, parsley and cayenne pepper (*sauce piquante*).

Lapereau. A young rabbit.

Lapin/Lièvre. Rabbit/hare.

> **Chasseur.** Rabbit sautéed with white wine, mushrooms, shallots, brown sauce (*demi-glace*) and tomato sauce, then sprinkled with parsley.
> **Grandmère.** Rabbit sautéed with butter, onions, mushrooms, bacon, potatoes, Madeira wine, herbs and seasonings.
> **À la Moutarde.** Rabbit in a mustard sauce enriched with cream and seasoned with lemon juice, salt and pepper.
> **À la Royale.** Rabbit, boned and stuffed with foie gras and truffles, then braised in red wine and brandy.

Limande. Lemon (usually sole).

Lotte. Monkfish.

> **Aux Poireaux.** With leeks.

Loup (de mer). Mediterranean sea bass, lit. "sea wolf."

Magret de Canard. Duck breast. Boned and sliced, usually grilled or gently pan-fried. Served rare.

Maquereaux. Mackerel.

Matelote. A stew of different freshwater fish, particularly eel and carp, pike or perch; in wine with mushrooms and onions.

Merlin (frit). Whiting (fried).

Meurette. Red wine sauce.

Meunière. Herb-butter sauce. (See *Beurre.*)

Moelle. Bone marrow, usually beef.

Morilles. Wild mushrooms, morels.

Morue. Codfish. (Salt cod, as opposed to *cabillaud*, which is fresh codfish.)

Mousseline. A light, creamy purée.

Nantua. A light crayfish-flavored cream sauce.

Navarin. Lamb or mutton stew with vegetables. Usually served with turnips and potatoes.

> **D'agneau Printanier.** Lamb stew with a variety of spring vegetables such as new potatoes, onions, carrots, turnips, tomatoes, peas, string beans. Seasoned with garlic and herbs.

Navet. Turnip.

Noisette. Hazelnut. But also refers to anything small and round, especially a medallion of meat.

Noix. Nut, especially walnut. But also refers to the topside of veal. (See *Fricandeau* and *Veau.*)

Oie. Goose.

Oignon. Onion.

Ombre. A freshwater fish similar to trout.

Onglet. Steak (mitre-joint from the strip encasing the ribs). Like strip steak, the cut is juicy and flavorful. Usually grilled or sautéed with shallots.

Os. Bone.

> **À l'Os.** With bone marrow.

Oreille. Ear, usually pig.

Oseille. Sorrel.

Panée. Coated with breadcrumbs.

Palette. Blade bone. A thin circular cut from the top of the shoulder blade, usually pork.

Palombe. Wild dove, wild pigeon.

Pavé. A term for various thickly sliced items, lit. "paving stone," e.g. thickly sliced beef steak.

Perdreau. Young partridge.

Perdrix. Adult partridge.

Petits Pois. Green peas.

Petit Salé. Lightly salted pork tenderloin.

> **Aux Choux Braisés.** Salt pork poached and served with braised cabbage.
>
> **Aux Lentilles.** Salt pork simmered with garlic, onions, and herbs. Served with green lentils, and garnished with butter and chopped parsley.
>
> **De Canard.** Duck that has been marinated for several days in salt brine, herbs and spices, then cooked and served with vegetables.

Pieds. Feet or trotters.

> **De Mouton.** Sheep's trotters. Prepared in ways similar to those described below for pigs' feet.
>
> **Poulette.** Poached sheep's trotters in a rich sauce made with pan juices, cream and egg yolks flavored with lemon and parsley. Sometimes mushrooms are added.
>
> **De Porc (pané).** Pigs' feet (breaded). Usually grilled.
>
> **Farci et Pané.** Poached pigs' feet, stuffed, breaded and grilled. Served with potatoes and a spicy sauce or mustard.
>
> **Ste. Menehould.** Pigs' feet poached for 24–36 hours in a stock of white wine, cloves and herbs to soften the bones, making them edible. They are then breaded and grilled until crisp. Served plain with mustard or a pungent sauce and often accompanied by potatoes or lentils.

Pieds et Paquets. Stuffed lamb's trotters and tripe. The "packets" are little rolls made from a sheep's stomach stuffed with a seasoned salt pork mixture. These are braised with lamb's feet in white wine, with skin of beef and veal, onions, tomatoes, garlic, herbs, parsley and orange peel. This is a specialty of Marseilles.

Pigeon. Pigeon.

Pigeonneau. Squab.

Pintade. Guinea fowl.

Pinteadeau. Young guinea fowl.

Pipérade. A Basque preparation consisting of an omelette or scrambled eggs with onions, Bayonne ham, sweet peppers and tomatoes.

Piquant(e). Spicy, pungent.

Poêlé. Pan-fried.

Poivre. Pepper.

Pomme de Terre (pomme). Potato.

Porc. Pork. The principal cuts of pork are: *Carré:* Rack, ribs. *Côte:* Chop. *Échine:* Shoulder. *Filet:* Tenderloin. *Jambon:*

Ham. *Jamboneau:* Knuckle/shoulder. *Longe:* Top half of the loin. *Palette:* Shoulder. *Pied:* Trotter. *Poitrine:* Breast.

Porcelet. Piglet.

Potage. A thick soup which may be a purée of vegetables, a creamy soup made with cream or milk, or a soup based on creamy white velouté sauce made with stock, eggs and cream.

Pot-au-Feu. Boiled dinner (soup, meat and vegetables). Usually various cuts of beef simmered with bone marrow, turnips, leeks, cabbage and carrots. A *pot-au-feu* is traditionally served with the soup first followed by a platter of the vegetables and meat garnished with marrow. Served with mustard, *cornichons* and coarse salt. No two chefs agree on the ingredients. Sausage, ham, fowl, mutton, bacon, etc. may be used.

Potée. A substantial soup of meat and vegetables. The basic ingredients are fresh or salt pork with cabbage, beans or lentils and sausage, but there is a wide latitude as to what may be included and the ingredients vary according to region.

> **Alsacienne/aux Haricots Rouges.** Soup made with red kidney beans, sausage and pork.

> **À l'Auvergnate.** Soup made with sausage, bacon, cabbage, onions, carrots, garlic and sometimes lentils or other beans.

> **Bourguignonne.** Cubes of beef, chicken, salt pork, garlic sausage, cabbage, potatoes, leeks, celery and turnips. The soup is poured over slices of bread and the meat and vegetables are served separately.

Poularde. A roasting chicken, fattened hen, pullet. Often used interchangeably with *capon, coq* and *poulet.*

> **À la Crème au Vinaigre de Xérès.** With sherry vinegar from Jerez.

> **Au Riz.** With rice.

Poule. Hen (boiling).

Poule au Pot. Chicken stuffed with a mixture of its own liver, ham, bread, eggs, garlic and herbs then poached in bouillon made with aromatic vegetables. The vegetables (turnips, carrots, leeks and celery) are removed before poaching the chicken and transferred to a skillet where they are simmered in stock. Meanwhile some of the stuffing ingredients are wrapped in cabbage leaves and cooked with the chicken. The chicken is served accompanied by the vegetables and a sauce made from some of the stock, thickened with cream and egg yolks. The rest of the stock is served separately as a soup. Coarse salt and *cornichons* may also accompany this dish.

Poulet. Chicken.

> **De Bresse.** Corn-fed free-range chicken from Bresse in Eastern France. Very high in quality.
>
> **Fermier.** Free-range.
>
> **À l'Estragon.** Roasted or sautéed chicken with tarragon. Served with either a cream sauce or a brown sauce flavored with tarragon.
>
> **Rôti.** Roasted.

Poulette. A rich white sauce made from stock thickened with egg yolks and cream. Sometimes button mushrooms, onions and white wine are added. *Poulette* is also the name for a young chicken.

Poulpe. Octopus.

Poussin. Young spring chicken, baby chicken.

Pré(s) Salé(s). Salt marsh mutton. This is the most prized mutton in France because the sheep are grazed in meadows saturated with salt from ocean winds, giving the meat a special salty taste.

Quenelles. Forcemeat dumplings. A purée of meat, poultry or fish is mixed with fat, eggs and pastry dough or crumbs, then made into light dumplings. These are usually poached and served with a simple cream sauce.

> **De Brochet.** Pike dumplings, often served in a *beurre blanc* sauce.
>
> **Nantua.** Dumplings served with a crayfish-flavored cream sauce made with white wine, fish stock, a few drops of cognac, and cayenne pepper. Sometimes mushrooms or truffles are added.
>
> **De Volaille.** Chicken dumplings.

Queue de Boeuf. Oxtail.

Queues et Oreilles de Cochon Grillées. Grilled pigs' tails and ears.

Râble de Lièvre (Lapin). Saddle of hare (rabbit). The word *selle* is used for larger animals.

Raie. Skate.

> **Au Beurre Noir.** With black butter. Poached or grilled skate served in a sauce of blackened butter, vinegar, lemon and parsley. Sometimes garnished with capers.

Raifort. Horseradish.

Rascasse. Scorpion fish.

Ravigote. A thick, spicy vinaigrette mixed with vinegar, chopped cornichons, herbs, capers and onions.

Rémoulade. Spicy mustard mayonnaise mixed with chopped herbs, capers, *cornichons* and sometimes anchovies.

Ris. Sweet breads, usually braised or sautéed.

    D'Agneau. Lamb.

    De Veau. Calf.

Riz. Rice.

Rognons (d'Agneau, de Veau). Kidneys (lamb, veal), usually grilled or sautéed.

    Poêle de Rognons. Sautéed kidneys.

Rôti. Roasted.

Rouget. A mediterranean fish similar to red mullet.

Rouille. Hot red-pepper mayonnaise. (See *Bouillabaisse.*)

Saint-Pierre. John Dory, a firm, white-fleshed ocean fish with dark spots (the thumb marks of St. Peter!) on each side.

Sandre. Pike-perch, a freshwater river fish.

    À l'Oseille. With sorrel.

Sanglier. Wild boar.

Sauge. Sage.

Saumon. Salmon.

    Fumé. Smoked.

    Grillée à l'Unilateral. Grilled on one side.

    Mariné. Marinated.

    Saumuré. Salted.

Sauté. A preparation of meat, game, fish or fowl lightly pan-fried in oil and butter over high heat. The pan juices are used as a garnish and sometimes vegetables are added. In some *sautés* the meats are braised or baked to complete the cooking.

Selle. Saddle, back (of meat).

Sole Meunière. Sole (pan-fried) with butter sauce.

Soupe. Soup, usually refers to a thick country-style soup with pieces of meat and vegetables.

Sucré(e). Sweetened.

Tabliers de Sapeur. Pan-fried tripe. Ox tripe is pounded into a flat sheet, cut into small squares, breaded and pan-fried until crisp. Served with garlic butter, tartar sauce or béarnaise. This is a specialty of Lyon.

Tête. Head, especially calf's head, usually served hot with vinaigrette (see *Tête de Veau*). Can also mean brawn, as in *fromage de tête*.

Tête de Veau. Head of veal, poached in an herbal stock with spices, white wine, carrots and onions. It is boned, sliced and served hot or cold in a sauce, often with slices of the tongue and brains. When the head is lean and tender and served very hot in a tasty warm vinaigrette, it can be quite good. Otherwise, it can have a repellent and gristly texture.

Sauce Gribiche. With a creamy vinaigrette flavored with tarragon, chopped hard-boiled egg yolks, capers, and *cornichons*.

Sauce Ravigote. With a vinaigrette seasoned with *chervil*, tarragon, capers, and onions.

Thon. Tuna.

Thym. Thyme.

Tiède. Warm, tepid.

Tomate. Tomato.

    Farci. Stuffed.

Tournedos. Steak from the best part of the fillet.

    Rossini. Tournedos sautéed and served on a crust topped with a slice of foie gras then covered with pan juices mixed with red wine.

Tranche. A slice.

Tripe. Ox tripe.

    À la Mode/À la Mode Caen. The classic Norman preparation for tripe, in which it is boiled and braised for several hours with calf's foot, salt pork, carrots, onions, herbs and seasonings in apple cider, wine, and Calvados.

Tripous/Tripoux. Pieces of veal or mutton tripe wrapped round a stuffing mixture of minced pork and veal seasoned with cloves. The stuffing ingredients may vary, but cloves are always used. The tripe is then made into small rolls and simmered for several hours in an airtight casserole.

Truffade. A large fried pancake made with layers of potato, Cantal cheese, bacon and garlic. A specialty from Auvergne.

Truffe. Truffle.

Truite. Trout.

    Au Bleu. A method of cooking trout by first plunging it into boiling water with vinegar then removing it to a court bouillon to finish the cooking.

Turbot. Turbot, a flat white sea fish with a subtle flavor.

Vapeur (à la). Steamed.

Veau. Veal. The principal cuts of veal are: *Carré:* Rib, rack. *Côte:* Chop. *Cul:* Rump. *Escalope:* Thin slice from the fillet. *Jarret:* Knuckle. *Longe:* Top half of the loin. *Noisette:* Medallion, small round steak. *Noix:* Topside, from the upper part of the leg. *Poitrine:* Breast. *Tendron:* Cartilage from the end of the breast. *Tête:* Head (see *Tête de Veau*).

Vert(e). Green.

Poivre Vert. Green peppercorns.

Sauce Verte. Green herb mayonnaise.

Volailles. Poultry.

Xérès: A dry white sherry produced in Jerez de la Frontera, Spain.

Vinaigre de. Vinegar made from this wine.

DESSERTS

Abricot. Apricot.

Ananas. Pineapple.

    Au Kirsch (Rhum). Sliced pineapple sprinkled with sugar and Kirsch (rum).

Baba au Rhum. Sponge cake with rum-flavored syrup.

Banane. Banana.

Bombe. A moulded, layered ice cream dessert. Usually two flavors layered together in a spherical mold.

Cafe (Chocolat) Liégeois. Cold coffee (chocolate) poured over coffee (chocolate) ice cream. Served in tall glasses topped with whipped cream.

Caprice. A dessert, lit. "whim."

Cerises. Cherries.

Charlotte. A molded dessert of which there are two kinds. One is a pudding mixture made from fruit and sugar, baked in a mold lined with white buttered bread or sponge cake and served hot. The other is a cold custard cream or mousse (e.g. chocolate) chilled in a mold lined with lady fingers.

Citron. Lemon.

Clafoutis. A thick custard tart made with egg yolks and a kind of pancake batter poured over preserved fruit (traditionally cherries but any available fruit may be used), and baked. This is a specialty from the Limousin.

Compôte. Fresh or dried fruit stewed in wine.

Corbeille. A basket of fresh fruit.

Coupe. A glass or bowl. Often refers to one serving, e.g. one scoop or *boule,* of ice cream.

Crème Anglaise. Light egg and vanilla custard sauce.

Crème Brûlée. Egg custard topped with brown sugar which is "burnt" to form a hard dark coating.

Crème Caramel. Egg custard in a sauce of caramelized sugar.

Cremet. Fresh unsalted cream cheese eaten with fruit, jam or cream and sugar.

Crème de Marrons. Sugar-sweetened chestnut purée.

Crème Renversée. Upside-down *crème caramel.*

Delice. Lit. "Delight," a menu description of a dessert.

Douce (Doux). Sweet(s).

Flan. A baked custard tart or open pie; sometimes refers to *crème renversée.*

Frais/Fraîche. Fresh.

Fraises. Strawberries.

Framboises. Raspberries.

>   **Au Sucre.** With sugar.

Fromage. Cheese.

>   **Blanc.** Fresh cream cheese with a salty taste and the consistency of smooth cottage cheese. Served plain or with sugar, cream, fruit or salt and pepper.

>   **Brebis.** Sheep's milk cheese.

>   **Cervelle de Canut.** A soft, fresh cream cheese made with herbs, vinegar, white wine, oil and garlic. A specialty of Lyon.

>   **Crottin (de Chavignol).** A small dry goat's milk cheese with a strong sharp taste.

Au Fruits Rouges. With berries.

Gâteau. Cake.

Gâteau de Noix. Walnut cake.

Gâteau de Riz. Rice is cooked in vanilla-flavored milk, moulded into a cake and served with whipped cream and/or sauce. Sometimes fruit is added to the rice.

Glace. Ice cream.

Île Flottante. "Floating island." Poached egg whites are caramelized with sugar and vanilla beans and served in a vanilla custard sauce. Sometimes used interchangeably with *Oeufs à la Neige.*

Marquise au Chocolate. A mousse-like chocolate sponge cake with a butter cream filling.

Marrons Glacés. Candied chestnuts.

Mille-Feuille. A Napoleon. Layers of puff pastry, filled with cream or custard, cut into rectangles, glazed and frosted.

Mirabelle. A kind of yellow plum.

Mont Blanc. A mound of puréed chestnuts topped with whipped cream.

Mousse au Chocolat. A light chocolate pudding, often served with whipped cream.

Mûres. Mulberries/blackberries.

Myrtilles. Huckleberries/blueberries.

Mystère. A "mystery." An ice cream dessert, often vanilla ice cream in meringues with chocolate sauce.

Oeufs à la Neige. "Snow eggs." Caramelized egg whites served in a vanilla custard sauce. (See *Île Flottante.*)

Oranges. Oranges.

Panaché(e). Mixture.

Parfum. Flavor.

Pâtisseries. Pastries.

Pêches. Peaches.

    Melba. Poached peaches with vanilla ice cream and raspberry sauce.

Poires. Pears.

    Belle Helène. Poached pears with vanilla ice cream and chocolate sauce.

    Au Vin. Pears poached in sugar and red wine or Port.

Pommes. Apples.

    Au Four. Baked apples.

Profiteroles. Small cream puffs filled with ice cream (or pastry cream), covered with chocolate or coffee sauce and served with whipped cream.

Pruneau(x). Prune(s).

Raisins. Grapes.

Riz au lait. (See *Gâteau de Riz.*)

Sorbet. Fruit ice, sherbet.

Tarte-Tatin. Caramelized upside-down apple tart, served hot or cold.

Tartes. Open-faced pies. Fruit tarts may or may not be made with pastry cream but are usually coated with an apricot or currant glaze.

Tartelettes. Small or individual tarts.

GLOSSARY

Afternoon	*Apres-midi*
An amusement— something to nibble while waiting for food to be served	*Amuse-bouche*
Ashtray	*Cendrier*
Beer	*Bière*
Draft Beer	*À la pression (bière)*
Beverages	*Boissons*
Bread	*Pain*
Breakfast	*Petit déjeuner*
Butter	*Beurre*
The check	*l'addition*
Cider	*Cidre*
Closed*	*Fermé*
Coffee	*Café*
black	*noir*
decaffeinated	*déca/décafeiné*
espresso	*express*
very strong, black	*filtre*
with milk	*au lait/crème*
Cover charge	*Un couvert***
Cup	*Tasse*
Dinner	*Dîner (8:00–10:30)*
Evening	*Soir*
This evening	*Ce soir*
Every day	*Tous les jours (TLJ)*
An extra charge	*Supplément*
Fork	*Fourchette*
Full, no more room for customers	*Complet*
Glass	*Verre*
Half bottle	*Demi-bouteille*
Head waiter	*Maître d'hôtel*

*Most restaurants close for a summer holiday and for one or two days a week throughout the year.
**This charge is for a place setting. Sometimes, but not always, bread is included.

Horseradish	*Raifort*
Jug, pitcher	*Pichet*
Juice (fruit juice)	*Jus (des fruits)*
Fresh squeezed orange (lemon) juice	*Orange (citron) pressé*
Orange (lemon) fruit drink	*Jus d'orange (de citron)*
Knife	*Couteau*
Large bottle	*Grande bouteille*
Lemon	*Citron*
Lunch	*Déjeuner (12:30–2:00)*
Midday/Noon	*Midi*
Milk	*Lait*
Mustard	*Moutard*
Napkin	*Serviette*
Night	*Nuit*
Oil	*Huile*
Open	*Ouvert*
Pepper	*Poivre*
Pepper mill	*Moulin de poivre*
Pickle	*Cornichon (small, tart gherkin)*
Plate	*Assiette*
Please	*S'il vous plaît*
Proprietor	*Patron (ne)*
Reservation	*Réservation*
Salt	*Sel*
Serving until (9:30)	*Jusqu'à (21h30)*
Spoon	*Cuillère*
Sugar	*Sucre*
Tea (Chinese)	*Thé (de Chine)*
Herb tea	*Infusion*
Thank you	*Merci*
Tip included	*Service Compris*
Tip not included	*Service Noncompris*
Today	*Au jour d'hui*
Tomorrow	*Demain*
Tooth pick	*Cure-dent*
Vinegar	*Vinaigre*
Waiter	*Garçon*
Waitress	*Serveuse****
Water	*Eau*
Hot water	*Eau chaude*

***Not a form of address "Madame" or "mademoiselle" is appropriate.

Ice water	*Eau glacé*
Mineral water(s)	*Eau(x) minerale(s)*
Non-Sparkling/flat	*Non-gazeuse/plate (e.g. Vittel, Evian)*
Pitcher of tap water	*Une carafe d'eau*
Plain tap water	*Eau fraiche*
Sparkling	*Gazeuse (e.g. Perrier, Vichy, Badoit)*
Week	*Semaine*
Monday	*Lundi*
Except Monday	*Sauf Lundi*
Tuesday	*Mardi*
Wednesday	*Mercredi*
Thursday	*Juedi*
Friday	*Vendredi*
Saturday	*Samedi*
Sunday	*Dimanche*
Wine steward	*Sommelier*

PART III

Ratings of the Best Bistro Dishes

*T*he dishes that follow portray a cross section of the most typical bistro cuisine. These are the foods for which bistros are famous and, while many establishments may serve these items, the restaurants appearing under each heading offer outstanding versions and are listed in order of their preparation's merit. In each case our favorite is listed first, however, all may be considered part of an honor roll of restaurants where meals of exceptionally high quality or originality—truly the great bistro classics of Paris—may be enjoyed.

ANDOUILLETTE
(Smoked Pork Sausage)

RESTAURANT PIERRE AU PALAIS ROYAL	1er	CHEZ ROGER	20e
		À SOUSCEYRAC	11e
		PERRAUDIN	5e
JOSÉPHINE (CHEZ DUMONET)	6e	LE BISTROT D'ANDRÉ	15e
CHEZ FRED	17e	LE POUILLY-REUILLY	19e
AUX CHARPENTIERS	6e		
		LE CHARDENOUX	11e
AU GOURMET DE L'ISLE	4e	LA TOUR DE MONTHLÉRY (CHEZ DENISE)	1er
CHEZ MARCEL (ANTOINE)	12e		
		LE BISTRO D' À CÔTÉ	17e
LES BACCHANTES	9e		
LA FOUX	6e	AU MOULIN À VENT (CHEZ HENRI)	5e
ASTIER	11e		
AU PETIT RICHE	9e	AU DUC DE RICHELIEU	2e
MOISSONNIER	5e		
LES GOURMETS DES TERNES	17e		

(BABA)
(Yeast Cake with Rum Syrup)

CHEZ ANDRÉ	8e	LE MONDE DES CHIMÈRES	4e
POLIDOR	6e		
LES GOURMETS DES TERNES	17e	CHEZ GEORGES	2e
		PAUL	1er

BEURRE BLANC
(White-Wine Butter Sauce for Seafood)

LA GRILLE	10e	AU PETIT RICHE	9e
ALLARD	6e	SAVY	8e
CHEZ MAÎTRE PAUL	6e	LA VIGNE (CHEZ SABINE)	1er
RESTAURANT PIERRE AU PALAIS ROYAL	1er		

BLANQUETTE DE VEAU
(Veal Stew in White Cream Sauce)

SAVY (THURSDAYS)	8e	CHEZ RENÉ (FRIDAYS)	5e
À L'IMPASSE (CHEZ ROBERT)	4e	LA VIGNE (CHEZ SABINE) (THURSDAYS)	1er
BENOÎT	4e		
À LA POMPONNETTE	18e	POLIDOR	6e
LE ROND DE SERVIETTE	2e	LES PETITES SORCIÈRES	14e

BOEUF BOURGUIGNON
(Beef Stew with Red Wine)

CHEZ PAULINE	1er	AU MOULIN À VENT (CHEZ HENRI)	5e
CHEZ RENÉ	5e		
JOSÉPHINE (CHEZ DUMONET)	6e	CHEZ PIERROT	2e
		AUX CRUS DE BOURGOGNE	2e
LA GRILLE	10e		
POLIDOR	6 e	PERRAUDIN	5e
LESCURE	1er	LE BISTROT D'ANDRÈ	15e
LES GOURMETS DES TERNES	17e		

BOEUF EN DAUBE
(Beef with Red Wine and Vegetables)

CHEZ LA VIELLE	1er	AUX CHARPENTIERS	6e
AU PIED DE FOUET	7e		
LE CAMÉLÉON	6e		

BOEUF À LA FICELLE
(Poached Fillet of Beef)

RESTAURANT PIERRE AU PALAIS ROYAL	1er	AU MOULIN À VENT (CHEZ HENRI)	5e
CARTET	11e	AUX CHARPENTIERS	6e
BENOÎT	4e	CHEZ CLOVIS	1er

BOEUF MIROTON
(Leftover Beef Stew with Onions)

CHEZ LA VIELLE	1er	LE BRIN DE ZINC	2e
MOISSONNIER	5e	. . . ET MADAME	
		AU PETIT RICHE	9e

BOEUF À LA MODE
(Pot Roast with Vegetables)

BENOÎT	4e	ALLARD	6e
CHEZ FRED (FRIDAYS)	17e	AUX CHARPENTIERS (TUESDAYS)	6e
CHEZ LA VIELLE	1er		
CHEZ RENÉ (THURSDAYS)	5e		

BOUDIN
(Sausage)

LA FERMETTE DU SUD-OUEST	1er	AU PIED DE FOUET	7e
		CHEZ YVETTE	15e
JEAN DE CHALOSSE	8e	LE PETIT ZINC	6e
BENOÎT	4e	CHEZ ANDRÉ	8e
AUX CHARPENTIERS	6e	THOUMIEUX	7e
		LE POUILLY-REUILLY	19e
MOISSONNIER	5e		
L'ARTOIS (ISIDORE)	8e	AU GOURMET DE L'ISLE	4e
CHEZ MARCEL (ANTOINE)	12e		

BRANDADE
(Purée of Cod)

CARTET	11e	L'AUBERGE DU CENTRE	14e
PIERRE VEDEL	15e		
JEAN DE CHALOSSE (FRIDAYS)	8e	LE MONDE DES CHIMERES	4e
ASTIER	11e	AU PETIT RICHE	9e
L'OEUF À LA NEIGE	17e		

CASSOULET
(White Bean Casserole)

AUBERGE PYRÉNÉES CÉVENNES (CHEZ PHILIPPE)	11e	LE FERMETTE DU SUD-OUEST	1er
		LA GITANE	15e
AUX FINS GOURMETS	7e	THOUMIEUX	7e
		AU PASSÉ RETROUVÉ	15e
JOSÉPHINE (CHEZ DUMONET)	6e	AUX BEC FINS	20e
À SOUSCEYRAC	11e	CHEZ CASIMIR	10e

CHOU FARCI
(Stuffed Cabbage)

RESTAURANT PIERRE AU PALAIS ROYAL	1er	AUBERGE PYRÉNÉES CEVÉNNES (CHEZ PHILIPPE)	11e
SAVY (TUESDAYS)	8e		
CHEZ PAULINE	1er	AUX CHARPENTIERS (SATURDAYS)	6e
AU PASSÉ RETROUVÉ	15e		
RESTAURANT BLEU	14e	LA GITANE	15e
LA TOUR DE MONTHLÉRY (CHEZ DENISE)	1er		

CIVET DE PORC ET PORCELET
(Pig Stew)

AU GOURMET DE L'ISLE	4e	CHEZ MARCEL (ANTOINE)	12e

COCHONNAILLES
(Assorted Pork Products)

LA FERMETTE DU SUD-OUEST	1er	LA TOUR DE MONTHLÉRY (CHEZ DENISE)	1er
CARTET	11e		
ALLARD	6e	LE TRUMILOU	4e
CHEZ MAÎTRE PAUL	6e	LE CAMÉLÉON	6e
		L'ARTOIS (ISIDORE)	8e
CHEZ MARCEL (ANTOINE)	12e	CHEZ GEORGES	17e
		CHEZ FRED	17e
LE PETIT MARGUERY	13e	CHEZ RENÉ	5e
AU PASSÉ RETROUVÉ	15e		

COQ AU VIN
(Chicken Stewed in Wine)

❖

AUBERGE PYRÉNÉES	11e	**AUX FINS GOURMETS**	7e
CÉRVENNES (CHEZ PHILIPPE)		**AUX CRUS DE BOURGOGNE**	2e
L'ARTOIS (ISIDORE)	8e	**CHEZ L'AMI JEAN**	7e
CHEZ RENÉ	5e	**AU DUC DE RICHELIEU**	2e
CHEZ MAÎTRE PAUL	6e	**ALLARD**	6e

CÔTES DE BOEUF
(Ribs of Beef)

❖

L'AMI LOUIS	3e	**PIERRE VEDEL**	15e
CHEZ GEORGES	17e	**LES GOURMET DES TERNES**	17e
CHEZ PAULINE	1er	**LE BOEUF BISTROT**	13e
AU MOULIN À VENT (CHEZ HENRI)	5e	**AUX CHARPENTIERS**	6e
LE CHÂTELET GOURMAND	1er		

FOIE GRAS

❖

L'AMI LOUIS	3e	**LA FONTAINE DE MARS**	7e
JOSÉPHINE (CHEZ DUMONET)	6e	**PIERRE LE LYONNAIS**	16e
PIERRE VEDEL	15e	**AU MOULIN À VENT (CHEZ HENRI)**	5e
À SOUSCEYRAC	11e	**AUX BEC FINS**	20e
LE BRISSEMORET	2e	**CHEZ L'AMI JEAN**	7e
AUX CRUS DE BOURGOGNE	2e	**CHEZ CASIMIR**	10e
LE PETIT MARGUERY	13e		

276 ▪ **RATINGS OF THE BEST BISTRO DISHES**

GATEAU DE RIZ (RIZ AU LAIT)
(Rice Pudding)

❧

CHEZ LA VIELLE	1er	POLIDOR	6e
CHEZ RENÉ	5e	MOISSONNIER	5e
LE BRIN DE ZINC ... ET MADAME	2e	LE POUILLY-REUILLY	19e
CHEZ PAULINE	1er		

GIBELOTTES ET CIVETS DE LAPIN/LIÈVRE
(Rabbit /Hare Stew)

❧

LE PETIT MARGUERY	13e	CHEZ MARCEL (ANTOINE)	12e
L'OULETTE	4e	À L'IMPASSE (CHEZ ROBERT)	4e

GIGOT D' AGNEAU
(Leg of Lamb)

❧

CHEZ GEORGES	17e	LE TRUMILOU	4e
JOSÉPHINE (CHEZ DUMONET)	6e	CHEZ RABU	3e
		CHEZ ANDRÉ	8e
L'AMI LOUIS	3e	LE CHÂTELET GOURMAND	1er
LE PETIT ZINC	6e		
AUX FINS GOURMETS	7e	LA FONTAINE DE MARS	7e
CARTET	11e	PERRAUDIN	5e
CHEZ GEORGES	2e	BISTROT D'ANDRÉ	15e

GRAS-DOUBLE
(Inner Stomach of Ox)

LA FERMETTE DU SUD-OUEST	1er	PIERRE LE LYONNAIS	16e
AUX BECS FINS	20e	CARTET	11e
LA FOUX	6e	LE PETIT MÂCHON	15e
MOISSONNIER	5e	LE BISTROT DE L'ETOILE	17e
ALLARD	6e		
AUX LYONNAIS	2e		

HACHIS PARMENTIER
(Meat-and-Potato Casserole)

CHEZ LA VIELLE (MUST BE ORDERED IN ADVANCE)	1er	LE ROND DE SERVIETTE	2e
		CHEZ GEORGES	17e
L'OEUF À LA NEIGE (TUESDAYS)	17e	CHEZ RABU	3e

HARICOT DE MOUTON
(Lamb Stew with White Beans)

CHEZ GEORGES	17e	AUX FINS GOURMETS	7e
LA TOUR DE MONTHLÉRY (CHEZ DENISE)	1er	CHEZ LA VIELLE	1er
		CHEZ RENÉ (TUESDAYS)	5e

JAMBON
(Ham)

❖

REGIONAL HAMS

CHEZ FRED	17e
LA FERMETTE DU SUD-OUEST	1er
JOSÉPHINE (CHEZ DUMONET)	6e
L'ARTOIS (ISIDORE)	8e
CHEZ L'AMI JEAN	7e
AUX FINS GOURMETS	7e
LES BACCHANTES	9e

COOKED HAMS
(JAMBONS CUITS)

CHEZ MAÎTRE PAUL	6e
AUBERGE PYRÉNÉES CÉVENNES (CHEZ PHILIPPE)	11e

JAMBON PERSILLÉ
(Parslied Ham)

❖

AUBERGE PYRÉNÉES CÉVENNES (CHEZ PHILIPPE)	11e	RESTAURANT PIERRE AU PALAIS ROYAL	1er
CHEZ PAULINE	1er	ALLARD	6e
		CARTET	11e
		CHEZ GEORGES	2e

LAPIN À LA MOUTARDE
(Rabbit in Mustard Sauce)

❖

ASTIER	11e	CHEZ GRAND-MÈRE	13e
POLIDOR	6e		
LA TOUR DE MONTHLÉRY (CHEZ DENISE)	1er		

LIÈVRE À LA ROYALE
(A Complex Preparation of Hare; see "Les Plats")

À SOUSCEYRAC	11e	BENOÎT	4e
CHEZ PAULINE	1er		

RABLE DE LIÈVRE/LAPIN (LAPEREAU)
(Saddle of Hare/Rabbit)

PIERRE VEDEL	15e	LES PETITES	14e
AU PETIT RICHE	9e	SORCIÈRES	
		L'OULETTE	4e

MAQUEREAU
(Mackerel)

RESTAURANT PIERRE AU PALAIS ROYAL	1er	LESCURE	1er
		CARTET	11e
		CHEZ PIERROT	2e
LA GRILLE	10e	LE ROND DE SERVIETTE	2e
À LA POMPONNETTE	18e		
LE PETIT MARGUERY	13e	LE BRISSEMORET	2e
		AU PIED DE FOUET	7e
CHEZ MARCEL (ANTOINE)	12e		

NAVARIN
(Lamb Stew)

ALLARD	6e	SAVY	8e
PERRAUDIN	5e	CHEZ GERMAINE	7e
JOSÉPHINE (CHEZ DUMONET)	6e	(BABKINE)	
		CHEZ ANDRÉ	8e
CHEZ EDGARD	8e	AU PIED DE FOUET	7e
CHEZ LA VIELLE	1er		

PETIT SALÉ
(Lightly Salted Pork Tenderloin)

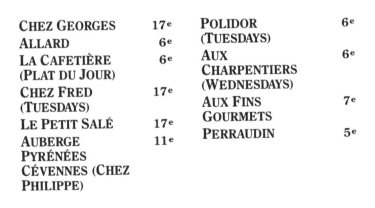

CHEZ GEORGES	17e	POLIDOR (TUESDAYS)	6e
ALLARD	6e		
LA CAFETIÈRE (PLAT DU JOUR)	6e	AUX CHARPENTIERS (WEDNESDAYS)	6e
CHEZ FRED (TUESDAYS)	17e		
LE PETIT SALÉ	17e	AUX FINS GOURMETS	7e
AUBERGE PYRÉNÉES CÉVENNES (CHEZ PHILIPPE)	11e	PERRAUDIN	5e

PIEDS DE PORC
(Pigs' Feet)

À SOUSCEYRAC	11e	AUX CHARPENTIERS	6e
MOISSONNIER	5e		
CHEZ MARCEL (ANTOINE)	12e	LA TOUR DE MONTHLÉRY (CHEZ DENISE)	1er
L'OEUF À LA NEIGE	17e		
AUX CRUS DE BOURGOGNE	2e	THOUMIEUX	7e
		LE PETIT MÂCHON	15e

POT-AU-FEU/BOEUF GROS SEL
(Beef with Vegetables and Coarse Salt)

❦

LE SANCERRE (WEDNESDAYS)	19e	LA GITANE	15e
CHEZ GORISSE	17e	LA TOUR DE MONTHLÉRY (CHEZ DENISE)	1er
LA FOUX (WEDNESDAYS)	6e	CHEZ GEORGES (WEDNESDAYS)	17e
CHEZ LA VIELLE (ORDER IN ADVANCE)	1er	LE ROND DE SERVIETTE	2e
L'OEUF À LA NEIGE	17e	CHEZ GRAND-MÈRE	13e
LE ROI DU POT-AU-FEU	9e	LA CAFETIÈRE (PLAT DU JOUR)	6e
CHEZ FRED (THURSDAYS)	17e	SAVY (FRIDAYS)	8e

POULE-AU-POT
(Poached Stuffed Chicken)

❦

LA POULE-AU-POT	7e	LE MONDE DES CHIMÈRES	4e
POLIDOR	6e	LE PETIT ZINC	6e
LESCURE	1er		
SAVY (TUESDAYS)	8e		

RAIE
(Skate)

❦

CHEZ PAULINE	1er	RESTAURANT PIERRE AU PALAIS ROYAL	1er
LA CAGOUILLE	14e	AUX LYONNAIS	2e
LE PETIT MARGUERY	13e	AUX CRUS DE BOURGOGNE	2e
CHEZ FERNAND (LES FERNANDISES)	11e	LE POUILLY-REUILLY	19e

SAUCISSON CHAUD
(Hot Garlic Sausage)

❖

BENOÎT	4e	POLIDOR	6e
CHEZ GEORGES	17e	CARTET	11e
CHEZ MAÎTRE PAUL	6e	L'ARTOIS (ISIDORE)	8e
CHEZ RENÉ	5e	LE BISTROT DU XXe	20e
JEAN DE CHALOSSE	8e	À SOUSCEYRAC	11e
RESTAURANT PIERRE AU PALAIS ROYAL	1er	CHEZ MARCEL (ANTOINE)	12e
		MOISSONNIER	5e
LE SANCERRE	19e	LE BISTROT DE L'ÉTOILE	17e
LE PETIT MÂCHON	15e		

SAUTÉS/RAGOUTS D'AGNEAU
(Lamb)

❖

POLIDOR	6e	CHEZ LA VIELLE	1er
CHEZ FRED (SATURDAYS)	17e		

SAUTÉS/RAGOUTS DE PORC
(Pig)

❖

POLIDOR	6e	LA FERMETTE DU SUD-OUEST	1er
CHEZ EDGARD	8e	LES PETITES SORCIÈRES	14e
CARTET	11e		

TABLIERS DE SAPEUR
(Lyonnaise, Pan-Fried Version of Gras-Double)

MOISSONNIER	5e	LA FOUX	6e
LE PETIT MÂCHON	15e	LES BACCHANTES	9e

TÊTE DE VEAU
(Calf's Head)

PIERRE VEDEL	15e	L'OEUF À LA NEIGE (THURSDAYS)	17e
BENOÎT	4e		
CHEZ PAULINE	1er	LE ROND DE SERVIETTE	2e
CHEZ GEORGES	17e		
LE BRIN DE ZINC ... ET MADAME	2e	LA FONTAINE DE MARS	7e
JEAN DE CHALOSSE	8e	CHEZ CLOVIS	1er
CHEZ GORISSE	17e		

TRIPE
(Tripe)

LA TOUR DE MONTHLÉRY (CHEZ DENISE)	1er	PAUL	1er
		CHEZ FERNAND (FERNANDISES)	11e
LA FOUX	6e	LE CHARDENOUX	11e
CHEZ MARCEL (ANTOINE)	12e	THOUMIEUX	7e
		POLIDOR	6e

TRIPOUX
(Auvergnat Preparation of Veal or Mutton Tripe)

LE SANCERRE	19e	AU PASSÉ RETROUVÉ	15e
L'ARTOIS (ISIDORE)	8e		
LA LOZÈRE	6e	LE PETIT MÂCHON	15e
RESTAURANT BLEU	14e		

BOOKS OF INTEREST

*F*or those interested in further reading, we recommend the following books:

Bond, Michael. *The Pleasures of Paris, A Gastronomic Companion.* New York: Clarkson M. Potter, Inc., 1987.

Chadwick, Brian and Klaus Boehm ed. *The Taste of France, A Dictionary of French Food and Wine.* Boston: Houghton Mifflin Co., 1982.

Delthil, Françoise and Bernard. *The Good Value Guide to Paris.* Edison, N.J.: Hunter Publishing, Inc., 1986.

Escaig, Roland and Maurice Beaudon. *The French Way, An Insider's Guide to the Hotels and Restaurants of France.* New York: Warner Books Inc., 1988.

Escaig, Roland. *La Petite Bible de Roland Escaig, Paris 1990.* Paris: Éditions Roland Escaig, 1990.

Gardner, Carl and Julie Sheppard. *Eating Paris, A Guide to Moderate Priced Eating in Paris.* London: Fontana Paperbacks, 1987.

Gault/Millau. *The Best of Paris.* New York: Crown Publishers, 1986.

Le Guide du Routard, 1990/91, Restos & Bistrots de Paris. Paris: Hachette, 1990.

Gustafson, Sandre. *Cheap Eats in Paris.* San Francisco: Chronicle Books, 1990.

In and Around Paris. Collier World Travelers Series. New York: Macmillan Publishing Co., 1986.

Laffont, Robert. *Le Guide Lebey 1990 Des Restaurants de Paris.* Paris: Éditions Robert Laffont, Sa., 1990.

Laffont, Robert. *Le Petit Lebey/1990 des Bistrots Parisiens, Brasseries et Bars à Vins.* Paris: Éditions Robert Laffont, 1990.

Laffont, Robert. *Le Petit Lebey/1987 des Bistrots Parisiens.* Paris: Éditions Robert Laffont, Sa., 1987. (English edition.)

Lazareffe, Alexandre. *Paris Rendez-Vous, 1990/91.* Paris: Guides Hachette, 1990.

Paris in Your Pocket. New York: Barron's Educational Series, Inc., 1987.

Siedeck, Wolfram. *Die Schönsten und Besten Bistros von Paris.* Munich: Wilhelm Heyne Verlag, 1990.

Travant, Warren and Jean. *Paris Confidential.* Baltimore: Agora, Inc., 1987.

Turner, Miles. *Paupers' Paris.* London: Pan Books, 1984–85.

Wells, Patricia. *The Food Lover's Guide to Paris.* New York: Workman Publishing, 1988.

Wurman, Richard Saul. *Richard Saul Wurman's Ultimate Guide.* Paris: Access Press, New York, 1990.

INDEX OF BISTROS

A

À Sousceyrac	11e
Allard	6e
Chez l'Ami Jean	7e
L'Ami Louis	3e
Chez André	8e
Antoine (Chez Marcel)	12e
L'Artois (Isidore)	8e
Astier	11e
L'Auberge du Centre	14e
Auberge Pyrénées Cévennes (Chez Philippe)	11e

B

Babkine (Chez Germaine)	7e
Les Bacchantes	9e
Aux Bec Fins	20e
Benoît	4e
Le Bistrot d' À Côté "Flaubert"	17e
Le Bistrot d'André	15e
Le Bistrot d'Henri	6e
Le Bistrot de Clémence	4e
Le Bistrot de l'Étoile	17e
Le Bistrot du XXe	20e
Le Boeuf Bistrot	13e
Boeuf Gros Sel	20e
Le Brin de Zinc . . . et Madame	2e
Le Brissemoret	2e

C

La Cafetière	6e
Le Caméléon	6e
La Cagouille	14e
Cartet	11e
Chez Casimir	10e
Chardenoux	11e
Aux Charpentiers	6e
Le Châtelet Gourmand	1er

La Cigale (Chez Pierre et Micheline)	7e
Chez Clovis	1er
Aux Crus de Bourgogne	2e

D

Chez Denise (Tour Monthléry)	1er
Au Duc de Richelieu	2e
Chez Dumonet (Josephine)	6e

E

Chez Edgard	8e

F

La Fermette du Sud-Ouest	1er
Chez Fernand (Les Fernandises)	11e
Aux Fins Gourmets	7e
La Fontaine de Mars	7e
La Foux	6e
Chez Fred	17e

G

Chez Georges	2e
Chez Georges	17e
Chez Germaine (Babkine)	7e
La Gitane	15e
Chez Gorisse	17e
Au Gourmet de l'Îsle	4e
Les Gourmets des Ternes	17e
Chez Grand-Mère	13e
La Grille	10e

H

Chez Henri (au Moulin à Vent)	5e

I

A l'Impasse (Chez Robert) 4e
Isidore (l'Artois) 8e

J

Jean de Chalosse 8e
Joséphine (Chez Dumonet) 6e

L

Lescure 1er
La Lozère 6e
Aux Lyonnais 2e

M

Chez Maître Paul 6e
Chez Marcel (Antoine) 12e
Moissonnier 5e
Le Monde des Chimères 4e
Le Montalivet 8e
Au Moulin à Vent (Chez Henri) 5e

O

L'Oeuf à la Neige 17e
L'Oulette 4e

P

Au Passé Retrouvé 15e
Paul 1er
Chez Pauline 1er
Perraudin 5e
Le Petit Mâchon 15e
Le Petit Marguery 13e
Au Petit Riche 9e
Le Petit Salé 17e
Le Petit Zinc 6e
Les Petites Sorcières 14e
Chez Philippe (Auberge Pyrénées Cévennes) 11e
Au Pied de Fouet 7e
Pierre le Lyonnais 16e

Chez Pierre et Micheline (La Cigale) 7e
Chez Pierrot 2e
Polidor 6e
À La Pomponnette 18e
Le Pouilly-Reuilly 19e
La Poule-au-Pot 7e

R

Chez Rabu 3e
Chez René 5e
Restaurant Bleu 14e
Restaurant Pierre au Palais Royal 1er
Chez Robert (À l'Impasse) 4e
Chez Roger 20e
Le Roi du Pot-au-Feu 9e
Le Rond de Serviette 2e
La Rôtisserie du Beaujolais 5e

S

Chez Sabine (La Vigne) 1er
Le Sancerre 19e
Savy 8e
Le Scheffer 16e
À Sousceyrac 11e

T

Thoumieux 7e
La Tour de Monthléry (Chez Denise) 1er
Chez Toutonne 5e
Le Trumilou 4e

V

Pierre Vedel 15e
Chez la Vieille 1er
La Vigne (Chez Sabine) 1er

Y

Chez Yvette 15e

ABOUT THE AUTHORS

*R*obert and Barbara Hamburger were born and raised in New York City. Robert received a bachelor of arts degree from Columbia University; Barbara was graduated from St. Lawrence University, also with a bachelor of arts degree. Following college, they were married and entered the family bridal gown manufacturing business together, with Robert as president and Barbara as designer of their company. For the past thirty years they have holidayed in France, admiring the countryside, the towns, and the French way of life, while developing a special interest in French food and wine. Though they remain active in the apparel business, Robert has become a private art dealer, and Barbara is the author of *Zooming In* (Harcourt Brace Jovanovich, 1974).